EVERY ★ ★ THING ★ ★ ★ PROSPERS ★

American Furniture

AMERICAN FURNITURE 2010

Edited by Luke Beckerdite

Published by the CHIPSTONE FOUNDATION

Distributed by University Press of New England

Hanover and London

Cover Illustration: Crest of a side chair, possibly Portsmouth, New Hampshire, 1730–1750. Maple. (Chipstone Foundation; photo, Gavin Ashworth).

Design: Wynne Patterson, Pittsfield, VT
Copyediting: Fronia Simpson, Bennington, VT
Typesetting: Aardvark Type, Hartford, CT
Printing: Meridian Printing, East Greenwich, RI

Published by the Chipstone Foundation
Distributed by University Press of New England
1 Court Street
Lebanon, New Hampshire 03766
upne.com

© 2010 by the Chipstone Foundation
All rights reserved
Printed in the United States of America   5 4 3 2 1
ISSN 1069–4188
ISBN 0–9767344–7–5

Contents

Editorial Statement

American Furniture is an interdisciplinary journal dedicated to advancing knowledge of furniture made or used in the Americas from the seventeenth century to the present. Authors are encouraged to submit articles on any aspect of furniture history, essays on conservation and historic technology, reproductions or transcripts of documents, annotated photographs of new furniture discoveries, and book and exhibition reviews. References for compiling an annual bibliography also are welcome.

Manuscripts must be typed, double-spaced, illustrated with black-and-white prints, transparencies, or high resolution digital images, and prepared in accordance with the *Chicago Manual of Style*. The Chipstone Foundation will offer significant honoraria for manuscripts accepted for publication and reimburse authors for all photography approved in writing by the editor.

Luke Beckerdite

Dedication

In Memory of Dudley J. Godfrey, Jr.

▼ MY FIRST ENCOUNTER with Dudley Godfrey was a phone conversation regarding a late seventeenth-century Massachusetts table that Sumpter Priddy and I had for sale when we were in the antique business in the late 1980s. In my mind's eye, I envisioned the person at the other end of the line as being tall and thin with compulsively groomed gray hair and a somewhat gruff personality. When I met Dudley and his wife Constance a couple years later, I discovered I was wrong on all accounts. He was a robust 5' 10", follicly challenged, and had a big smile and hearty handshake that made the newest of acquaintances feel like old friends. Over the next few years, I came to discover that many of the people who knew Dudley, myself included, considered him their best friend.

To many who will turn the pages of this volume, Dudley is remembered as a collector of colonial American furniture and early English pottery, silver, and needlework. Although he and his wife Constance assembled one of the finest collections in this country, their contributions to the decorative arts field and their community went much deeper. As a trustee of the Chipstone Foundation from 1966 to 2004, Dudley was instrumental in the development of its collection and educational initiatives, including *American Furniture* and *Ceramics in America*. He and Constance were also major donors to the Milwaukee Art Museum and generous supporters of publications, exhibitions, and conservation projects at other institutions. Most of the Godfreys' gifts were made anonymously, but their impact on decorative arts scholarship is substantial and continues today. Their philanthropy was not solely limited to the arts, however, and extended to providing numerous college scholarships and medical care to those in need and supporting a broad range of social service organizations.

The trustees and staff of the Chipstone Foundation dedicate this issue of *American Furniture* to Dudley Godfrey in recognition of the many contributions he and Constance have made to our field and to us personally.

Luke Beckerdite

American Furniture

Figure 1   Pier table attributed to Thomas Seymour with decoration by John Penniman, Boston, Massachusetts, 1809. White pine and white ash; brass mounts. H. 34½", W. 48", D. 23". (Courtesy, Nichols House Museum, Boston; photo, David Bohl.)

*Robert Mussey and
Christopher Shelton*

John Penniman and the Ornamental Painting Tradition in Federal-Era Boston

▼ A RECENTLY DISCOVERED pier table bearing the inscription "Painted in M ____ 1809 by John P___niman" is the only piece of furniture signed and dated by John Penniman (1782/83–1841), Boston's most important decorative painter of the federal period (figs. 1, 2). The table is attributed to the shop of cabinetmaker Thomas Seymour (1771–1848) and is also the only Boston example with painted and gilded decoration in the "antique taste." It may have been part of a suite that included at least one other identical table, a card table, and a set of chairs decorated by Penniman or a craftsman associated with him. The table's ornament is based on two plates in Thomas Sheraton's *The Cabinet-Maker and Upholsterer's Drawing-Book* (1793), but its unique form and novel adaptation of published designs reflect the penchant of both Seymour and Penniman for experimentation. The sophisticated application of the decoration indicates that Penniman was at the height of his abilities at the age of twenty-seven. Based on the distinctive style and painting techniques manifest in this work, several other pieces of Boston furniture with painted and gilded decoration can now be tentatively attributed to him.[1]

Figure 2   Detail of the pier table in fig. 1. At least two other tables by Thomas Seymour have two pairs of similarly shaped supports.

Furniture Painting and Painters

At a time when Baltimore, Philadelphia, and New York painters led the new nation in the production of fancy furniture, their Boston counterparts tended to focus on clock dials, reverse-glass tablets, carriages, Masonic regalia, military banners, shop signs, floor carpets, window shades, transparent illuminations for public celebrations, and fire buckets—the "thousand etceteras" of decorative painting. In 1823 Boston painter Charles Hubbard advertised "coach and chaise Bodies ornamented with Arms, Initials, Borders, &c." as well as "Military Standard Painting, Sign Painting, Masonic and fancy Painting, Landscape and marine do, Clock and Timepiece Do, Gilt and painted ornaments for ships." Boston craftsmen did produce fancy-painted seating but in lesser quantity than chair makers and decorators in most other urban centers. In addition, most Boston fancy chairs are stylistically conservative in comparison with contemporary examples made in the Middle Atlantic region and the South.[2]

Boston newspapers from the first decade of the nineteenth century document the importation of thousands of fancy-painted chairs. In the February 23, 1805, issue of the *Columbian Centinel*, furniture warehouse-man William Leverett reported that he had just received as "great a variety of Furniture as was ever offered for sale in the United States; fancy japanned Chairs, and other Furniture to match, suitable for a Room, constantly arriving from Philadelphia. Orders executed for any article in the fancy Japanned line, from the first Japanners, in Philadelphia, by the above." Two years later, he advertised chairs "in the latest styles, as good as may be had in Philadelphia." In 1807 the furniture warehousing firm Nolen & Gridley imported three hundred fancy chairs "of different patterns" from "one of the first manufactories in New-York." It claimed that aside from a surcharge for shipping, the prices were the same as those of the manufacturer. Among the fancy seating forms mentioned in Nolan & Gridley's advertisement were chairs with "white and gold double shells and green Tops, cane color Scroll Back[s], coquilico and gold Grecian border[s], green and gold double Cross Backs, Tulip tops, white and gold double cross do. Bronzed Tops, Coquilico do. Eagle Tops, Salmon do. Grape leaf, Orange and Red."[3]

Although imported fancy furniture set a standard for style and quality in Boston, painted and gilded seating, tables, and case pieces were less popular there than in New York, Philadelphia, and Baltimore, where immigrant artisans appear to have contributed to the taste for fancy furniture. In Baltimore, Irish émigrés John (1777–1851) and Hugh Finlay (1781–1831) dominated the market for painted objects in the neoclassical, or "antique," taste. English immigrant George Bridport (b. England before 1794–d. 1819) worked in a similar style for prominent Philadelphia patrons like William Waln. A few British painters and gilders were active in Boston during the federal period. "J. White" advertised chair japanning and ornamental painting of signs, architecture, and furniture from his shop "near the Common" at 45 Pleasant Street: "He having been employed in the first professional houses, both in England and India—the latter of which exceeds every other country, in the art of japaning; and he flatters himself capable of adducing work equal in point to any yet imported; and with greater dispatch than any other person in this State. . . . N.B. Bamboo and fancy chairs re-painted, as new." White's career in Boston was brief, however, possibly owing to lack of demand for sophisticated neoclassical painted decoration and the economic decline following President Thomas Jefferson's embargo on trade with Britain from 1807 to 1808.[4]

Fifteen or fewer immigrant decorators are known to have worked in Boston during the federal period. Moreover, several of these craftsmen were principally gilders and looking-glass makers who occasionally did reverse glass–painted tablets for looking glasses and clocks. James Sharp is the only one who achieved success as a furniture decorator but not until the 1820s. Prior to that, Jefferson's embargo and the War of 1812 ruined the local market for luxury goods. Most of the immigrant decorators who went to Boston left after a short period, seeking greater opportunities in New York, Baltimore, Norfolk, Charleston, Savannah, or other coastal Atlantic urban style centers whose economies were less adversely affected by the embargo and the war. There is no evidence that an ornamental painter as skilled as Bridport or the Finlays ever worked in Boston, and that city's apparent aversion to the French taste precluded the introduction of *verte antique* and decorative gilt finishes like those associated with New York cabinetmaker Charles Honoré Lannuier.[5]

Boston Painted Furniture in the Antique Style
Although the pier table illustrated in figure 1 may have been part of a suite of paint-decorated furniture, its early provenance remains unclear. Boston landscape designer and women's rights advocate Rose Nichols (1872–1960) probably purchased the table during or after the 1930s (fig. 3). There is no documentary evidence that she inherited it from her parents, Arthur and

Figure 3 Taylor Greer, *Rose Standish Nichols*, Massachusetts, ca. 1912. Watercolor on paper. 4¾" x 3⅜". (Courtesy, Nichols House Museum.) Nichols was forty when she sat for this miniature. She probably acquired the pier table illustrated in fig. 1 after 1930.

Figure 4 Lyman White, tracing, Boston, Massachusetts, probably before 1835. Graphite on paper. 9¹⁵/₁₆" x 8". (Courtesy, Winterthur Library; Joseph Downs Collection of Manuscripts and Printed Ephemera.) White probably traced one of the supports on the pier table illustrated in fig. 1 when he repainted the top.

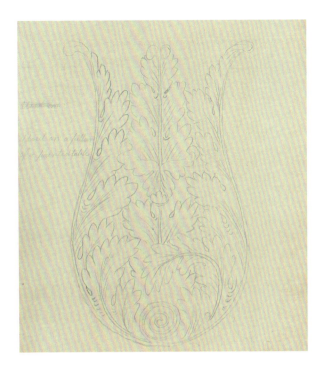

(fig. 4) and bears the penciled notation "used on a pillar of a painted table." White may have done the sketch while the table was in his shop for repainting of worn and stained top surfaces. If so, this work would probably have occurred before 1838, when he became foreman for the Chickering Piano Company.[6]

The 1809 date on the pier table is significant, for in that year Penniman rented shop space in Thomas Seymour's warehouse on Common Street. Other facts and features supporting the theory that Seymour's shop made the table include his and Penniman's collaboration on other furniture in that year, the table's distinctive stamped sheet-brass hardware, and the use of ash as a secondary wood. John and Thomas Seymour are the only Boston cabinetmakers known to have used ash before circa 1817. Also typical of Thomas's work are scrolled feet that form a slightly asymmetric, flattened oval; the use of two pairs of supports; and a thick front-to-back medial rail that is dovetailed to the front and rear rails and secured to the tops of the supports with wedged mortise-and-tenon joints. Although "lyre base" is the term commonly used to describe tables of this type, Boston newspaper advertisements of the period occasionally refer to examples with a "harp base."[7]

The decoration on the front rail of the pier table depicts a pair of classical griffins and arabesques of scrolling leafage flanking a burning pyre. It was copied from a design on pl. 56 in Sheraton's *Drawing-Book* (fig. 5). Similar

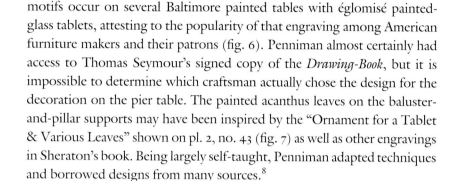

Figure 5 Ornament for a Frieze or Table illustrated on pl. 56 in Thomas Sheraton's *The Cabinet-Makers and Uphosterer's Drawing-Book* (1793; reprinted, 1802). (Courtesy, Winterthur Library; Printed Book and Periodical Collection.) The identical design in Thomas Seymour's copy of the first edition was Penniman's source for the decoration on the frieze on the pier table illustrated in fig. 1.

motifs occur on several Baltimore painted tables with églomisé painted-glass tablets, attesting to the popularity of that engraving among American furniture makers and their patrons (fig. 6). Penniman almost certainly had access to Thomas Seymour's signed copy of the *Drawing-Book*, but it is impossible to determine which craftsman actually chose the design for the decoration on the pier table. The painted acanthus leaves on the baluster-and-pillar supports may have been inspired by the "Ornament for a Tablet & Various Leaves" shown on pl. 2, no. 43 (fig. 7) as well as other engravings in Sheraton's book. Being largely self-taught, Penniman adapted techniques and borrowed designs from many sources.[8]

Penniman's painting style is distinctive. The acanthus leaves on the supports have organic, rounded tips, and some curl as they terminate, leaving "eyelets" along their edge. The leaves were articulated with five different shades of brown oil glaze, ranging from very pale, transparent sienna to a

Figure 6 Églomisé and gilt glass panel on the frieze of a card table, Baltimore, Maryland, 1805–1815. (Private collection; photo, Robert Mussey Associates.)

Figure 7 Ornament for a Tablet & Various Leaves illustrated on pl. 2 in Thomas Sheraton's *Cabinet-Makers and Upholsterer's Drawing Book* (1802). (Courtesy, Winterthur Library; Printed Book and Periodical Collection.) Penniman may have used the leaf decoration at the bottom of this plate as inspiration for the decoration on the supports of the pier table illustrated in fig. 1.

Figure 8   Detail of the gilt and glazed leafage on the right front support of the pier table illustrated in fig. 1. (Photo, Robert Mussey Associates.) Penniman built up several layers of transparent oil glaze, beginning with the palest color, with successively darker layers applied at an angle or at right angles to the previous one.

Figure 9   Detail of the gilt and glazed leafage on the right front support of the pier table illustrated in fig. 1. (Photo, Robert Mussey Associates.)

very dark, opaque brown umber (fig. 8). Layers of glaze were built up with parallel, curving brushstrokes, with each layer oriented roughly at right angles to the previous layer. These techniques, which create the illusion of shadows, depth, and flow, are related to cross-hatching used by contemporaneous engravers. It is conceivable that engravers' techniques, which were manifest in the *Drawing-Book* and other period sources, influenced Penniman's handwork as much as his designs. He is the only Boston decorator known to have used short, fluid brushstrokes to apply layers of glaze at right angles to one another. This idiosyncratic technique is also used in his signed watercolor depicting a stringer of three fish.[9]

To give his work volume and dimension, Penniman used shades of pale or drab gray paint to simulate shadows on the right and below his leafage, figures, and panel bordering. This technique, which gives the illusion of a light source at the upper left, is manifest in all his work (fig. 9). The primary components of the pier table are highlighted with stripes of the same pale gray, a darker gray, and a separating line of dark reddish brown. On the top, the stripes are graduated in depth of color and "mitered" at the corners to simulate the applied beaded moldings on English Regency furniture.[10]

A card table and set of four painted and gilded fancy chairs—one bearing the stenciled name "Holden"—display similar techniques and can tentatively be attributed to Penniman or one of the workmen in the decorator's

Figure 10   Card table attributed to Thomas
Seymour with decoration attributed to John
Penniman, Boston, Massachusetts, 1808–1815.
Maple and white pine with white pine. H. 30⅜",
W. 35¾", D. 18⅛". (Private collection; photo,
Robert Mussey.) This card table is one of the
earliest examples with a top that rotates around
a threaded iron pivot rod to reveal an inner well
for cards and game pieces. The interior wells are
repainted with a pale "sky blew." The upper edges
of the rails are faced with thin undyed morocco
leather instead of the customary wool baize.

Figure 11 Side chair, Boston, Massachusetts, 1808–1815. Mahogany. H. 20¾", W. 19", D. 25⅜". (Courtesy, Winterthur Museum.)

shop (figs. 10, 11). The decoration on this suite is also related to that on the pier table, although the leaf designs on the card table and chairs are somewhat less refined (figs. 12, 13). All have moldings simulated with sienna and umber striping and detailed with layers of brown glaze. The seating was formerly attributed to New York chair maker Asa Holden, but it is more likely that they are from the shop of Joshua Holden, a Boston chair maker and chair painter.[11]

The card table has several painted and gilt designs that are virtually identical to those on the chairs: a stylized shell surrounded by leafage (fig. 14), acanthus leaves with prominent central veins, roundels, and shadowing in two shades of gray (fig. 12). The shading of the leaves and shell and the use of several hues of brown glazing provide further evidence that the same hand decorated these objects. Attribution of the table to Thomas Seymour's shop is supported by its fastidious construction, square shaping of the legs,

Figure 12 Detail of the painted decoration on the right front leg of the card table illustrated in fig. 10.

Figure 13 Detail of the decoration on the front legs and seat rail of the side chair illustrated in fig. 11. (Courtesy, Winterthur Museum.) The decoration is not as refined as that on the pier table illustrated in fig. 1. Its incorporation of pale gray shadowing, rounded leaf tips, faux reeding, and several tints of transparent brown glaze over gold-leaf designs suggest that the work is by Penniman or one of his apprentices or journeymen.

Figure 14 Detail of the center panel on the front rail of the card table illustrated in fig. 10.

Figure 15 Detail of the kerfed and bent glue blocks on the underside of the card table illustrated in fig. 10.

paneled therm foot design, and distinctive use of kerfed and bent glue blocks on the underside (fig. 15). Small beaded moldings are set into precisely cut grooves around the ankles and below the cyma-shaped elements of the legs—another feature associated with Seymour's furniture (fig. 12).

Joshua was probably the son of David Holden, born April 3, 1781, at Townsend, Massachusetts. The younger Holden first appeared in Boston tax records in 1807, when he was described as a chair maker in partnership with Asa Jones in Ward 12. Assessments from 1808 to 1811 listed Holden as an independent craftsman on Washington Street, which was just over a block from Seymour's furniture warehouse.[12]

Newspaper advertisements and other primary documents pertaining to Thomas Seymour reveal that he frequently hired other artisans to make furniture that he sold under his own name. From 1804 to 1805, he was in partnership with Samuel Tuck, a chair maker and painter who probably supplied the showrooms with fancy seating. Tuck may have made the set of "8 White fancy chairs" for which Seymour charged Salem merchant and shipowner Joseph Peabody $32.00 on December 2, 1807 (fig. 16). Tuck left the partnership in 1807 and opened a "Paint Warehouse." That business

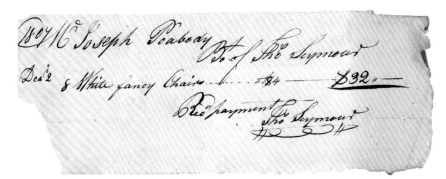

Figure 16 Joseph Peabody's receipt for white fancy chairs from Thomas Seymour, Boston, Massachusetts, 1807. (Private collection; photo, Robert Mussey Associates.) Peabody was a successful Salem ship captain who became a merchant.

prospered until the financial decline preceding and during the War of 1812 forced him out of business. From 1808 to 1809, Seymour was in partnership with James Cogswell, a cabinetmaker who is not known to have made chairs. It is plausible that they turned to Joshua Holden to provide fancy seating like that previously furnished by Tuck.[13]

It is also possible that the chairs and matching card table (figs. 10, 11) were actually decorated by one of the many painters whom Penniman either trained or employed over his long career. Alvan Fisher (1792–1863), who began his term in 1810, recalled his attempts to learn academic landscape painting techniques: "In consequence of this determination to be an artist I was placed with a Mr. Penniman who was an excellent ornamental painter. With him I acquired a style which required many years to shake off—I mean a mechanical ornamental touch and manner of coloring." Other Penniman apprentices included Thomas Badger, Charles Bullard, Thomas Cunningham, Charles Hubbard, Henry Loring, Nathan W. Munroe, Nathan Negus, Henry Nolen, Asa Parks, and Moses Swett. Several of these men were working independently during the period when the chairs and card table were made, but except for clock dials, none of their furniture work is documented.[14]

If Penniman did not decorate the suite himself, a leading candidate would be Nathan W. Munroe, who was nearing the end of his apprenticeship in 1809. In the August 25, 1810, issue of the *Columbian Centinel*, Munroe reported: "[Munroe] . . . has taken the Shop in the North end of the Boston Furniture Warehouse, near the bottom of the Mall, lately occupied by Mr. John R. Penniman, with whom he served his apprenticeship. . . . He offers his services as Painter of Standards, Signs, Window and Bed Cornishes, Chairs, Toilets, tables, and articles in the Furniture Line." These dates and qualitative differences between the painting on the pier table and chairs suggest that Penniman may have assigned decoration of the seating to the less-skilled Munroe.

A group of Boston card tables has gilt acanthus leaves with multiple brown glazes applied in a manner almost identical to that on the signed pier table (figs. 17, 18). These painted motifs echo the carved leaves on other card tables attributed to Seymour as well as the English Regency examples that inspired them. Furniture historian Edwin Hipkiss established the connection between Penniman and Seymour when he discovered a receipt for a

Figure 17   Card table attributed to Thomas Seymour with decoration attributed to John Penniman, Boston, Massachusetts, 1810–1815. Rosewood and rosewood veneer with white pine, birch, ash, and mahogany; brass mounts, stringing inlays, and moldings. H. 29¾", W. 36", D. 17⁹⁄₁₆". (Courtesy, Historic New England; photo, David Bohl.)

Figure 19 Detail of the painted decoration on the top of a commode chest, Boston, Massachusetts, 1809. (Courtesy, Museum of Fine Arts, Boston, the M. and M. Karolik Collection of Eighteenth-Century American Arts, 23.19.)

Figure 20 Workbox attributed to Thomas Seymour with decoration by John Penniman, Boston, Massachusetts, 1808–1814. Satinwood and bird's-eye maple veneer, with mahogany and satinwood. H. 3½", W. 8", D. 10⅝". (Private collection.)

demilune commode chest the cabinetmaker made for Elizabeth Derby of Salem, Massachusetts. Dated the same year as the pier table, the receipt lists Seymour's charges for making the chest, English immigrant Thomas Wightman's charges for carving leaves and moldings, and Penniman's charges for painting a panel depicting shells and seaweed at the rear of the top (fig. 19). The exceptional artistry evident on the panel of the commode and on the ornament on the signed pier table suggests that Penniman was Seymour's decorator of choice for the finest work.[15]

A small lady's workbox bearing the painted initials "J R P" is the only other piece of furniture known that is marked by Penniman (fig. 20). Reputedly made for Elizabeth Derby, the box is decorated on top with a painted shell that is closely related to that on the panel of the commode chest. The refined construction, mahogany lining, and bird's-eye maple and curly satinwood veneers suggest that Seymour's shop made the box, possibly in the same year as the commode. All other documented, signed, or initialed examples of Penniman's work are either clock dials, painted-glass tablets for clocks, landscape or portrait paintings, heraldry panels, engravings, or prints.[16]

Several pieces of furniture attributed to Seymour's shop have painted decoration that was probably executed by Penniman or, at the very least, influenced by his work. Included in this group are a number of lady's dressing tables with elegant gilt leafage and striping (fig. 21). He also appears to

Figure 21 Dressing table attributed to Thomas Seymour with decoration attributed to John Penniman, Boston, Massachusetts, 1808–1814. Mahogany, bird's-eye maple and satinwood veneers, with white pine, mahogany, ash, and soft maple. H. 73", W. 45", D. 25". (Courtesy, Peabody Essex Museum; photo, Gavin Ashworth.) The table reputedly descended from Elizabeth Derby (West) of Salem.

Figure 22 Worktable attributed to Thomas Seymour with top decoration attributed to John Penniman, Boston, Massachusetts, 1808–1814. Maple and bird's-eye maple veneer, with eastern white pine and cherry. H. 29", W. 20½", D. 15¼". (Private collection; photo, David Bohl.) The decoration of the drawer fronts and side rails appears to be by a schoolgirl. This table is one of five with similar floral decoration on the top.

Figure 23 Detail of the top of the worktable illustrated in fig. 22. (Private collection; photo, Robert Mussey.)

have been responsible for the decoration on at least six lady's worktables with refined flower and leaf painting (figs. 22, 23) and a set of quartetto, curly-maple side tables with bamboo-turned legs and elaborate tops. The painter's naturalistic representation of the flowers, which he probably observed from life, allows for the identification of fifteen different species, all of which were grown contemporaneously in New England.[17]

Figure 24 Dressing table, Boston, Massachusetts, 1808–1815. Soft maple with eastern white pine. Dimensions not recorded. (Private collection; photo, David Bohl.)

A dressing table bearing the label of Boston looking-glass maker Stillman Lothrop (1780–1853) features a gilt version of the shell and seaweed motif associated with Penniman (fig. 24). The painter's use of silver leaf and gold-tinted glazing on the looking-glass balls complements the gilt shell and gives the decoration a bold yet idiosyncratic appearance. Penniman may have first met Lothrop while doing minor decorative painting for Dorchester cabinetmaker Stephen Badlam, in whose shop Stillman and his younger brother Edward apprenticed. In 1822 Penniman's shop was directly above Stillman Lothrop's, providing easy opportunity for their collaboration.[18]

Figure 25   Side chair from the shop of Samuel Gragg with decoration attributed to John Penniman, Boston, Massachusetts, 1808–1812. Birch, white oak, and beech. H. 34⅜", W. 18⅛", D. 25⅜". (Courtesy, Winterthur Museum.) The chair is branded "S.GRAGG / BOSTON" under the front rail and "PATENT" under the back rail. Gragg and John Penniman both leased space in Thomas Seymour's Boston furniture warehouse in 1809.

Figure 26   Detail of the decoration on the front legs and seat rail of the side chair illustrated in fig. 25. The use of faux-fluted panels with "mitered" corners, four colors of sienna and umber brown glazes, and faux-shadowing from the upper left resemble Penniman's work on the pier table illustrated in figs. 1, 2, and 8.

Samuel Gragg, who patented "elastic" bentwood chairs, was another important Boston furniture maker who appears to have contracted work to Penniman (fig. 25). As is the case with the Nichols pier table (fig. 1), many of Gragg's chairs have fluting simulated with multiple lines of shadowed striping (fig. 26). Some Gragg chairs also have gilt leaves and scrolls similar to those associated with Penniman. Others display spectacular peacock feathers composed of layers of three colors of gold powder applied in opposing directions (fig. 27).[19]

Figure 27   Side chair from the shop of Samuel Gragg, Boston, Massachusetts, 1808–1812. White oak with unidentified woods. Dimensions not recorded. (Private collection; photo, Robert Mussey Associ- ates.) The chair is branded "S.GRAGG / BOSTON" under the front rail. It has been repainted to match evidence from pigment analysis and microscopy of related chairs.

Other Painting Associated with Penniman

John Penniman began painting on a wide variety of surfaces during his teens and early twenties. He was born in the small rural town of Milford, Massachusetts, and claimed to have been self-taught. Penniman's earliest known work is a painted clock dial, which he signed and dated 1794. Fewer than a dozen of his documented dials are known, and the highest number he recorded next to his signature is sixteen. Since these numbers do not appear to have been chronological, they may have referred to account book entries.[20]

Penniman's use of relatively pale, unsaturated colors on moon dials and the style of his signature and numbering have cognates in the work of John Minott (1772–1826) and William Trescott. Since Penniman and Trescott were about the same age, it is possible both men trained or worked with Minott, who was one of the leading decorative painters in Boston and

Figure 28 Hood of a clock attributed to Thomas Seymour with decoration attributed to John Penniman, Boston, Massachusetts, 1809-1812. Mahogany, bird's-eye maple, and mahogany veneers, with white pine. H. 11¾", W. 22¼", D. 9⅞". (Courtesy, Metropolitan Museum of Art; photo, Peabody Essex Museum.) The movement is by Scottish immigrant clock maker James Doull. He worked for Aaron Willard from 1807 to 1808 before establishing his own shop in Charlestown in 1809. The brass finials are replaced.

Roxbury. Several of Penniman's painted dials also incorporate thick foliage branches or twigs as part of the fruit-painted decoration on dial corners, a feature found occasionally on English dials but not on those of other Boston painters. His favorite subject, however, was the Four Seasons (fig. 28).[21]

The scarcity of Penniman's signed dials suggests that he did clock work only early in his career, probably to support himself while endeavoring to become a portrait and landscape painter. His apprentices Alvan Fisher and Charles Codman followed a similar career path. Penniman's earliest known painting is a miniature self-portrait dated 1796 and inscribed "John R. Penniman age 14 years." An early photograph of the miniature bears the notation "From John R. Pennimans First Portrait age 14 years From a boys first Portrait taken from a looking glass age 14—the work of John R Penniman, Hardwick, Mass."[22]

Eight years later and with considerably more skill, Penniman painted at least four portraits of the Willard family. Aaron Willard Jr.'s portrait is signed, dated 1804, and inscribed with the sitter's age (fig. 29). Willard is shown sitting in a painted, bamboo-turned Windsor side chair wearing a high-collared, ruffled shirt and formal waistcoat. Although Penniman's

Figure 29   John Penniman, *Aaron Willard Jr.*, Boston, Massachusetts, 1804. Oil on canvas. 28" x 23". (Willard Clock Museum; photo, Gavin Ashworth.) Willard became a clockmaker like his father, Aaron Sr. Penniman painted at least six members of Willard's extended family between 1804 and 1810. Although the artist's shading of the face and hands displays subtle gradation, the background foliage is similar to that on Penniman's furniture painting.

portrait is reasonably realistic, the treatment of leafage in the background retains the distinctive hard-edged style of a decorative painter. Similar portraits of Aaron Sr., his daughter Nancy, and his house and clock-manufacturing complex also date circa 1804. The following year Penniman painted a portrait of Aaron Sr.'s wife, Susan (Bartlett), and in 1806 he provided a likeness of Willard's son-in-law, painter Spencer Nolen.

Between April 1803 and April 1805, Penniman purchased at least eight gilt picture frames from Boston gilder John Doggett. The latter's account books show that in return he received at least seventeen reverse glass–painted tablets from Penniman. The painter is not mentioned in subsequent entries, which suggests that he found another source for his frames. Penniman reputedly took instruction from Gilbert Stuart after the

Figure 30 Trade card of John Penniman, Boston, Massachusetts, 1822. Engraving on paper. 3" x 4". (Courtesy, American Antiquarian Society.) William B. Annin and George Girdler Smith based this engraving on a painted design by Penniman.

Figure 31 John Penniman, preparatory painting for a membership certificate for the New England Society for South Carolina, Boston, Massachusetts, 1820. Pen, ink, and wash on paper. 11⅝" x 15⅝". (Courtesy, American Antiquarian Society.) The painting is inscribed at the lower left "Design'd & Drawn by J. R. Penniman. Boston." Much of Penniman's known work between 1815 and 1830 consists of preparatory drawings and paintings for Boston's publishing industry.

Figure 32 John Penniman, *Circular Saw*, Boston, Massachusetts, 1826. Lithograph on paper. 3½" x 7". (Courtesy, American Antiquarian Society.) The lithograph is inscribed "the first original Drawing on Stone, in the United States by / J. Pendleton Boston J. R. Penniman / 1826." The earliest documented lithograph in the United States was done in 1819.

portraitist returned from England. Although there is no documentation for Penniman's training, he clearly admired Stuart and named his first son Gilbert Stuart Penniman (1811–1812).[23]

Penniman's oeuvre widened in the following years to include copies of portraits by artists such as Gerritt Schipper, classical and biblical scenes derived from printed sources, landscapes, and family groups. As Boston's printing and publishing industry expanded to become the city's fourth-largest employer by 1840, Penniman did paintings for engravings and lithographs (figs. 30, 31). One of his images, which served as the basis for a giant early sawmill blade, bears the pencil inscription "the first original Drawing on Stone, in the United States by / J. Pendleton Boston J. R. Penniman / 1826" (fig. 32). Penniman anticipated the importance of stone lithographic reproduction, which soon became dominant in printing. Like other Boston artists, he also produced paintings for patent applications, such as "Pianoforte in the shape of a Bentside Spinet," possibly an invention of innovative Boston piano maker Alpheus Babcock (fig. 33).[24]

Penniman painted a variety of subjects in Milton. In one of his landscapes, he pictured that town's most famous house, Unquety (Unquity)

Figure 33   John Penniman, *Pianoforte in the Shape of a Bentside Piano*, Boston, Massachusetts, 1829–1834. Watercolor on paper. 17" x 12". (Courtesy, Museum of Fine Arts, Boston.) The painting is inscribed "Drawn by Jnº. R. Penniman." He may have painted the watercolor to accompany a patent application by Boston pianoforte maker Alpheus Babcock. The fly is a reference to Mary Howitt's popular poem "The Spider and the Fly," published in 1829.

Figure 34 John Penniman, *Unquety House*, Milton, Massachusetts, 1827. Watercolor on embossed French writing paper. 7½" x 9¼". (Courtesy, Milton Historical Society; photo, Robert Mussey.) Penniman's name is written on the reverse.

(fig. 34), originally the summer home of loyalist governor Thomas Hutchinson. The latter's property was seized when he fled Massachusetts during the Revolutionary War and subsequently sold to James and Mercy Otis Warren. According to Milton historian Albert Teele, Penniman, with his plein air painter's tools, accompanied Boston's Light Infantry when it encamped on Hutchinson's Field (then the pasture of wealthy Boston merchant Barney Smith who had since bought Unquity) opposite Unquity in 1827. The artist also appears to have painted name boards for pianos made by Benjamin Crehore, who lived on Adams Street just four houses down (fig. 35).[25]

Figure 35 Detail of a name board on a pianoforte by Benjamin Crehore with decoration attributed to John Penniman, Milton, Massachusetts, 1815–1830. (Private collection; photo, Robert Mussey.)

In 1827 Penniman advertised that he was auctioning his stock-in-trade, tools, and art supplies and retiring to "follow his inclination in the higher branches of his art." The sale also included his "Sportsman's Basket containing a great variety of Marine Shells." By the mid-1830s he had moved his studio to West Brookfield, Massachusetts, west of Boston, evidently to be near his or his wife's family. His tendency to alcoholism had caught up to him. In the next few years, he apparently wandered the countryside soliciting work as a portrait and heraldic painter. Penniman's portraits from the early 1830s may be his finest work, but he never became successful enough as a fine art painter to support himself exclusively with that prestigious and better-paid genre. Throughout his career, he was forced to fall back on decorative painting.[26]

Figure 36   Detail of the painted peacock feathers on the back of a side chair from the shop of Samuel Gragg. (Private collection; photo, David Bohl.)

It is hard to escape the conclusion that the greatest achievements in Penniman's diverse career occurred during his collaboration with Thomas Seymour, James Cogswell, and Samuel Gragg (fig. 36). The Nichols pier table is a testament to his tremendous skill. The discovery of Penniman's signature and date on that table should allow scholars to identify other examples of his work and significantly broaden the identifiable body of his oeuvre.

ACKNOWLEDGMENTS   For assistance with this article, the authors thank Carol Damon Andrews, Gavin Ashworth, Georgia Barnhill, David Bohl, Flavia Cigliano, Wendy Cooper, Stuart Feld, Paul Foley, Rebecca Garcia, Linda Kaufman, Alexandra Kirtley, Darcy Kuronen, Johanna McBrien, Bill Pear, Sumpter Priddy III, Albert Sack, Anthony Sammarco, John Stephens, Page Talbott, Gerald W. R. Ward, and Gregory Weidman.

1. The pencil inscription was discovered by furniture conservator Christopher Shelton when the table was in the studio of Robert Mussey Associates for conservation under a grant from the Institute of Museum and Library Services. Portions are extremely difficult to read, and some small areas are worn from abrasion. Infrared photography and manipulation of a mosaic of enlarged image sections with various filters and enhancements with Photoshop© software allowed us to transcribe most of the script. Enough of Penniman's name remains to allow him to be clearly identified as the signer. Penniman frequently signed or initialed and often dated his paintings. His *Portrait of a Man* (Worcester Art Museum) is inscribed on the reverse "Painted by / John Ritto Penniman / Boston Jany 30 / 1804."

2. For more on Boston-area painters, see Alice Knotts Cooney, "Ornamental Painting in Boston, 1790–1830" (master's thesis, University of Delaware, 1978). Among the artisans she identified were Daniel Bartling, Charles Bullard, Charles and William Codman, Robert Cowen, Benjamin B. Curtis, George Davidson, Samuel Gore, Charles Hubbard, Spencer Nolen, Rea & Johnston, and Aaron Willard Jr. Irving W. Lyon, *The Colonial Furniture of New England* (Boston: Houghton, Mifflin & Co., 1891), pp. 53, 110, as cited in Cooney, p. 10.

3. *Columbian Centinel*, February 23, 1805; April 13, 1807; December 5, 1810.

4. For the Finlays, see Gregory R. Weidman, *Furniture in Maryland, 1740–1940: The Collection of the Maryland Historical Society* (Baltimore: Maryland Historical Society, 1981), nos. 53–57, 122, 133, 134, 150, 171, 172; and Lance Humphries, "Furniture, Patronage, and Perception: The Morris Suite of Baltimore Painted Furniture," in *American Furniture*, edited by Luke Beckerdite (Hanover, N.H.: University Press of New England, for the Chipstone Foundation, 2003), pp. 138–212. For the Waln furniture, see Jack Lindsey, "An Early Latrobe Furniture Commission," *Antiques* 139, no. 1 (January 1991): 208–19. Beatrice B. Garvan first attributed the Waln furniture and woodwork to Bridport in *Federal Philadelphia, 1785–1825: The Athens of the Western World* (Philadelphia: Philadelphia Museum of Art, 1987), pp. 90–93. For more on Bridport, see Alexandra Alevizatos Kirtley, "The Painted Furniture of Philadelphia: A Reappraisal," *Antiques* 169, no. 5 (May 2006): 134–45. *Columbian Centinel*, December 19, 1807.

5. Immigrant painters include Robert Cowen, William Cunnington, George Graham, Francis Lloyd, John McDuell, James McGibbon, James Sharp, Joseph Stokes, William Tolman, and John Worrall. Painters possibly of British origin include Thomas Benson, William Bittle, Nathaniel Bodge, William Dearborn, and Samuel Hastings. The authors compiled these names from Boston tax assessors' taking records, newspaper advertisements, Suffolk County Court dockets, and Paul J. Foley, *Willard's Patent Time Pieces: A History of the Weight-Driven Banjo Clock* (Norwell, Mass.: Roxbury Village Publishing, 2002), pp. 178–98.

6. The authors thank Bill Pear and Flavia Cigliano for providing access to the Nichols House archives and collection. "Inventory of Furniture, Rugs, Paintings, Tapestries, Etc. / [Arthur] H. Nichols Boston 1906"; Inventory of the Nichols House prepared after his wife Elizabeth's death in 1929; Inventory of the Nichols House prepared by Miss Rose Nichols, ca. 1930; Inventory of the Nichols House by Helen Homer, caretaker and wife of Rose's executor, 1960. In this latter inventory, the table illustrated in fig. 1 is identified as "painted and stencil decorated Empire console table that once belonged to John Hancock." Although

the latter history is implausible because Hancock died in 1793, the table could have belonged to his widow, Dorothy (Quincy), and her second husband, Capt. James Scott, and sold at one of three sales of Hancock House objects. The drawings are included in White's papers at the Winterthur Library and Museum. The authors thank Wendy Cooper for bringing these drawings to their attention. For more on White, see Rebecca Garcia, "Pigments and Pianos: Painter and Varnisher Lyman White" (master's thesis, University of Delaware, 2007). White became a member of the Massachusetts Charitable Mechanic Association in 1837. His stencils, designs, sketches, and pricked patterns indicate he was a competent artisan, although his designs were occasionally mechanical and geometric; Garcia, "Pigments and Pianos," p. 9.

7. Boston Tax Taking Records, Boston Public Library, Rare Books and Manuscripts Division. After circa 1817, ash began to appear as a secondary wood in the furniture of other leading craftsmen including (George) Archibald & (Thomas) Emmons and Isaac Vose. The mounting of the top assembly to the base assembly was modified somewhat during an earlier repair. The net effect was to lower the overall height of the top by 1". The reason for this change is not clear, but it resulted in making the signature more accessible to us once the top was unscrewed and removed.

8. Seymour's copy of the *Drawing-Book* is at the Museum of Fine Arts, Boston.

9. Carol Damon Andrews, "John Ritto Penniman, 1782–1842: An Ingenious Artist," *Antiques* 120, no. 1 (July 1981): 159, pl. 10.

10. The top was overpainted in the nineteenth century, possibly by Lyman White. The restorer approximately replicated the original colors and striping pattern.

11. Furniture scholar Wendy Cooper first noticed that the painting on these chairs was similar to that on the Nichols House pier table and generously shared her research with the authors. Four chairs from this set are known. Israel Sack, Inc. sold them to a private collector who subsequently lent the chairs to the New York State Museum. Sack later bought back two examples from the set. One of the privately owned examples remains in the New York State Museum, and the other was donated to the Winterthur Museum. The chairs are cited in Israel Sack, Inc., *American Antiques from Israel Sack Collection*, 10 vols. (New York: Highland House, 1988), 7: 1818, no. 5011; 9: 2439, no. 5011; 10: 2705, no. 6341. Another chair with an upholstered seat is pictured in Kinnaman & Ramaeker's advertisement in *Antiques* 78, no. 3 (March 1985): 506. The Winterthur chair is marked "I" on both the underside of the chair and on the caned seat frame and has "$6" written in pencil on the inner surface of the rear seat rail. The chair at the New York State Museum, which bears the inscription "Holdens," is marked with "II" in the same locations as the numeric marks on the Winterthur chair. Both chairs are made of birch, a wood more commonly used in Boston than in New York.

12. Joshua Holden married Mary Armstrong Mitchell (1782–1863) on April 27, 1802, and died at Westminster, Vermont, on December 17, 1852. The authors thank John Scherer of the New York State Museum for this genealogical information. According to the 1850 census, Holden's eldest son, Joshua, was a "painter" in Gardner, Massachusetts. Joshua Holden worked on Orange Street in Boston from 1813 to 1818. Tax assessments indicate that he occupied space in a building owned by cabinetmaker Isaac Vose. Holden employed several journeyman chair makers and chair painters. His tax valuations rose steadily, suggesting that he ran a successful shop; Boston Tax Taking Books, Ward 12, Boston Public Library, Rare Books and Manuscripts. Holden was on Orange Street in 1821 and Washington Street after 1824; Page Talbott, "The Furniture Industry in Boston, 1810–1835" (master's thesis, University of Delaware, 1974), p. 213.

13. *Columbian Centinel*, July 31, 1805. Joseph Peabody receipt, private collection. *Columbian Centinel*, September 12, 1809.

14. *Columbian Centinel*, August 25, 1810. As quoted in Mabel Swan, "John Ritto Penniman," *Antiques* 39, no. 5 (May 1941): 247.

15. Mabel Swan, "A Seymour Bill Discovered," *Antiques* 51, no. 4 (April 1947): 244. The receipt is illustrated in Vernon Stoneman, *John and Thomas Seymour: Cabinetmakers in Boston, 1794–1816* (Boston: Special Publications, 1959), p. 248, fig. 159.

16. Wendy A. Cooper, *Paul Revere's Boston, 1735–1818* (Boston: Museum of Fine Arts, 1975), p. 171, no. 207.

17. One dressing table is painted white, but the paint appears to be new, and the current location of the object is unknown; Dean A. Fales Jr., *American Painted Furniture, 1660–1880* (New York: E. P. Dutton, 1972), p. 106, fig. 177. Other examples of the form have mahogany exteriors but with beautifully developed gilt leafage, scrollwork, and striping ornamenting the

lyre supports for the mirrors. Dressing tables with gilt leafage on mirror brackets are in the collection of the Newark Museum and illustrated in Sack, *Antiques from Israel Sack Collection*, 8: 2130, no. 5581. For a dressing table owned by the Peabody Essex Museum and two work-tables, see Robert D. Mussey Jr., *The Furniture Masterworks of John & Thomas Seymour* (Salem, Mass.: Peabody Essex Museum, 2003), pp. 258, 314, 315, nos. 62, 90, 91. For the quartetto tables, see ibid., pp. 370–71, cat. no. 118, collection of Mrs. Linda Kaufman.

18. The table illustrated in fig. 24 may be the same example shown in Page Talbott, "Boston Empire Furniture, Part II," *Antiques* 109, no. 5 (May 1976): 1004, fig. 1. Stephen Badlam, "Remarkable Occurrences," private collection. This diary mentions the names of thirty-one of Badlam apprentices, including both of the Lothrops and John Doggett, and the dates of their terms. *Eastern Argus* (Portland, Maine), July 9, 1822, as cited in Andrews, "John Ritto Penniman," p. 161, n. 19. The address was 73 Market Street at the "Sign of the Red Cross Knight directly over the Gilding Manufactory of Mr. Stillman Lothrop." This article was republished with additional information and illustrations by the Worcester Art Museum in 1982. See also Carol Andrews, "The Penniman Coat-of-Arms Painted by John Ritto Penniman," typescript, 2003, New England Historic Genealogical Society, Boston.

19. Gragg was a tenant in Thomas Seymour's Boston furniture warehouse from 1808 to 1811; Boston Tax Taking Books, Boston Public Library. The former was listed in the 1801 tax records as "journeyman to Samuel Tuck," who was one of Seymour's business partners in the warehouse from 1804 to 1805; Mussey, *Furniture Masterworks*, p. 53. Several scholars have suggested that Penniman may have painted some Gragg chairs. See Michael Podmaniczky, "The Incredible Elastic Chairs of Samuel Gragg," *Antiques* 163, no. 5 (May 2003): 138–45. Advertisements in the *Columbian Centinel* (Boston) indicate that white furniture became fashionable for parlors and bedchambers beginning circa 1805. In the April 22, 1807, edition of that paper, the "Broad-Street Cabinet and Chair Manufactory" advertised "White and Gilt fancy Chairs, with cane seats, very elegant." Three years later (April 11, 1810) an auction at the house of "the late Charles Paine" included "white and gilt Settees and chairs." The most detailed account of white-painted furniture was in the November 21, 1810, edition, which listed "articles of rich Furniture, viz. White and gilt Bedsteads, with Cornices to match; white and gilt Bureaus; do do Toilet Tables; do do Wash Stands; do do fancy Chairs, various patterns and fabrics. The above are painted by a finished workman." Two years later (January 29, 1812), the paper reported on a sale featuring "white Bureaus," presumably for a bedchamber. White and gilt fancy chairs were the most commonly advertised forms.

20. Foley, *Willard's Patent Time Pieces*, p. 296. David Wood, "Concord, Massachusetts, Clockmakers, 1811–1831," *Antiques* 159, no. 5 (May 2001): 762–69. All of the information on Penniman's painted dials comes from Foley's book or personal communication with him.

21. Foley, *Willard's Patent Time Pieces*, pp. 178–79, 283–84, 300. This source lists Trescott incorrectly as Prescott.

22. Penniman's first shop was next to Simon Willard's (1803) and his second was at the rear of Aaron Willard's; Andrews, "John Ritto Penniman," p. 161 n. 18. The portrait is illustrated and discussed on p. 149, fig. 2.

23. John Doggett Account Books, Winterthur Library. Doggett had recently completed his apprenticeship with Stephen Badlam; Badlam, "Remarkable Occurrences." Quoted in Andrews, "John Ritto Penniman," from William Dunlap, *The History of the Rise and Progress of the Arts of Design in the United States*, 3 vols. (New York: George P. Scott, 1834), 2: 215. Andrews also cites James Flexner, *Gilbert Stuart: A Great Life in Brief* (New York: Alfred A. Knopf, 1955), p. 165, who states that Penniman was Stuart's favorite drapery painter.

24. The painting includes the anomalous image of a small fly, and its companion painting includes a spider. These are visual references to Mary Howitt's 1829 poem "The Spider and the Fly." The painting was reputedly found in the attic of a house built by Samuel Crehore on Adams Street in Milton. Samuel's house was across the street from the shop and house of his brother Benjamin, a pianoforte maker.

25. Albert K. Teele, *The History of Milton, Massachusetts, 1640–1887* (Boston: Rockwell & Churchill, 1887), pp. 134–44. The watercolor is executed on a fine French paper with floral embossed border and with French poetry quotations in the corners, each transcribed on the reverse in pencil; frame is not original. The house was destroyed in the 1950s.

26. *Columbian Centinel*, April 12, 1827. Andrews, "John Ritto Penniman," p. 156.

Figure 1 Campeche chair, probably New Orleans, Louisiana, ca. 1803–1810. Cherry, mahogany, and light wood inlay. H. 42½", W. 28¼", D. 33". (Private collection; photo, Gavin Ashworth.)

Diane C. Ehrenpreis

The Seat of State: Thomas Jefferson and the Campeche Chair

▼ THOMAS JEFFERSON (1743–1826) has long been associated with the Campeche chair, a lounging form with a curved, reclined back and a *sella curulis* base (fig. 1). Decorative arts historians have interpreted the example Jefferson owned as a reflection of his knowledge of classical design sources and his refined taste, in addition to its being an object that provided physical comfort during his later years. Recent research now ties Jefferson to the Campeche chair much earlier than previously thought and suggests that the form held multiple layers of meaning for him. Evidence indicates that he probably became interested in the Campeche chair after the Louisiana Purchase of 1803, when he acquired an example and used it as part of the furnishings in the President's House during his residency from 1801 to 1809. For Jefferson and his contemporaries, this chair form no longer alluded to its Roman imperial past but served as a reminder of the Louisiana Purchase and Jefferson's pivotal role in securing the West for the new nation.[1]

The Campeche chair traces its origins back to folding or cross-legged stools used in ancient Egypt and later Greece and Rome. In his *History of Rome*, Livy indicated that Roman officials had borrowed the *sella curulis* from their neighbors the Etruscans. An example can be seen on the silver denarius coin illustrated in figure 2. This version of the chair has curule legs situated laterally, with a boss at the intersection, and ball feet. These chairs became such a significant sign of power in the Roman Republic that their use was confined to consuls, praetors, and, eventually, Roman emperors. The *sella curulis* evolved into an emblem of authority and majesty and can be found on coins, medals, and monuments of the age.[2]

From its Roman origins, the cross-stool retained its function as a symbol of authority in Europe through the Middle Ages and into the Renaissance. One of the best-known survivals is Dagobert's Throne (fig. 3), once thought to be the throne of King Dagobert I of France (r. 623/29–639). This chair started out as a stool, and a back and armrests were added later in its life. It eventually entered the treasury of the abbey of St.-Denis outside Paris, where Abbot Suger (1081–1155) noted, "We also restored the noble throne of the glorious King Dagobert, on which, as tradition relates, the Frankish kings sat to receive the homage of their nobles after they had assumed power. We did so in recognition of its exalted function and because of the value of the work itself." The stool remained at St.-Denis until 1791, when the turmoil of the French Revolution led to its removal to the Cabinet of Antiquities and eventually to its current home, the Bibliothèque nationale de France.[3]

Figure 2 Silver denarius of P. Cornelius P.f.L.n. Lentulus, Rome mint, ca. 74 B.C. Diam. ⁹⁄₁₆". (Courtesy, Yale University Art Gallery, Numismatic Collection Transfer; photo, Alex Contreras.)

During the Renaissance, the curule stool evolved into a chair with a back and attained widespread popularity throughout Europe and Britain. By the sixteenth and seventeenth centuries, a variation of the *sella curulis* known as the *sillon da cadera* (fig. 4) was widely used in Spain. In addition to having a superstructure of posts, arms, and a low back, the *sillon da cadera* also had crossed legs oriented to face forward. The Spanish conquistadors brought the *sillon da cadera* to the New World, and the Campeche chair developed in Mexico from those antecedents. The chair took on the name of the port city of Campeche on the Yucatán Peninsula, which was a primary export center for this form as well as for logwood, a dyewood commonly known as Campeche wood. From Mexico, the Campeche chair made its way to the Spanish territory of Louisiana.[4]

North American chair makers began producing these chairs around 1800. In New Orleans, where the form was in considerable demand, the archetypal Campeche chair has a tall demilune crest, a leather back and seat, flat arms with scrolled terminals, shaped arm supports, a flat front stretcher, and a curule base. The chair illustrated in figure 1 is an early example distinguished by having twelve inlaid stars on its crest. Inlaid crests are relatively common on New Orleans Campeche chairs, but typically the ornament is floral. Although the basic form of the New Orleans Campeche chair remained relatively unchanged, later examples often have turned arm supports and stretchers and occasionally finials with plinths (fig. 5).[5]

Figure 4 Folding chair (*sillon de cadera*), Granada, Spain, ca. 1500. Walnut, ivory, bone, mother-of-pearl, tin. H. 36½", W. 24", D. 19½". (Courtesy, Metropolitan Museum of Art, Fletcher Fund, 1945; photo, Art Resource, NY.)

Figure 5 Campeche chair, probably New Orleans, Louisiana, 1810–1825. Mahogany with white oak and satinwood. H. 37", W. 26¾", D. 27½". (Courtesy, Louisiana State University Museum of Art, gift of D. Benjamin Kleinpeter; photo, David Humphreys.) New Orleans Campeche chairs are often made of mahogany, but some are constructed of local woods, particularly walnut.

Figure 6 Thomas Sully, *Thomas Jefferson*, 1856. Oil on canvas. 34½" x 27½". (Courtesy, Thomas Jefferson Foundation, Monticello; photo, Edward Owen.) Sully made this copy after his earlier full-length life portrait of Jefferson done for the United States Military Academy at West Point in 1821.

It is well documented that a New Orleans Campeche chair was part of the eclectic furnishings with which Thomas Jefferson (fig. 6) surrounded himself, especially during his lengthy retirement at Monticello (fig. 7) and Poplar Forest (fig. 8). In the summer of 1819, when the seventy-six-year-old Jefferson was ill at Poplar Forest, he asked his daughter Martha Jefferson Randolph (1772–1836) to send him a Campeche chair, because "While too weak to set up the whole day, and afraid to increase the weakness by lying down, I longed for a Siesta chair which would have admitted the medium position. I must therefore pray you send by Henry the one made by Johnny Hemings." Forty years later, Jefferson's granddaughter Ellen Randolph Coolidge (1796–1876) recalled that chair's location in Monticello, noting, "In the large Parlour, with it's parquetted floor, stood the Campeachy chair, made of goat skin, sent to him from New Orleans, where, in the shady twilight, I was used to seeing him resting." Indeed, Ellen not only observed his rest but was one of his favorite evening companions. Shortly after Ellen's marriage in 1825, her sister Virginia Randolph Trist (1801–1882) wrote: "Grandpapa's health is steadily improving, but I fear he misses you sadly

Figure 7   Monticello, Charlottesville, Virginia. (Courtesy, Thomas Jefferson Foundation, Monticello; photo, Peter Hatch.) Jefferson may have sat in one of his Campeche chairs under this portico.

Figure 8   Poplar Forest, Lynchburg, Virginia. (Courtesy, Thomas Jefferson's Poplar Forest; photo, Les Schofer.) Campeche chairs made up part of the furnishing plan at Jefferson's retreat Poplar Forest.

Figure 9   Parlor, Monticello, Charlottesville, Virginia. (Courtesy, Thomas Jefferson Foundation, Monticello; photo, Edward Owen.) Jefferson used two Campeche chairs in the parlor, one on either side of the door to the portico. One chair was next to a bust of Napoleon Bonaparte.

Figure 10   Gilbert Stuart, *Thomas Jefferson*, 1805. Oil on wood. 26¼" x 21¾". (Courtesy, National Portrait Gallery, Smithsonian Institution, and Thomas Jefferson Foundation; photo, H. Andrew Johnson.)

every evening when he takes his seat in one of the campeachy chairs, & he looks so solitary & the empty chair on the opposite side of the door is such a melancholy sight to us all, that one or the other of us is sure to go to occupy it." Virginia's letter is evidence that two Campeche chairs were in the parlor, placed on either side of the door that led to the west portico and the lawn beyond (fig. 9). This proximity to the door, coupled with their relatively lightweight frames, meant that these Campeche chairs could also have been used outdoors. None of the family documents mentions what drew Jefferson to this form, but recent research indicates that his association with the chairs began during his presidency and that he most likely sought them out because of their unique ties to New Orleans and the Louisiana Territory.[6]

After being sworn in as president in March 1801, Thomas Jefferson (fig. 10) faced the troubling issue of France and Spain using the Louisiana Territory as a colonial pawn and the possibility that these imperial powers would block American trade into the port of New Orleans. To address this concern, President Jefferson authorized Robert Livingston (1746–1813), United States minister to France, and envoy James Monroe (1758–1831) to negotiate the purchase of what was known as the Isle of Orleans and part of West Florida from France. In April 1803, to the astonishment of these diplomats, Napoleon Bonaparte (1769–1821) offered to sell the whole of the Louisiana Territory, an area far larger and more expensive than originally proposed. Livingston and Monroe swiftly agreed to the $15,000,000 price, however, because the advantages for the United States were too numerous to deny. In addition to gaining control of New Orleans, which was Jefferson's original intent, the purchase would double the size of the United States at a cost of less than 3¢ per acre. Charles Talleyrand-Périgord (1754–1838), Napoleon's minister of foreign affairs, told Livingston, "You have made a noble bargain for yourselves, and I suppose you will make the most of it."[7]

On July 3, 1803, Jefferson received word that the treaty had been signed in Paris on April 30, 1803. The American public learned the news on July 4, a propitious day associated with Jefferson as author of the Declaration of Independence. His friend Caspar Wistar (1761–1818) recorded that Jefferson and his contacts considered the Louisiana Purchase "the most important & beneficial transaction which has occurred since the declaration of Independence, & next to it, most like to influence and regulate the destinies of our Country." France handed New Orleans over on December 20, 1803, with word reaching Jefferson on January 15, 1804. As scholar Junius P. Rodriguez noted, Jefferson was among the first "to comprehend the coast-to-coast notion of American identity that would come to be called Manifest Destiny by the 1840s." This singular presidential decision opened up the West to the young nation, offering the potential for growth and greatness to future generations.[8]

After appointing William C. Claiborne (1775–1817) territorial governor, Jefferson immediately set as a priority the exploration of these vast new lands. He sent the now-famous Lewis and Clark Expedition into the North-

UNDER MY WINGS EVERY THING PROSPERS

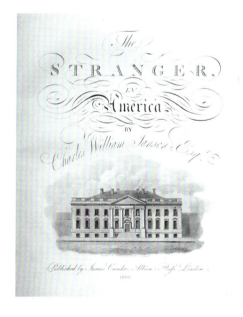

Figure 11 John L. Boqueta de Woiseri, *A View of New Orleans Taken from the Plantation of Marigny*, New Orleans, Louisiana, 1804. Aquatint on paper. 11⅝" x 21⁷⁄₁₆". (Courtesy, Historic New Orleans Collection, Museum/Research Center.)

Figure 12 "The President's House," title page engraving. Chas. W. Janson, *Stranger in America* (London: J. Cundee, 1807). (Courtesy, Rare Book and Special Collections Division, Library of Congress.) This illustration shows how the house looked during Jefferson's term.

west, but he was equally interested in the smaller Territory of Orleans to the south, which included the city of New Orleans (fig. 11). In 1804 Jefferson deputized William Dunbar (1749–1810), a scientist, inventor, and planter from Natchez, to explore the southern Mississippi Valley, in what came to be known as the Red River Expedition. Jefferson himself researched and wrote a report titled *The Limits and Bounds of Louisiana* (1804), which reviewed the region's history of exploration and ownership by Spain and France in order to delineate the boundaries of the new territory. The report was not widely circulated, but the newspapers of the day gave the content considerable coverage. While some federalist commentators criticized Jefferson's report for overstating the merits of the region, it offered preliminary information to a nation eager to learn more about the new territory and its history. Moreover, it demonstrates the high level of interest and personal attention Jefferson gave to the acquisition of the Louisiana territory.[9]

Jefferson was not satisfied with just written reports on the new territory, he wanted specimens, objects, and visitors to come to the President's House (fig. 12). On November 29, 1804, Pierre Derbigny (1769–1829), Jean Noël Destrehan (1754–1823), Pierre Sauve (1749–1822), and the territorial governor, William Claiborne, dined with Jefferson. The French Louisianans had gone to Washington to protest the Governance Act of 1804, which had not created any elected offices or representation for the new American territory. There is no mention of this meeting in Jefferson's papers, but New Hampshire Senator William Plumer (1759–1850), a federalist, wrote "that [Jefferson] . . . has not made enquires of them relative either to their government, or the civil or natural history of their country—That he studiously avoided conversing with them upon every subject that had relation to their mission here." Despite his curiosity about the new territory, Jefferson may have felt that it would have been imprudent to discuss the delegation's demands while the appointed governor sat at the table. After dining at the President's House just a few days later, Plumer noted that Jefferson had "on the table two bottles of water brought from the river Mississippi." Whether the New Orleans contingent or Governor Claiborne presented the river water to Jefferson as a curiosity is unknown, but it is likely that one or both brought other objects representative of their region, perhaps including a Campeche chair.[10]

In addition to receiving specimens brought from the new territory by explorers and visitors, Jefferson requested items of specific interest. On August 18, 1808, he wrote to William Brown, collector of the customs for the District of Mississippi, asking for a "campeachy hammock, made of some vegetable substance netted, [which] is commonly to be had at New Orleans. Having no mercantile correspondent there, I take the liberty of asking you to procure me a couple of them & to address them to New York, Philadelphia, or any port in the Chesapeake, to the care of the Collector." Brown was likely entrusted with this task by virtue of his ties to Jefferson through mutual Trist family in-laws. By October 10, 1808, Brown had fulfilled his commission, but the schooner carrying the hammocks was lost at sea. Although some scholars have posited that the term "campeachy hammock" might be interchangeable with "campeachy chair," a recently discovered Trist family letter notes that the former was a woven-fiber sling. When he ordered the hammocks in early 1809, Jefferson was nearing the end of his second presidential term and looking forward to his return to private life. Although it is not known what he intended to do with the hammocks, he may well have planned to install them at either Monticello or Poplar Forest.[11]

Jefferson also procured objects from Thomas Bolling Robertson (1779–1828), a Virginian who moved to the Territory of Orleans after finishing his law studies in 1806. A year after Robertson's arrival in the territory, Jefferson appointed him to the office of secretary of the Territory of Orleans. In 1819 Robertson wrote Jefferson:

> I transmit to you a small volume of letters. . . . I hope you will give it the advantage of an agreeable attitude while seated in your Campeachy chair. Many years ago you asked me to send you a few of these chairs; embargo, war, the infrequency of communication between N.O. and the ports of Virginia and my being in Congress prevented me from complying with your request. Meeting with some two weeks ago on the Levee and hearing that there was a vessel then up from Richmond I had them put on; one I sent to my father and the other to you, two men on earth whom I most highly respect. I hope it may answer your expectations; if you wish for more I can now at any time procure and forward them to you.

Although Robertson was not able to send the chairs until nearly a decade after Jefferson left office and after encountering what may have been venture cargo examples on the levee (fig. 13), his letter is proof that Jefferson first asked for Campeche chairs before the Embargo Act, which took effect in December 1807. This indicates that Jefferson knew about the Campeche chair form and was seeking an example for his own use, either publicly or privately, while he resided in the President's House.[12]

Figure 13 Benjamin Henry Latrobe, *View from the Window of My Chamber at Tremoulet's Hotel, New Orleans*, 1819. Pencil, ink, and watercolor on paper. 9" x 11⁷⁄₁₆". (Courtesy, Maryland Historical Society.)

Figure 14 Editorial, *Daily National Intelligencer*, July 28, 1827. From *19th Century U.S. Newspapers*. (Courtesy, Gale/Cengage Learning.)

TO THE EDITORS.

GENTLEMEN : Passing down the Avenue yesterday, I was attracted by an article which was standing in the Cabinet Warehouse of Mr. Henry V. Hill. It is a large *Writing and Reading Chair*, made, as I understood, for the Department of State ; and, for convenience and ingenuity, it excels any I have ever seen. It is of mahogany, made in the form of those Spanish Chairs introduced here by Mr. Jefferson. The legs are short and firm, the back high, and the seat formed of a large sheet of leather suspended from the top of the back, and coming round in a sweep to the front of the frame below, being regulated in its degree of tension by a roller with rack and pinion. The chair has two elbows, made low, and on the outside of that on the right side is an upright iron pillar, from which proceeds a strong arm of iron with a double join, carrying at its extremity a small convenient writing desk, which may be drawn round in front of the person who sits in the chair, or thrown back, or drawn in close to the right hand, at pleasure. The height of this desk is capable of being varied by a screw, so that by means of this double motion, it may be brought into almost any position that the ease of the writer may require Placed before a bright winter fire, this most convenient establishment secures to a studious man the utmost luxury of comfort, and I feel confident that its general adoption will well reward the ingenuity of the deserving artist who constructed it.

                        S.

The New Orleans Campeche chair that Robertson sent to Monticello in August 1819 was not the first example Jefferson had owned. A July 28, 1827, editorial in the *Daily National Intelligencer* reported (fig. 14):

> Passing down the Avenue yesterday, I was attracted by an article which was standing in the Cabinet Warehouse of Mr. Henry V. Hill. It is a large *Writing and Reading Chair*, made, as I understood, for the Department of State; and, for convenience and ingenuity, it excels any I have ever seen. It is of mahogany, made in the form of those Spanish Chairs introduced here by Mr. Jefferson. The legs are short and firm, the back high, and the seat formed of a large sheet of leather suspended from the top of the back, and coming round in a sweep to the front of the frame below, being regulated in its degree of tension by a roller with rack and pinion. The chair has two elbows, made low, and on the outside of that on the right side is an upright iron pillar, from which proceeds a strong arm of iron with a double join, carrying at its extremity a small convenient writing desk, which may be drawn round in front of the person who sits in the chair, or thrown back, or drawn in close to the right hand, at pleasure. The height of this desk is capable of being varied by a screw, so that by means of this double motion, it may be brought into almost any position that the ease of the writer may require. Placed before a bright winter fire, this most convenient establishment secures to a studious man the utmost luxury of comfort, and I feel confident that its general adoption will well reward the ingenuity of the deserving artist who constructed it. S.

The author's intent may have been to promote cabinetmaker Henry V. Hill's warehouse, located on Pennsylvania Avenue between 4½ and 6th Streets Northwest, but the notice offers substantial historical information. The chair described in the editorial is clearly of the Campeche form. In reference to seating, the descriptors "Spanish" and "Campeche" were synonymous in the nineteenth century.[13]

The source of Hill's knowledge of Campeche chairs is not known. He appears to have begun his career at least five years after Jefferson left office and is not mentioned in the latter's financial accounts or correspondence. If

Hill's Campeche chair was commissioned by the Department of State, as the editorial suggests, that form may have been specified because of its association with Jefferson, who was the first secretary of state under George Washington. The author's reference to "those Spanish chairs introduced here by Mr. Jefferson" suggests local familiarity with the seating form and reverence for the former president, who by 1827 was considered an icon of the American Revolution and a leading architect of the new republic. Since Jefferson left office eighteen years earlier and never returned to Washington, his introduction of Campeche chairs must have occurred during his presidential term—supporting the hypothesis that a Campeche chair sat in the President's House and was seen by Jefferson's visitors. How and when Jefferson acquired his first example is not known, but the most likely scenario is that it arrived after the Louisiana Territory came under American control in 1803.[14]

Jefferson's family preserved two Campeche chairs as relics of their famous ancestor, but both are too late to be the example that he presumably used in the President's House. The first chair (fig. 15) has a mahogany frame with a curule base, a flat front stretcher, baluster-shaped arm supports mounted to the outside of the side rail, and flat, S-curved arms, but no turned com-

ponents. The most striking feature is the extremely tall back and integral upholstered crest. Earlier Campeche chairs typically have applied demilune crests made of wood. The pared-down design of this example suggests that it dates 1815–1820. It may well be the chair that Robertson acquired for Jefferson in New Orleans in August 1819 and that the latter's granddaughter Ellen Randolph Coolidge described several years later as "made of goat skin . . . [and] from New Orleans."[15]

After Jefferson's death, the chair illustrated in figure 15 passed to his grandson Thomas Jefferson Randolph (1792–1875) of Edgehill in Albemarle County, Virginia. Randolph's December 1875 estate inventory listed "1 arm chair (upright tall back) 4.00," which could refer to this chair. The Campeche chair remained at Edgehill until circa 1894, when Randolph's granddaughter Jane Randolph Harrison Randall (1862–1926) took it to Baltimore. Jane's husband and son subsequently sold the chair and several other family objects to Monticello.[16]

The other Campeche chair (fig. 16) came down in the family of Virginia Randolph Trist who, with her husband, Nicholas (1800–1874), and young children, was the last Jefferson descendant to live at Monticello. In 1828 her sister Cornelia Randolph (1799–1871) wrote that Virginia's daughter

Martha "begs to be put in the 'yed [yard] chair' (the campeache) she is also very affectionate." Cornelia's use of "yed chair" and "campeache" as interchangeable terms lends credence to the theory that Campeche chairs were occasionally taken outdoors. About 1828 Nicholas Trist accepted a position at the Department of State and went to Washington, D.C., ahead of his family. On May 8, 1829, he wrote Virginia: "I shall want you to send . . . the low chair (like the one Jefferson gave Mrs. Carr) wh. I left in the pavilion." Although Campeche chairs are not often described as "low chairs," Trist may have been referring to the height of the seat rather than the height of the back. Since he did not use the proper term for such seating, he offered a comparison to a chair given by his wife's brother to a Mrs. Carr. A Campeche chair reputedly owned by a Mrs. Carr, a cousin and neighbor of the Randolphs, remains in the family (fig. 17). The Carr chair is a slightly later version of the Campeche form, featuring turned stretchers in the front and back, simplified arms, and terminal bosses on the crest and curule base.[17]

Figure 17 Campeche chair, probably Albemarle County, Virginia, 1815–1830. Cherry. H. 41", W. 23½", D. 51½". (Courtesy, Thomas Jefferson Foundation, Monticello; photo, Gavin Ashworth.)

The Trist chair in figure 16 is made of mahogany and follows the traditional Campeche form fairly closely. Two notable deviations are the tapering arm supports mounted on top of the seat rails and the scalloped crest rail. Another nearly identical Campeche chair is known but has no history. Because of its unusual design and family history, decorative arts scholars have suggested that the Trist chair is the one described as "made by Johnny Hemings" in Jefferson's 1819 letter. However, it now appears these chairs were made in the New Orleans area and sent to Nicholas P. Trist in 1818, when he lived at Monticello as a guest of Thomas Jefferson.[18]

After Jefferson's death, his family struggled with the loss of their patriarch and the crushing debt he left behind. In an effort to stave off financial ruin, Jefferson's heirs sold slaves, livestock, farm equipment, and furnishings from Monticello at public auction in January 1827. A document titled "Inventory of the furniture in the house at Monticello" appears to be a list of the items intended for sale rather than a complete inventory of the house's contents, since it does not mention certain furnished rooms or such common furniture forms as desks. The sale inventory lists two Campeche chairs, both located in the drawing room. Tradition maintains that David Fowler, a Charlottesville cabinetmaker and coffin maker, purchased one of the chairs, but no documentation verifying that history is known. However, his signature on a petition asking the Virginia General Assembly to save a bust of Jefferson and place it at the University of Virginia's library confirms his presence at the sale.[19]

George Blaetterman (1788–1850), a professor of languages at the University of Virginia and one of the five original professors hired by Jefferson, clearly purchased one of the Campeche chairs in the 1827 sale (fig. 18). Other purchases included a large marble-top table, two dumbwaiters, artwork, and nine chairs, the latter totaling $21.37. By comparison, the Campeche chair cost $18.00. In 1902 George Walter Blatterman (1820–1910), who changed the spelling of his last name, noted that "Dr. Blaetterman purchased a quantity of second hand furniture, at the sale [including] . . . a 'siesta' chair which came from Spain—covered in red leather and with 13 stars at the head." The professor kept the chair at his home outside Charlottesville until his death in 1850. His estate inventory listed parlor furnishings including "1 Jefferson's chair" valued at $1.50 and a marble table valued at $10.00. The

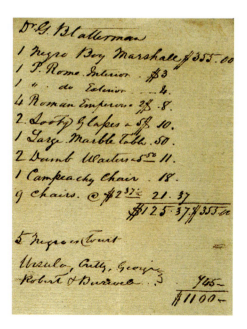

Figure 18 "File of Unsettled Bills to Purchase Articles at the Sale at Monticello, January 1827". (Courtesy, Albert and Shirley Small Special Collections Library, University of Virginia.)

table may have been the example Blaetterman purchased at Monticello. An account of Blaetterman's estate sale suggests that Thomas Jefferson Randolph purchased both objects, which were described as "1 Marble Table . . . $6.00/ 1 Chair . . . $4.00." Randolph may have taken the chair and table back to Edgehill, but there is no definitive mention of either piece in his estate records.[20]

A New Orleans Campeche chair that descended in the Trist-Gilmer families (fig. 1) appears to be similar to the example Blaetterman purchased at Monticello. The twelve inlaid stars on the crest of the Trist-Gilmer chair possibly represent the original twelve parishes that made up the Territory of Orleans (fig. 19). Although George Walter Blatterman wrote that the chair

Figure 19 Detail of the star inlays on the crest of the Campeche chair illustrated in fig. 1. (Photo, Gavin Ashworth.)

his foster father purchased at Monticello had "13 stars at the head," it is likely that there were only twelve. Blatterman's memory could have been flawed, or he may have associated the number of stars with the number of original colonies, which would have been logical, given Jefferson's involvement in the American Revolution.[21]

Little is known about the early history of the chair illustrated in figure 1, except that it descended in the Gilmer family, who had multiple connections to Jefferson, the Trist family, and the Louisiana Territory. Elizabeth House Trist (ca. 1751–1828) was Jefferson's lifelong friend, and her son Hore Browse Trist (1775–1804) moved to New Orleans and was appointed by Jefferson collector of the customs for the District of Mississippi in 1803. A year later he died of fever, leaving two sons, his widow, and his widowed mother alone in Louisiana. After her return to Virginia in 1809, Elizabeth House Trist lived with her niece Mary House Gilmer (1785–1853) and her husband, Peachy Gilmer (1779–1836), in Henry and later Bedford counties, but she also spent long spells with friends in Albemarle County. Her grandson Nicholas Philip Trist became Jefferson's private secretary and in 1824 married the latter's granddaughter Virginia Randolph.[22]

Writing from his home in Liberty, Virginia, on January 14, 1821, attorney Peachy Gilmer asked Jefferson: "Mrs. Trist some time ago presented me a campeachy chair, which had been sent for her to Monticello, and informed me that you had been so obliging, as to offer it sent to Poplar Forest." A few days later Jefferson wrote: "the chair which is the subject of your letter . . .

was sent to Poplar Forest the last summer, and has only awaited the order of Mrs. Trist or yourself. I write Mr. Yancy this day to deliver it to any person under your order." Jefferson's letter to Yancy described the chair as being "crosslegged covered with red Marocco" and noted that it could be "distinguished from the one of the same kind sent up last by wagon as being of a brighter fresher colour, and having a green ferret across the back, covering a seam in the leather." From Jefferson's description, he is concisely expressing details to help Yancy distinguish between two very similar chairs, ones not likely made at Monticello, only transshipped from there. This rules out examples made by John Hemmings and indicates that there were two imported Campeche chairs very similar in appearance at Poplar Forest in 1820. This exchange might reference the Campeche chair illustrated in figure 1 and Jefferson's missing chair with inlaid stars. However, these chairs, which may date to about 1803, were approximately a decade old at the time. Other possible candidates are the Trist chair shown in figure 16 and its near mate that has no provenance.[23]

The Campeche Chair through Jefferson's Eyes
When he took office, Jefferson introduced a tone at the President's House and public events that was considerably less aristocratic than that of his federalist predecessors. Through his Republican platform, he sought to establish a less-restrictive social hierarchy and usher in an era of simplicity in politics as well as in everyday life. On January 30, 1804, the *National Intelligencer* alluded to the egalitarian spirit of his administration in its description of a ball celebrating the transfer of the Louisiana Territory:

> The plain unembellished walls of our rooms, the want of splendor, and of that admiration which painting, and gilding, & all artful scenery of architecture can produce, and the still plainer quality of our manners, may, perhaps, to a foreign eye, and to foreign habits, place the grade of such a public festival far below the spectacles that celebrate the achievements of Warriors, or the peace that only suspends . . . destruction—But what humanity rejoices in the extension of the empire of freedom, and of peace, the superficial effects of the arts of the painter, and of the gilder, vanish before the splendor of the event, and put place and form out of consideration.

The Republicans were proud that they had found a peaceful way to expand the nation, while shunning "spectacles that celebrate the achievements of Warriors." From their perspective, the Louisiana Purchase was majestic in and of itself.[24]

As wonders from the new territory arrived in Washington, Jefferson displayed them at the President's House so that visitors would be edified and entertained. Depending on when they came, the public could have seen Native American weapons, furs, antlers, skeletons, exotic plants, and live animals, including a magpie and grizzly bear cubs. Many of these specimens were collected during the Lewis and Clark Expedition into the upper Louisiana Territory, shipped south to New Orleans, and from there carried to Washington, Philadelphia, or Monticello. Additional material came from William Dunbar's Red River Expedition of 1804. The public may have

Figure 20 Southeast wall of the entrance hall at Monticello. (Courtesy, Thomas Jefferson Foundation, Monticello; photo, Charles Shoffner.)

Figure 21 Dining room at Monticello. (Courtesy, Thomas Jefferson Foundation, Monticello; photo, Philip Beaurline.) Jefferson kept a volume by Livy on the mantelpiece.

been introduced to the Campeche chair through one of Jefferson's exhibits, since the novelty of that lounging form and its allusions to Spanish culture would have made it appropriate for display. Jefferson's penchant for natural history exhibits was well known even before his retirement, as the entry, or Indian, hall at Monticello attests (fig. 20). At the President's House and Monticello, citizens had the opportunity to learn about the Louisiana Territory and embrace it as an exciting and accessible addition to the nation.[25]

From Jefferson's perspective, the Campeche chair was more than a totem of the Louisiana Purchase. His classical education meant he had not only read Livy, whose history of Rome mentioned the *sella curulis*, but considered that text essential reading for students, including his own granddaughters. In 1814 Boston visitor Francis Calley Gray (1790–1856) noted that the mantel in Jefferson's dining room (fig. 21) was furnished with "many books of all kinds, Livy, Orosious, Edinburgh Review, 1 vol. of Edgeworth's Moral Tales, etc., etc."[26]

Jefferson had many opportunities to see curule stools when he served as minister to France from 1784 to 1789. In 1785 he toured the Gothic basilica of St.-Denis, the burial place of French kings and the repository of the treasury, which at that time included Dagobert's throne (fig. 3). From this relic, Jefferson would have learned that curule seating was not limited to Republican or Imperial Rome but had survived to become a symbol of authority in Europe into the Middle Ages and beyond.[27]

While visiting Versailles and other royal palaces, Jefferson would have encountered *pliants*, which are a variation of the *sella curulis* (fig. 22). *Pliants*, made as either folding or fixed versions of the crossed-legged stool, became

Figure 22 Jean-Baptiste-Claude Sené, folding stool, Paris, France, 1786. Beech. H. 18¼", W. 27", D. 20¼". (Courtesy, Metropolitan Museum of Art, gift of Mr. and Mrs. Charles Wrightsman; photo, Art Resource, NY.) This stool is from a set of sixty-four commissioned for the palaces of Fontainebleau and Compiègne in 1786. Examples from this set or similar stools may have been at the Hôtel du Garde-Meuble when Jefferson visited in September 1786.

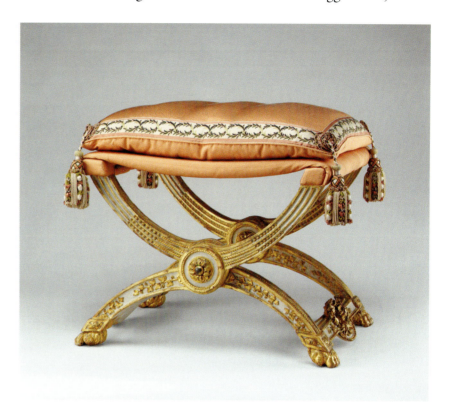

common fixtures in public apartments, where court etiquette established by Louis XIV (1638–1715) mandated that only persons of suitable rank were allowed to sit in the presence of the king or queen. When such permission was granted, the recipient typically sat on a *pliant*. Through such use, the *pliant* became a powerful symbol of imperial authority.[28]

Jefferson may have seen an evocative representation of a *pliant* when he attended the Paris Salon of 1787. As Pietro Antonio Martini's (1738–1797) *Exposition au Salon du Louvre en 1787* indicates, Adélaïde Labille-Guiard's (1749–1803) portrait *Adélaïde of France, Daughter of Louis XV, Known as Madame Adélaïde* (1787) was prominently displayed at the exhibition (fig. 23). Madame Adélaïde (1732–1800) was the daughter of Louis XV (1710–1774)

Figure 23 Pietro Antonio Martini, *Exposition au Salon du Louvre en 1787*. Engraving on paper. 12¾" x 19¼". (Courtesy, Bibliothèque nationale de France, Paris.)

and aunt of the increasingly unpopular King Louis XVI (1754–1793). The carved and gilded *pliant* in the foreground of Madame Adélaïde's portrait (fig. 24) and the medallion profiles of her parents and brother associate her with the stability and majesty of the royal family's earlier generation. Although Jefferson never mentioned this painting, he may have seen it when he visited Labille-Guiard's Paris studio. A September 9, 1786, entry in his memorandum book recorded, "Pd. Mlle. Guyard for picture 240f."[29]

On the same day, Jefferson "Paid seeing Gardes meubles 12f." The Hôtel du Garde-Meuble held the workshops and administrative arm responsible for furnishing the royal palaces and served as a warehouse for fine furniture, art, the crown jewels, and other historic relics. During his visit, Jefferson may have seen furniture commissioned for the nobility, including neoclassical versions of the *pliant* (fig. 22), which were enjoying a revival at that time.[30]

Although Jefferson furnished many rooms in his Paris house, no *pliants* or other curule forms were listed among the furniture he brought back to

Figure 24 Adélaïde Labille-Guiard, *Adélaïde of France, Daughter
of Louis XV, Known as "Madame Adélaïde,"* Paris, France, 1787. Oil
on canvas. 106¾" x 76¼". (Courtesy, Châteaux de Versailles et de
Trianon, Versailles; Réunion des Musées Nationaux /Art
Resource, NY; photo, Gérard Blot / Jean Schormans.)

America in 1790. At that date, this class of seating may not have appealed to
Jefferson because of its association with absolutism. By the time he acquired
a Campeche chair, however, more than a decade had passed since the fall of
the Bourbon monarchy, and the Campeche chair's classical lineage and later
popularity in the Louisiana Territory offered rich possibilities as an emblem
of Jefferson's republican vision for America.[31]

   After serving his term, Jefferson made sure that his role in the Louisiana
Purchase was demonstrated through his arrangement of art and furniture at
Monticello. He kept two Campeche chairs in the large parlor on either side

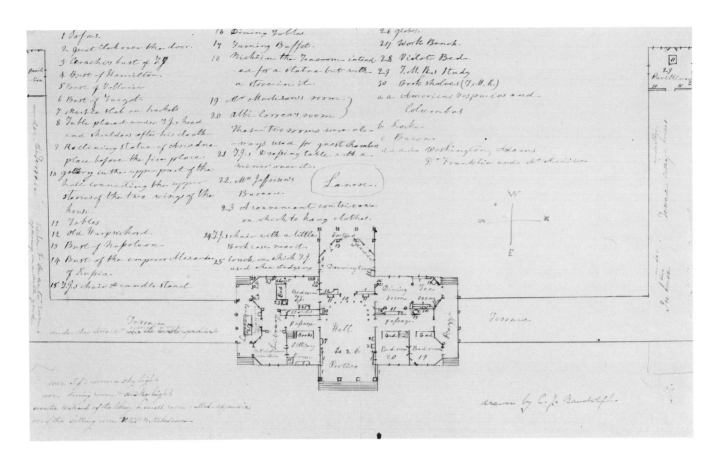

Figure 25 *Plan of the first floor of Monticello
Drawn by Cornelia J. Randolph*, ca. 1826. Ink on
paper. 8¼" x 13". (Courtesy, Albert and Shirley
Small Special Collections Library, University of
Virginia.) Cornelia Jefferson Randolph's floor
plan includes major works of art and large pieces
of furniture on the first floor, but it does not
mention movables like Campeche chairs.

of the portico doors. A floor plan drawn by his granddaughter Cornelia
Randolph (fig. 25) indicates that he displayed a bust of Napoleon (fig. 26)
behind the chair to the left and a bust of Emperor Alexander of Russia behind the chair to the right. The juxtaposition of a Campeche chair, especially
if it was the one embellished with stars, with the bust of Napoleon would
have reminded guests and family members of the political victory Jefferson
achieved with the Louisiana Purchase.[32]

Jefferson understood that objects could become revered relics and lasting
symbols of historic events. Near the end of his life, he sent his granddaughter Ellen Randolph Coolidge the lap desk that he used when drafting the
Declaration of Independence (fig. 27), intending it as a gift for her husband,
Joseph Coolidge (1798–1879). Jefferson wrote, "if then things acquire a
superstitious value because of their connection with particular persons,
surely a connection with the great Charter of our Independence may give a
value to what has been associated with that [document]. . . . Its imaginary
value will increase with the years . . . he [Mr. Coolidge] may see it carried

Figure 26   Bust of Napoleon Bonaparte after Antoine-Denis Chaudet, probably France, ca. 1807. Marble. H. 24½", W. 13", D. 10". (Courtesy, Thomas Jefferson Foundation, Monticello; photo, Edward Owen.)

Figure 27   Lap desk attributed to Benjamin Randolph, Philadelphia, Pennsylvania, ca. 1776. Mahogany. H. 9¾", W. 14⅜", D. 3¼". (Courtesy, Division of Political History, National Museum of American History, Smithsonian Institution.)

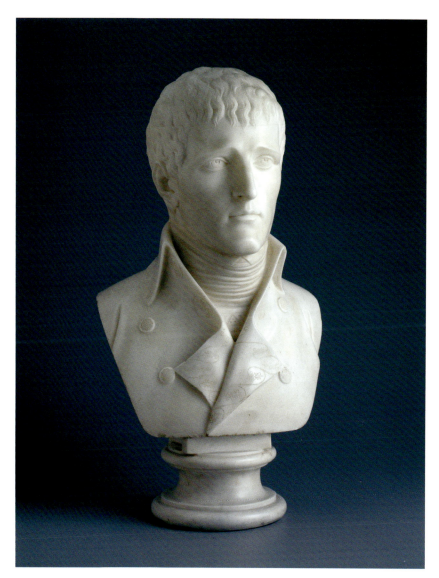

in the procession of our nation's birthday, as the relics of the saints are in those of the churches." Jefferson's words proved prophetic, as the lap desk is now one of the most famous historic objects in the collection of the Smithsonian Institution. For Jefferson, the Campeche chairs in his parlor may have been equally symbolic as totems of his role in the Louisiana Purchase and the country's westward expansion.[33]

ACKNOWLEDGMENTS
For assistance with this article, the author thanks Kay Arthur, Gavin Ashworth, Luke Beckerdite, Anna Berkes, Jenny Burden, Elizabeth Chew, Jessica Dorman, Lisa Francavilla, Cybèle Trione Gontar, Ellen Hickman, Eric Johnson, Sue Perdue, Gail Pond, Sumpter Priddy III, Jack Robertson, Justin Sarafin, Mary Scott-Fleming, Robert Self, Leah Stearns, Susan R. Stein, Endrina Tay, Carrie Taylor, and Gaye Wilson. I am particularly indebted to David Ehrenpreis, who challenges me to reach and create, both in work and in life.

1. In Jefferson's correspondence as well as that of his family, the name "Campeche" is spelled phonetically, usually as "Campeachy." I have used "Campeche," the spelling for the port city in the Yucatán Peninsula of Mexico. I thank Sumpter Priddy III for reading this paper in its early stage and for his thoughts on the Campeche chair as a lounging form. See www.monticello.org for more on the modern reproduction of the Campeche chair.

2. See David L. Barquist and Ethan W. Lasser, *Curule: Ancient Design in American Federal Furniture* (New Haven, Conn.: Yale University Art Gallery, 2003), pp. 26–27. *Livy's History of Rome, Vol. 1*, edited by Ernest Rhys (London: J. M. Dent & Sons, 1905), as posted on http://mcadams.posc.mu.edu/tst/ah/Livy/Livy01.html. The most thorough recent work on the *sella curulis* in antiquity is Thomas Schafer, *Imperii Insignia: Sella Curulis und Fasces; Zur Repräsentation römischer Magistrate* (Mainz am Rhein: Von Zabern, 1989).

3. *Creating French Culture: Treasures from the Bibliothèque nationale de France*, edited by Marie-Hélène Tesnière and Prosser Gifford (New Haven, Conn.: Yale University Press, 1995), pp. 42–43. This throne is also illustrated in André Jacob Roubo, *L'art du menuisier* (Paris: L. F. Delatour, 1769–1775), part 3, section 2, pl. 222, 1772. Jefferson owned an unidentified volume of Roubo, noting it as part of his post-1815 retirement library, "#245. *Art du Menuisier*. Folio." Jefferson's Retirement Library, 1815, Thomas Jefferson Papers (hereafter TJP), Library of Congress (hereafter LC). The whereabouts of Jefferson's copy is unknown. Thanks to Endrina Tay for locating this reference.

4. For a complete survey of the history of the form, see Cybèle Trione Gontar, "The Campeche Chair in the Metropolitan Museum of Art," *Metropolitan Museum Journal* 38 (2003): 183–212. Also useful is the Getty Art and Architecture Thesaurus Online, www.getty.edu/vow/AATFullDisplay?find=campeche&logic=AND&note=&english=N&prev_page=1&subjectid=300265223. For more on logwood, see http://en.wikipedia.org/wiki/Haematoxylum_campechianum.

5. For more on the Campeche chair in the United States, see Cybèle Trione Gontar, "The American Campeche Chair," *Antiques* 175, no. 5 (May 2009): 88–95.

6. Thomas Jefferson to Martha Jefferson Randolph, August 24, 1819, TJP, LC. Ellen Randolph Coolidge to Henry Randall, May 16, 1857, Ellen Coolidge Letterbook, Jefferson-Coolidge Family Collection (hereafter JCFC), #9090, University of Virginia (hereafter UVa); Virginia Randolph Trist to Ellen Randolph Coolidge, June 27, 1825, JCFC, #9090, UVa.

7. Dumas Malone, *Jefferson, the President, First Term, 1801–1805* (Boston: Little, Brown and Co., 1970), pp. 253–59, 284–310. Malone is still one of the best sources for an overview of the complex political events that took place in 1803 and 1804. For the public response to the Louisiana Purchase, see Jerry W. Knudson, "The Jefferson Years: Response by the Press, 1801–09" (Ph.D. diss., University of Virginia, 1962), pp. 199, 207–9.

8. As quoted in Carolyn Gilman, *Lewis and Clark: Across the Divide* (Washington, D.C.: Smithsonian Books, in association with Missouri Historical Society, 2003), pp. 79–80. *The Louisiana Purchase: A Historical and Geographical Encyclopedia*, edited by Junius P. Rodriguez (Santa Barbara, Ca.: ABC Clio, 2002), pp. 161–62. Malone, *Jefferson, the President*, pp. 284, 337–38.

9. Rodriguez, ed., *The Louisiana Purchase*, p. 250. Claiborne served as governor from 1803 to 1812. "William Dunbar," in *American National Biography*, edited by John A. Garraty and Mark C. Carnes (New York: Oxford University Press, 1999), pp. 62–63. Knudson, "The Jefferson Years," pp. 225–29. Both Jefferson's and Dunbar's Louisiana reports are included in *Documents Relating to the Purchase and Exploration of Louisiana*, edited by Bruce Rogers (Boston: Houghton Mifflin & Co., 1904).

10. Charles T. Cullen, "Jefferson's White House Dinner Guests," in *White House History*, edited by William Seale (Washington, D.C.: White House Historical Association, 2008), p. 314. *William Plumer's Memorandum of Proceedings in the United States Senate, 1803–1807*, edited by Everett Somerville Brown (New York: Macmillan Company, 1923), pp. 222–23, 212. Knudson, "The Jefferson Years," p. 225.

11. Thomas Jefferson to William Brown, August 18, 1809, TJP, LC. See also Receipt from Gilbert H. Smith to William Brown, October 6, 1808, TJP, LC; William Brown to Thomas Jefferson, October 10, 1808, TJP, LC; and Thomas Jefferson to William Brown, May 22, 1809, TJP, LC. Little is written about Brown, who disgraced himself and his family by stealing funds under his care while in office. Diane C. Ehrenpreis, "Trist-Gilmer Chair Research Report," Curatorial Department, Thomas Jefferson Foundation (hereafter TJF), 2008. Gontar, "The Campeche Chair," pp. 204–6. For the definitive word on the nature of a Campeche hammock versus a Campeche chair, see Lewis Livingston to Nicholas P. Trist, June 6, 1819, Trist Papers,

University of North Carolina, Chapel Hill (hereafter UNC): "A gentleman who sails today, I believe in the ship Emma has taken charge of your Campeachy hammock and will deliver it [to] Mr. Thorp no 36 Water Street who is requested forward it [to] West Point addressed [to] Mr. O. G. Brandon. All this according [to] the directions I received from your Mother.—I trust it will arrive in time to relieve you from the disagreeable necessity of lying on the hard and stony surface on which your encampment is . . . made—It will undoubtedly tend much your comfort and I have always thought that hammocks of that description or resembling them ought be introduced in our armies as part of the outfit of every soldier—They are not expensive, very durable and easily carried and would free the men from all danger of those numerous complaints caused by the cold and moisture of the earth."

12. "Thomas Bolling Robertson," in *Dictionary of American Biography*, edited by Dumas Malone, 16 vols. (New York: Charles Scribner's Sons, 1935), 8: 28. Thomas Bolling Robertson to Thomas Jefferson, August 2, 1819, TJP, LC. The Robertson family chair, which may have been identical to the one sent Jefferson, has not been located.

13. Anne Castrodale Golovin, "Cabinetmaker and Chairmakers of Washington, D.C., 1791–1840," *Antiques* 102, no. 5 (May 1975): 914–15.

14. Ibid. On October 21, 1828, an editorial in the *Daily National Intelligencer* commented on a new way of "arranging mounted maps" that the contributor saw in a committee room at the Capitol. The improvement "was in part the contrivance of Mr. Jefferson, but has been much improved by Mr. Hill, an ingenious cabinetmaker of this city." Hill seems to have been familiar with some of the objects that Jefferson left behind in Washington. John D. Hill, a cabinetmaker and chair maker working in Washington at the same time as Henry V. Hill, was probably Henry's kin. John apprenticed with William Worthington Jr., a cabinetmaker working in Washington during Jefferson's era. The author thanks Sumpter Priddy III for sharing information on Hill and Worthington. Gontar, "The Campeche Chair," p. 207.

15. For more on chairs with a connection to Jefferson and Albemarle County, see Diane C. Ehrenpreis and Robert L. Self, "'I Hope it May Answer Your Expectations': Thomas Jefferson and the Campeachy Chair," in *Louisiana Furniture*, edited by Jessica Dorman (New Orleans: Historic New Orleans, forthcoming). H. Parrot Bacot to TJF, 1989, object file, 1946-1, TJF. Bacot's letter suggests that this is a New Orleans chair and may be the one sent in 1819. Ellen Randolph Coolidge to Henry Randall, May 16, 1857, Ellen Coolidge Letterbook, JCFC, #9090, UVa.

16. Object file, 1946-1, TJF. George Green Shackelford, "Ellen Wayles Randolph and William Byrd Harrison," in *Collected Papers of the Monticello Association of the Descendents of Thomas Jefferson*, edited by Shackelford, 2 vols. (Charlottesville, Va.: Monticello Association, 1984), 2: 81–84. It is not known exactly how Jane Randall came to own most of her relics. The most likely scenario is that they came from her mother, Ellen Randolph Harrison. Ellen and her maiden sisters inherited Edgehill and its furnishings. See Thomas Jefferson Randolph, Will, Inventory, and Estate Sale, Albemarle County Will Book 29, pp. 133–43. Ellen Randolph Coolidge to Henry Randall, May 16, 1857, Ellen Coolidge Letterbook, JCFC, #9090, UVa.

17. Cornelia Randolph to Ellen Randolph Coolidge, July 6, 1828, JCFC, #9090 UVa. Nicholas P. Trist to Virginia Randolph Trist, May 8, 1829, Trist Papers, UNC. The chair with the Carr family provenance is currently on loan to the TJF.

18. Object file, 1979-91, TJF. The Trist chair descended in the family until John H. Burke gave it to the Pennsylvania School for the Deaf. The chair was subsequently purchased by the TJF. See object file, 2005-13, TJF, for a related chair. Gontar, "The Campeche Chair," p. 186, fig. 5. Imported examples with a scalloped leather skirt on the front rail could have provided inspiration for the scalloped crest on the Trist chair. Thomas Jefferson to Martha Jefferson Randolph, August 24, 1819, TJP, LC. This letter was written from Poplar Forest, where at least one Campeche chair was in use by the late summer of 1819; S. Allen Chambers, *Poplar Forest and Thomas Jefferson* (Forest, Va.: Corporation for Jefferson's Poplar Forest, 1993), pp. 126–27, 158. Jefferson used the term "Siesta chair" as a synonym for a Campeche chair. There is little doubt that is what Jefferson meant, especially with the description of the posture it afforded and the use of the Spanish word for "nap." "Hemmings" is the accepted spelling for the family surname when discussing John or Priscella, based on their own usage. Other family members went by "Hemings." The family took at least one other object made by Hemmings with them to Washington. On August 31, 1829, Martha Jefferson Randolph wrote Ellen Randolph Coolidge: "We shall carry all our bedding, some dining tables, your press and Virginia's tall chest of drawers, and some other articles, including stained bedstead, made by John Hemmings,

neater than you would suppose, low post, with head and foot boards." JCFC, UVa. For more on Hemmings, see Robert L. Self and Susan R. Stein, "The Collaboration of Thomas Jefferson and John Hemings, Furniture Attributed to the Monticello Joinery," *Winterthur Portfolio* 33, no. 4 (Winter 1998): 231–48. C. Tournillon to Nicholas P. Trist, April 10, 1818, Trist Papers, UNC. Mary Trist Tournillon to Nicholas P. Trist, May 7, 1818, Trist Papers, UNC. John F. Dumoulin to Nicholas P. Trist, July 23, 1818, Trist Papers, UNC. In 1818 Nicholas Trist lived at Monticello as the guest of Thomas Jefferson. Tournillon, Trist's stepfather, ordered "les deux fauteuils de Campêche" for Nicholas. He arranged the commission in either La Fourche or New Orleans, taking care with the upholstery. It is probable that the pair of chairs remained at Monticello, an occasional base for the entire Trist family.

19. For more on the Monticello estate sale, see Susan R. Stein, *The Worlds of Thomas Jefferson at Monticello* (New York: Harry N. Abrams, in association with the Thomas Jefferson Memorial Foundation, 1993), pp. 117–20. The inventory is printed in its entirety in ibid., appendix 5, pp. 436–38. James A. Bear Jr., "The 1827 Estate Sale Research Binder," n.d., Thomas Jefferson Library, TJF. If Fowler did purchase one of Jefferson's Campeche chairs, he may have done so in order to acquire a prototype for his cabinet shop as well as to take home a relic of his iconic neighbor. Janet Strain McDonald, "Furniture Making in Albemarle County, Virginia, 1750–1850," *Antiques* 153, no. 5 (May 1998): 748, 750–51. There is no evidence that David Fowler worked for Jefferson. January 27, 1827, Legislative Petition, Albemarle County, as published in Edmund Berkeley Jr., ed., "Save Mr. Jefferson's Bust! An Albemarle Petition of 1827," *Magazine of Albemarle County History* 27–28 (1968–1970): 117–18.

20. "File of Unsettled Bills to Purchase Articles at the Sale at Monticello, January 1827," Jefferson-Kirk papers (hereafter JKP), MSS 5291, Albert and Shirley Small Special Collections Library, UVa. Memoirs of George Walter Clements Blatterman, ca. 1902, MSS 10233, Albert and Shirley Small Special Collections Library, UVa. For evidence of Blaetterman's purchases, see "Unsettled Bills, 1827," JKP, MSS 5291, Albert and Shirley Small Special Collections Library, UVa. Although scholars have traditionally assumed that George Blatterman II took objects from Monticello with him when he moved to Kentucky, that was not the case. He did relocate slaves who had been at Monticello. George W. Blatterman Inventory, Albemarle Will Book 19, p. 463; and Estate Sale Account, Albemarle Will Book 20, p. 13. See Thomas Jefferson Randolph, Will, Inventory, and Estate Sale Account, Albemarle County Will Book 29, pp. 133–43. Scholars have traditionally assumed that at least two other chairs that descended in the family of John Hartwell Cocke were purchased at Monticello in 1827, but recent research has proven otherwise. A transcription of Cocke's receipt from the sale survives, but no Campeche chairs are listed. Bear, "The 1827 Estate Sale Research Binder." The author thanks Robert L. Self for verifying the Cocke information.

21. Ehrenpreis, "Trist-Gilmer Chair Research Report." For a contemporary source on the founding of the Territory of Orleans, see C. C. Robin, *Voyage to Louisiana, 1803–1805*, edited by Stuart O. Landry Jr. (New Orleans: Pelican Publishing Co., 1966), p. 263. The original twelve parishes were Orleans, German Coast, Acadia, Lafourche, Iberville, Point Coupee, Atakapas, Opelousas, Natchiches, Rapides, Ouachita, and Concordia (http://en.wikipedia.org/wiki/List_of_parishes_in_Louisiana). The number of parishes rose to nineteen in 1807 and remained at that number at least until Louisiana became a state in 1812. If the stars on the Trist-Gilmer chair signify the original parishes, the chair probably dates 1803–1807. Memoirs of George Walter Clements Blatterman.

22. Gerald Morgan Jr., "Nicholas Philip and Virginia Jefferson Randolph Trist," in Shackelford, ed., *Collected Papers of the Monticello Association*, 2: 100–113.

23. Peachy R. Gilmer to Thomas Jefferson, January 14, 1821, Coolidge Collection of Thomas Jefferson Manuscripts (hereafter CCTJM), Massachusetts Historical Society, Boston (hereafter MHi); Thomas Jefferson to Peachy R. Gilmer, January 27, 1821, CCTJM, MHi; Thomas Jefferson to Joel Yancy, January 27, 1821, CCTJM, MHi. Peachy Gilmer attended the Monticello estate sale in 1827, but his only known purchase was "2 pr wine sliders @ 2.55—5.10." See "Unsettled Bills, Monticello," MSS 5291, Albert and Shirley Small Special Collections Library, UVa.

24. Knudson, "The Jefferson Years," pp. 222–23. *National Intelligencer*, February 2, 1804.

25. John Whitcomb and Claire Whitcomb, *Real Life at the White House* (New York: Routledge, 2000), pp. 15–16, 23. Dumas Malone, *Jefferson, the President, Second Term, 1805–1809* (Boston: Little, Brown and Company, 1974), pp. 184–89. Jefferson selected some of the artifacts for his use at Monticello, and some were sent to Philadelphia to Charles Willson Peale and the American Philosophical Society. An excellent source for the study of the original

Native American materials and the reinstallation of the hall at Monticello is Castle McLaughlin, *Arts of Diplomacy: Lewis and Clark's Indian Collection* (Cambridge, Mass.: Peabody Museum of Archaeology and Ethnology, Harvard University, 2003), pp. 312–15. For the most thorough source on the shipments, their destinations, and their ultimate fate over time, see Gilman, *Lewis and Clark: Across the Divide*, pp. 335–53. The author thanks Elizabeth Chew for providing these sources. A May 18, 1804, list from the Lewis and Clark shipment survives but does not mention Campeche chairs; Malone, *Jefferson, the President, Second Term*, p. 184. William Seale, *The President's House*, 2 vols. (Washington, D.C.: White House Historical Association, with the cooperation of the National Geographic Society, 1986), 1: 96–98. There is no mention of a Campeche chair on the furniture inventory of the President's House. "Furniture Inventory, President's House," February 19, 1809, TJP, LC. For more on the entrance hall at Monticello, see Stein, *The Worlds of Thomas Jefferson*, pp. 64–68; and Elizabeth Chew, "Indian Hall and Museum," in the *Thomas Jefferson Encyclopedia*, www.monticello.org/site/house-and-gardens/indian-hall-and-museum.

26. For more on the dining room at Monticello and related quotes, see www.monticello.org/site/house-and-gardens/dining-room. For Jefferson's recommended reading for children, which includes Livy, see www.monticello.org/site/childrens-reading.

27. James A. Bear Jr. and Lucia C. Stanton, eds., *Jefferson's Memorandum Books*, 2 vols. (Princeton: Princeton University Press, 1997), 1: 587 and 640. Although he did not comment on his experience, he definitely toured the landmark, noting in his memorandum book, "Pd. Breakfast at St. Denis 3f18—gave for seeing church 6f." In 1804 Napoleon Bonaparte had Dagobert's throne repaired to use at his coronation, appropriating a symbol of the French monarchy for himself. Todd Porterfield and Susan Siegfried, *Staging Empire: Napoleon, Ingres, and David* (University Park: Pennsylvania State University Press, 2006), pp. 26–32.

28. Pierre Verlet, *French Furniture of the Eighteenth Century*, translated by Penelope Hunter-Stiebel (Charlottesville: University Press of Virginia, 1991), pp. 64–65. See also www.metmuseum.org/Works_of_Art/collection_database/european_sculpture_and_decorative_arts/folding_stool_jean_baptiste_claude_sene//objectview.aspx?OID=120049831&collID=12&dd1=12, and www.metmuseum.org/Works_of_Art/collection_database/european_sculpture_and_decorative_arts/folding_stool_jean_baptiste_claude_sene//objectview.aspx?OID=120049832&collID=12&ddi=12.

29. Jean Cailleux, "Portrait of Madame Adelaide of France, Daughter of Louis XV," in "L'art du dix-huitième siècle: An Advertisement Supplement to The Burlington Magazine" 3, no. 22 (March 1969): i–vi. Laura Auricchio, "Self-Promotion in Adélaïde Labille-Guiard's 1785 'Self-Portrait with Two Students,'" *Art Bulletin* 89, no. 1 (March 2007): 56–59. Jefferson did not comment on the *Portrait of Madame Adélaïde*, but he was very taken with the history painting hung directly beneath it, Jacques-Louis David's *Death of Socrates*. He wrote, "The Salon has been open four or five days. I inclose [*sic*] you a list of its treasures. The best thing is the Death of Socrates by David, and a superb one it is." Thomas Jefferson to John Trumbull, August 30, 1787, TJP, LC. Bear and Stanton, *Jefferson's Memorandum Books*, 1: 638.

30. Howard C. Rice Jr., *Thomas Jefferson's Paris* (Princeton: Princeton University Press, 1976), p. 26. The Metropolitan Museum of Art recently acquired a study by David, *The Lictors Bringing Brutus the Bodies of His Sons*, ca. 1787. In this picture David used a *sella curulis* with inward-facing lion's-paw feet and legs. In the finished painting the artist replaced the stool with a klismos chair, another form from antiquity; see www.metmuseum.org/ah/hd/jldv/ho_2006.264.htm.

31. "Grevin Packing List," July 17, 1790, William Short Papers, LC. *The National Intelligencer and Daily Advertiser*, April 26, 1805. In the early Republic, seating forms were still associated with positions of authority. Newspapers frequently mentioned Jefferson taking the "Presidential Chair" or "the chair of state."

32. Jefferson, Randolph, Trist Family Papers, 1791–1874, MSS 5385-ac, UVa. For more on both sculptures, see Stein, *The Worlds of Thomas Jefferson*, pp. 225, 232–33. The circumstances of Jefferson acquiring the sculpture of Napoleon Bonaparte are not known.

33. H. M. Kallen, "The Arts and Thomas Jefferson," *Ethics* 53, no. 4 (July 1943): 275–76. As quoted in Stein, *The Worlds of Thomas Jefferson*, p. 364. James A. Bear Jr., "Declaration of Independence Desk," in *Thomas Jefferson Encyclopedia*, at www.monticello.org/site/research-and-collections/declaration-independence-desk.

Figure 1   Side chair, Boston, Massachusetts, 1710–1720. Maple. H. 45½", W. 18", D. 14¼". (Private collection; photo, Gavin Ashworth.)

ETHAN W. LASSER

Ethan W. Lasser

The Cane Chair
and Its Sitter

▼ C O M P A C T ,   D I M I N U T I V E in scale, and minimally ornamented with a truncated crest and a tiny beaded edge, the early-eighteenth-century Boston cane chair is easy to overlook (fig. 1). In a gallery filled with elaborately carved rococo surfaces and muscular baroque curves, the chairs read as simple and even underdeveloped—mere skeletons in comparison with the more robust seating furniture made later in the century. But the unassuming character of the chairs has encouraged rather than stymied scholarly interest.

Benno Forman was the first scholar to consider the chairs seriously. In *American Seating Furniture, 1630–1730*, he identified twenty-six examples of the form in museums and private collections, enumerated their shared stylistic features, and connected the chairs to a broader international taste for designer Daniel Marot and the Georgian aesthetic that came to fruition in seating furniture of the 1740s. Forman also speculated that the "I" on the back rail of nineteen of the chairs was the mark of a caner's shop.[1]

Forman's interpretation laid the groundwork for Glenn Adamson's consideration of the chairs' symbolic content. In a 2002 essay, Adamson drew a distinction between the high-backed late-seventeenth-century cane chair and its early-eighteenth-century Boston counterpart. As internationally traded commodities shipped from London to a variety of English and colonial ports, the former was tied to the economic theory of mercantilism. Elaborately carved, showy surfaces were consistent with mercantilism's drive to encourage middle-class consumption. By contrast, the latter form was more exclusive. Its nascent Georgian features "marked . . . the transition [to] a new concept of taste and fashionability" associated with the British elite.[2]

This essay builds on Forman's and Adamson's analyses and considers the one aspect of the early-eighteenth-century Boston caned chairs they overlooked: their function as seats (fig. 2). While both scholars discuss the people who owned and used the chairs (members of the Boston elite), and while they detail the places where the chairs were used (new social sites like the tea table), they pay virtually no attention to the physical relationship between user and object. This relation is the subject of the pages that follow.

Leading scholars of American art have long encouraged decorative arts historians to pursue questions about the embodied experience of furniture. In discussing his method for studying material culture, Jules Prown advises the interpreter to "imagine what it felt like to interact with the object." Literary historian Philip Fisher is even more forceful on this point:

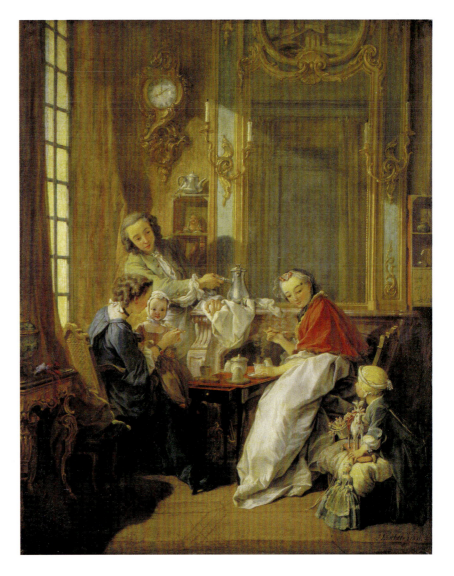

he argues that everyday objects "can only be understood by preserving the image of the user hovering nearby." "Most functional objects," he asserts, "imply the human by existing like jigsaw pieces whose outer surfaces only have meaning when it is seen that they are designed to snap into position against the body."[3]

Yet with a few important exceptions, furniture scholars—and specifically scholars of American decorative arts—have tended to avoid questions about how the object under study relates to the body that uses it. Essays, catalogues, and museum displays frame the historic piece of furniture as a self-contained unit of information—a code to be cracked—rather than as the jigsaw-puzzle pieces Fisher describes. The illustrations in most collection catalogues and material culture studies reflect this sensibility. They typically present the object alone on a bright white background, cut off from the context of use and bodily experience.[4]

This essay takes Prown's and Fisher's call as a starting point by inserting the embodied user into the history of the cane chair. The relation between sitter and chair took many different forms in the early eighteenth century.

Sitters moved chairs, moved around them, and perceived them. They put their feet up on the objects, knocked them over, and occasionally snapped them apart. They stood on chairs and threw clothing over their backs. But the chairs were built to accommodate a sitter, and the focus here is the experience of a seated body.

The body is a historically and culturally conditioned artifact—as much a part of its time as any material object—and the contemporary interpreter can never experience a chair in the manner of a sitter from the past. Yet using evidence gathered from close study of the surviving objects, images, and texts that depict the chairs in use and considering the social codes that governed the act of sitting, it is possible to understand the physical relationship that a chair was built to enter into and to facilitate. The I-chairs were designed to relate to the sitter's body in a way radically different from earlier chairs. This new relationship divested chairs of their earlier signification. Ultimately, the chairs reflect a new set of elite ideas about status and identity that emphasized the value of intrinsic qualities over and above extrinsic material objects.[5]

At the same time that this essay offers new insight into the early-eighteenth-century Boston caned chair, it also shows the value of adding an experiential lens to the furniture historian's interpretative toolkit. It is important to emphasize that this lens should augment rather than take the place of the standard questions furniture historians ask about manufacture and distribution. What follows is one interpretative strategy to help flesh out existing narratives about the connection between historic objects and the moment when they were produced.

The Disappearing Chair

Let us begin with the chairs themselves. The typical early-eighteenth-century Boston cane chair was diminutive in scale with a small seat and a short back, at least when compared with the high-backed cane chairs popular in the 1690s (fig. 3). The chairs had minimally ornamented carved crests, molded stiles, rectilinear seats with flat outside edges, turned legs tenoned into the bottom of the seats, and evidence of aprons (now missing in most of the objects). Estate inventories and upholsterers account books suggest that cushions were occasionally placed on the cane seats. The chairs were acquired in sets of six or twelve and were largely owned by members of Boston's merchant upper class. Urban and upwardly mobile, this elite group redefined the domestic interior as a flexible space. They stored pieces of furniture against the wall and brought them into the center of the room to furnish new social rituals like tea drinking (fig. 4). The cane chairs were well suited to this new environment because their lightweight materials made them easy to move.[6]

What was it like to sit in a cane chair and how did the physical relationship between sitter and chair differ from that which existed between sitters and earlier pieces of furniture? There is actually little evidence to suggest that sitting in a cane chair felt much different from sitting in earlier chairs. Historian Russel Lynes has distinguished between "passive" furniture on which we

Figure 3 Side chair, Boston, Massachusetts, 1710–1720. Maple. H. 45", W. 17½", D. 14½". (Private collection; photo, Gavin Ashworth.)

Figure 4 Thomas d'Urfey, *The Curtain Lecture*, London, England, ca. 1690. Etching on paper. 12½" x 13". (Courtesy, Lewis Walpole Library, Yale University.) A cane chair is pushed against the wall in the background.

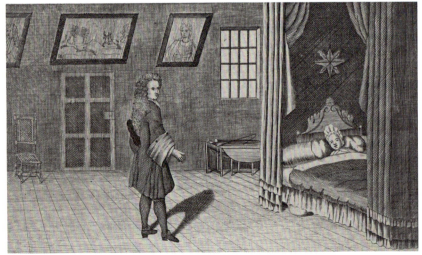

Figure 5 Detail of the right front leg and seat of a side chair, England, 1710–1720. Walnut. H. 44⅝", W. 20¼", D. 21½". (Courtesy, Wadsworth Atheneum Museum of Art, Wallace Nutting Collection, gift of J. P. Morgan.)

"impose our will to derive the greatest degree of comfort" and "disciplinary" furniture, which forces us into a particular posture or mode of behavior, and the seating furniture fashionable in the late seventeenth and early eighteenth centuries was almost all in the latter camp. The codes of gentility and politeness that pervaded social life across Europe and North America in the early modern era elevated the body—and the erect body and upright posture of the sitter—into a marker of class. As Mimi Hellman has explained in her analysis of eighteenth-century French furniture, chairs were designed to encourage the body to assume the proper elite position. They "refigured the body in much the same way as the system of clothing . . . through designs that shaped the body's movement and appearance." Boston cane chairs stand among the many British and colonial American objects that worked to this end. Their narrow backs, small seats, and fragile construction forced the sitter to sit bolt upright. Measuring fifteen to seventeen inches across, the chairs offered no support to sitters who leaned left or right. And if one did lean, the chairs were liable to break apart. In many examples of the form, the front legs are tenoned into the bottom of the seat rather than extending up as part of a mortise-and-tenon frame (fig. 5). Inherently unstable, this joint was prone to loosen and snap under the pressure of the sitter's shifting weight.[7]

While the restrictive agency of the early-eighteenth-century cane chair

Figure 6   Portrait of an Elderly Woman, attributed to
Jacob Backer, Holland, 1632. Oil on canvas. 50⅜" x
39⅛". (Courtesy, Trustees of the Wallace Collection,
London; photo, Art Resource, NY.)

was characteristic of earlier examples of seating furniture, there was nothing familiar about observing a person seated in such an object. Hellman
explains that the codes of gentility that governed social life in the eighteenth
century made every sitter into "a potential object of observation." For
observers, for friends seated across the tea table or rivals in cards, or for
servants waiting as master sat, the physical relationship between the I-chairs
and the sitter's body looked radically different from the way chairs and
bodies had looked in the past. Exploring this aspect of the relation between
sitter and chair offers the key into understanding the larger cultural pressures
at stake in these objects.[8]

Most of the seating furniture produced in the seventeenth century was
proportioned to enframe the body. Armchairs were always wide enough
to encompass their sitters (fig. 6), and the leather and upholstered side

Figure 7 Side chair, Boston, Massachusetts, 1660–1690.
Maple and oak. H. 37", W. 20½", D. 17½". (Courtesy,
Metropolitan Museum of Art, gift of Mrs. J. Insley Blair;
photo, Gavin Ashworth/Art Resource, NY.)

chairs fashionable in the period were often similarly scaled (fig. 7). Typically measuring twenty inches across, they were wide enough that their
corners remained in view even when sitters were attired in the period's
billowing garments. These proportions help to explain the tendency to
ornament the borders of the side chairs with bright brass nails or, in the
case of upholstered chairs, fabric fringe. This ornament remained in view
both when the chair was unoccupied and set against the wall and when it
functioned as a seat, as the ornamented edges of the chairs peeking out
from behind the sitter in paintings like Thomas Smith's *Self-Portrait* suggest (fig. 8). (The projecting finials on turned chairs and the projecting ears
on rococo chairs also were visible when the sitter leaned his back up against
the object.)[9]

One class of late-seventeenth-century chairs did not enframe the sitter:

Figure 8   Thomas Smith, *Self-Portrait*, Massachusetts, 1680. Oil on canvas. 24⅝" x 23⁹⁄₁₆". (Courtesy, Worcester Art Museum.)

the high-backed cane chairs popular between 1690 and 1715 (fig. 9). To encourage the proper upright posture, the backs of these chairs were only as wide as or in some cases narrower than the sitter's back. Period depictions of the chairs in use, like the English engraving *The Tea-Table*, show that the sitter's shoulders extended beyond the sides of the object (fig. 10).

If the high-backed cane chairs did not enframe the sitter as the side chairs of an earlier generation did, they still remained visible when occupied. What the chairs lost in width, they gained in height. Elevated fifty-three to fifty-five inches above the floor, the crests of the high-backed cane chairs are best understood as carved wooden crowns. As paintings like William Hogarth's *The Denunciation* and Ruben Moulthrop's portrait of an unknown man suggest, the crests were tall enough to perch just above the sitter's head even when the sitter donned one of the period's stylish tall wigs (figs. 11, 12). (Moulthrop depicts a derivative but similarly scaled and ornamented form, the banister-back chair.) The crests on the surviving corpus of high-backed chairs are elaborately decorated, often with motifs well suited to a position above the sitter. For example, the popular "boyes and crown" pattern presented a crown lifted by a pair of hovering cherubs

Figure 11 William Hogarth, *The Denunciation*, London, England, 1729. Oil on canvas. 19½" x 26". (Courtesy, National Gallery of Ireland, Dublin.)

(fig. 13). One exceptional sixty-six-inch-tall caned armchair built for the bishop of London was appropriately capped by a bishop's miter (fig. 14). Other motifs referenced the sitter's head more abstractly. For example, the C-scroll pattern on many crests could easily blend in with the curls of a male sitter's wig.[10]

Though there must have been exceptional cases in which a sitter extended over the sides of a leather-upholstered chair or a gentleman with a particularly elaborate wig obscured the crest of a high-backed object, it is safe to surmise that, generally speaking, late-seventeenth-century New England seating furniture remained visible when occupied. In a culture that knew the chair as an object that enframed and projected over its sitter's head, the early-eighteenth-century cane chair was a decided anomaly.

Averaging forty-two inches tall, seventeen inches wide, and fifteen inches

Figure 12   Ruben Moulthrop, *Portrait of an Unknown Man*, New England, 1770–1790. Oil on canvas. Dimensions not recorded. (Courtesy, Winterthur Museum.)

Figure 13   Detail of the crest of a side chair, England, ca. 1670. (Courtesy, Philadelphia Museum of Art.)

Figure 14   Armchair, London, England, 1709. Walnut. H. 66", W. 29⅞", D. 26". (Courtesy, St. Paul's Cathedral.) This chair originally had a caned seat and back.

deep, they were as narrow as the high-backed cane chairs, yet they were typically more than ten inches shorter. Though little comprehensive data exists about the height of Boston adults in the early eighteenth century, muster rolls indicate that the average height of the male soldiers stationed in New England in this period was five feet seven inches. (Unfortunately, no data exists on the height of women.) Extrapolating from this data to the approximate height of a sitter suggests that the backs of the I-chairs were just tall enough to jut into the base of the neck or, in the case of the "molded scoop" crests fashionable in English versions of the diminutive cane chairs, to dip

Figure 15   Side chair, Boston, Massachusetts, 1695–1705. Maple. H. 38⅜", W. 17¾", D. 14⅜". (Courtesy, Winterthur Museum.)

below the neck toward the shoulders (fig. 15). Thus, when viewed from the front, the back of the chair that had once projected over the body now disappeared behind it. (The chairs remained visible beneath the sitter when viewed from the side.)[11]

The new relationship between sitter and chair can be seen in period imagery. Before discussing this visual evidence, it is important to note that painters often had their own symbolic and iconographic agendas, and individual depictions of people using furniture must be considered carefully, and not simply admitted as fact. But when a consistent pattern emerges among multiple artists, the interpreter may be more willing to accept period representations as reliable evidence. Such is the case in the early eighteenth century. Artists in both Boston and London presented seated figures without any trace of a chair above or around them. For example, in John Smibert's iconic portrait *The Bermuda Group*, the women seated behind the table covered in a cupboard cloth seem almost to hover (fig. 16). The only indication that they are supported by chairs is the draped hand of the central standing figure, which appears to be gripping the back of a crest. Chairs are also absent in a trade card engraved for tobacconist Richard Lee (fig. 17). Though three low-backed cane chairs are visible in the foreground, no

Figure 16 John Smibert, *The Bermuda Group*, Boston, Massachusetts, 1729. Oil on canvas. 69½" x 93". (Courtesy, Yale University Art Gallery, gift of Isaac Lothrop; photo, Art Resource, NY.)

Figure 17 *Trade Card for Richard Lee*, after
William Hogarth, London, England, 1733–1745.
Etching on paper. 6⅛" x 8⅞". (Courtesy, Heal
Collection, British Museum.)

chairs are visible under the two men on the far side of the table at the left.
Hogarth presumably expected his viewers to be fluent enough with the
scale of period designs to understand that these men also occupied low-
backed chairs.[12]

Forman, Adamson, and the other scholars who have written about the
I-chairs always note that the objects were shorter than their predecessors. In
their object-centered focus, however, they overlook the profundity of this
shift. Boston chair makers not only broke away from the scale of earlier seating furniture; they created a group of chairs that related to the body in a radically different way than chairs from the past. To observe a person from the
front seated in a cane chair was not to see a body bordered in brass tacks and
fringe or crowned by a carved ornament. Instead, like viewing a person
seated on one of the stools that dominated New England homes in the early
seventeenth century, it was to see a body with no object surrounding it at all.

Excess

Why did chairs that disappeared behind their occupants come into fashion
in Boston in 1720? One way to answer this question is to return to the matter of style. In *American Seating Furniture*, Forman argued that the early-
eighteenth-century chairs were connected to a broader stylistic turn away
from the high baroque aesthetic that had dominated seating furniture in
seventeenth-century New England. In his words, they constituted a fourth
phase in the development of the cane chair and reflected "another idea about
the styling of chairs . . . inspired by the engravings of such men as Daniel
Marot." Marot's engravings presented chairs with low backs, and one could
argue that the shift engendered by the I-chairs was simply symptomatic of
the international adoption of his ideas. (It is also tempting to speculate that

Marot's designs responded to another set of changes in clothing or hairstyle that necessitated a lower-backed chair, though there is little evidence to support this claim.)[13]

Yet an explanation focused on stylistic shift is only partially satisfactory. While new aesthetic ideas certainly played a role in the affect the I-chairs engendered, these ideas do not account for what was lost when the part of the chair that projected beyond the sitter was eliminated. What was lost was nothing less than the signifying power of earlier objects.

Moving backward in time allows us to consider the symbolic role played by projecting crests and sides in earlier seating furniture. Just when they were fashionable in middle-class forms, these design elements were also common features of English royal thrones and chairs of state. In the discussion of furniture in his 1688 treatise *The Academy of Armory*, an encyclopedia of heraldic symbols and the "instruments used in all trades and sciences," Randle Holme identified the "throne or seat of majesty" as a "chair of gold richly imbossed, mounted upon steps, with the achievements of the sovergn set over head and under a rich canopy with valence curtains fringed and imbroidered with silk." The coronation chair that Thomas Roberts built for Queen Anne in 1702 fits this description (fig. 18). Capped by an elaborate gilded crest and bordered by red tassels, the object looks like a large-scale hybrid of a high-backed and an upholstered side chair. Its grandeur is matched by that of the thrones in period images. For example, in Thomas Hawker's depiction of King Charles II, the king sits in a giant

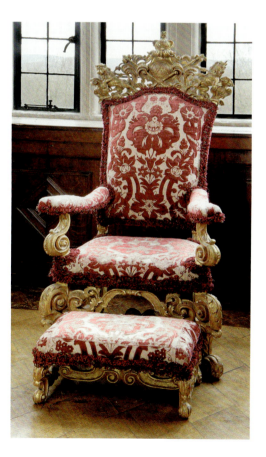

Figure 18 Thomas Roberts, coronation chair for Queen Anne, London, 1702. Carved beechwood and gilding, modern upholstery. H. 68⅛", W. 34⅜", D. 38¼". (Courtesy, Hatfield House.)

Figure 19 *King Charles II*, attributed to Thomas Hawker, England, ca. 1680. Oil on canvas. 89¼" x 53⅜". (Courtesy, National Portrait Gallery, London.)

throne dominated by a massive gilt and carved crown that surrounds him like a giant halo (fig. 19).[14]

The crests and projecting sides of these royal objects obviously did not serve any functional purpose. Neither played any role in supporting the sitter's weight. Instead, their function was communicative. In a culture where most people sat on the ground or on stools, they differentiated the king and conveyed what Holme described as his "immutability and authority." At the same time, as parts of the chair that stood in excess of the object's practical requirements, they marked the king's wealth in an era when most could only afford the bare necessities.[15]

Principally sold in sets and owned by members of the Boston and London middle class, the late-seventeenth-century domestic seating furniture did not convey any claim to royal power. But the projecting sides and crests of these chairs still expressed excess, the same way in the domestic sphere as it did in the royal one. As historian Timothy Breen, among many others, has explained, the "luxuries and superfluities of life . . . communicated claims to social status." Ornamented silver, expensive clothing, coaches, portraits, and elaborately decorated pieces of storage furniture "spoke to contemporaries of class and gender, identity and status" and defined one as a member of the middle class. The chairs stand among these symbolic objects. Indeed, one Boston writer in 1719 identified cane chairs among the fashionable objects like "fine costly shoes and pattoons, ribbons, rich lace, silk hankercheifs, fine hatts, gloves . . . and China ware . . . which have not been necessary, yet very costly." Among all of the period's symbolic goods, the chairs functioned most like pieces of clothing because their excess was designed to communicate in relation to the sitter's body. To observe a person crowned by a carved crest or enframed by brass tacks and silk fringe was to observe a person ensconced within a symbol of the expendable capital that marked a social position over and above that of the poorer, inferior ranks.[16]

This brings us back to the I-chairs. Lost when the chair was scaled to disappear behind the body was the part of the chair that conveyed and confirmed social identity when the chair was in use. Reduced in height and width, the I-chairs were shorn of the excess that possessed communicative power. Like the common stool, they were chairs that functioned on the most basic level. To observe a person seated in one of these objects was simply to observe a face, a face devoid of the signs of expendable wealth and social position that had surrounded sitters in the past (fig. 20).

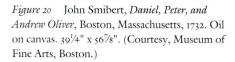

Figure 20 John Smibert, *Daniel, Peter, and Andrew Oliver*, Boston, Massachusetts, 1732. Oil on canvas. 39¼" x 56⅞". (Courtesy, Museum of Fine Arts, Boston.)

A Chair for the Boston Elite

At this point, we are in a position to rephrase the question posed above. Rather than ask why a chair that disappeared behind its sitter came into fashion in 1720s Boston, we can ask what cultural pressures made a chair desirable that was shorn of the identity-conferring excess that had traditionally surrounded the sitter. The best way to answer this question is to consider the chair's owners. On the basis of family histories, Adamson notes that these chairs were owned by members of the Boston elite, including the Aldens, Hancocks, and Holyokes. The beliefs and values of this group and their response to the rise in middle class consumption helps to explain the connection between the chairs and the moment when they were produced.[17]

Historians have shown that the growing economic power of the middle class at the beginning of the eighteenth century made elites uncomfortable. As Breen explained, this group viewed middle-class consumers "as a threat to their own social standing." Historically, only the elite could afford goods with superfluous qualities, and they acquired these goods to convey their position at the top of the social hierarchy. But once excess became a staple of middle-class objects like the high-backed cane chair, the elites feared that traditional social categories would be confused and their social authority weakened. "As more and more ordinary people purchased British manufactures, they inevitably transgressed the older boundaries of class and status. . . . In the new order almost anyone of moderate means seemed capable of presenting himself, at least in terms of material possessions, as a gentleman."[18]

Elites responded to this disruption in the social order by calling for a return to an older, medieval and Renaissance model of class distinction in which innate qualities like a distinguished name and family lineage rather than visible possessions defined social status. The argument for this model surfaced throughout early-eighteenth-century Britain and colonial America, but few writers expressed it as clearly and forcefully as Charles Rollin. Rollin was a French historian made famous by his multivolume histories of ancient Greece and Rome. In his 1726 work the *Traité des études*, which was available in English in both Boston and London, Rollin changed course to study education and emphasize the value of learning from the ancients. Most pertinent here are the lessons Rollin drew from the ancients' attitudes toward status and identity.[19]

At the beginning of a chapter entitled "Of Furniture, Dress and Equipage," Rollin observed that his contemporaries use objects to convey and uphold their social status. "The most part of mankind placed their greatness in [furniture, dress and equipage]. . . . They swell and enlarge the idea they form of themselves, as much as they can, from these outward circumstances." But this, Rollin argued, was a naïve practice. Things were hollow and artificial bearers of identity: "What renders a man truly great and worth of admiration is neither riches, magnificent buildings, costly habits or sumptuous furniture, neither a luxurious table." The model of the ancients showed that true greatness was vested in intrinsic qualities: "A man owes his real worth to his heart."[20]

Rollin bolstered his argument for the connection between greatness and intrinsic qualities by citing heroes from antiquity. Scipio Aemilianus, the ruler of Carthage who was "descended from one of the most illustrious families in Rome, and adopted into one of the richest," "never made any acquisition in his life." His "greatness" was defined and conveyed by "his person alone, without any other attendance than that of his virtues, his actions, and his triumphs." Similarly, Agesilaus, king of Lacedemon, "gained reverence" through "his name, his reputation and his victories." He traveled around "in a very plain dress" and "without further ceremony, sat himself down upon the grass."[21]

As these examples and others like them in the text suggest, "greatness" correlated to the position of the kings at the top of the social hierarchy, and the intrinsic qualities that defined greatness included the name and family lineage that people born into this position possessed. Rollin's argument, then, is far less democratic than it seems. What he meant by an identity defined by the "heart" was an identity to which the elite alone had access.

The *Traité des études* and the numerous other writings available in Boston and London that echoed Rollin's arguments help to explicate the desirability of the cane chairs. Shorn of the symbolic excess of earlier pieces of seating furniture, the chairs were well suited to a sitter who sought distance from the newly monied who "swell[ed] . . . themselves" with "outward circumstances." Proportioned to privilege the sitter's face, these objects were appropriate to elites who subscribed to the view that intrinsic qualities rather than external goods conveyed and upheld identity. Unencumbered by elaborately decorated borders or lavishly carved crests, members of the Alden, Hancock, or Holyoke families could lay claim to the greatness of Scipio and Agesilaus and show observers that their identities were vested in the face and by extension the name and family lineage to which they alone had access.

Rollin's language offers the best set of terms to articulate the chairs' cultural significance. At the conclusion of "Of Furniture, Dress and Equipage," he slightly shifted his focus and advised the reader on the best way to judge the identity of others:

> To pass a right judgment upon their greatness we should examine them in themselves and set aside for a few moments their train and retinue. Strip them of this advantage, and reduce them to their proper standard, or their just proportion. . . . Whatever is external to a man . . . does not make him truly valuable. We must judge of a man by the heart.[22]

The cane chairs allowed for this "right judgment." They "strip" the sitter of his "advantage" and "reduced" him to a "proper standard," a "just proportion." Obscured behind the sitter's back, they allowed the observer to "examine" sitters "in themselves" without the influence of "their train and retinue." They enabled the observer to "judge of a man by the heart."

This interpretation raises questions of intentionality, and it is important to be clear that eighteenth-century Boston chair makers were probably not reading Rollin and translating his ideas into material form. Instead, consumers were the conduits that carried the new ideas about identity into design. In all likelihood, this process was neither deliberate nor even conscious. With Rollin echoing somewhere in the back of their minds, members of the Boston elite found some inexpressible value in the short-backed chairs and continued to acquire and commission the objects.

Conclusion

Although this reading initially appears incompatible with Adamson's assertion that the early-eighteenth-century caned chair was a fundamentally communicative object, further research might reveal a more nuanced relation between these two interpretations. What if, unlike late-seventeenth-century seating furniture, the communicative function of the chairs depended on the physical position of the objects? What if the chairs communicated the class position of their owners when not in use but reflected Rollin's ideas about the intrinsic basis of elite identity when occupied? In other words, might the I-chairs function symbolically when they were stored against the wall but cease to communicate when they actually came into contact with the body? Were other furniture forms characterized by this duality?

These are all questions for a more extended study. Together with the larger interpretation put forward here, they illustrate the new issues and insights that follow from a consideration of the physical relationship between a historic piece of furniture and the body it was intended to serve. Though chairs, chests, and tables may constitute mysterious and compelling texts to contemplate in and of themselves, they were built to serve bodily needs and to participate within the fabric of sensuous bodily experience, and they are best understood—indeed, only understood, to return to literary historian Philip Fisher's eloquent phrasing—by imagining "the user hovering nearby."

ACKNOWLEDGMENTS The author thanks Glenn Adamson, Dennis Carr, Jon Prown, Kate Smith, and members of the Newberry Library Seminar in American Art for their comments on earlier versions of this article and Randall O'Donnell for his insights into the construction of the cane chair.

1. Benno Forman, *American Seating Furniture, 1630–1730* (New York: W. W. Norton, 1988), pp. 229–81. For English chairs, see Adam Bowett, *English Furniture: 1660–1714* (London: Antique Collectors' Club, 2002), pp. 84–85; David Dewing, "Cane Chairs: Their Manufacture and Use in London, 1670–1730," in *Regional Furniture* 22 (2008): 53–81; and R. W. Symonds, "The Export Trade of Furniture to Colonial America," *Burlington Magazine* 77 (November 1940): 152–63. See also Symonds, "English Cane Chairs, Part I," *Connoisseur* (March 1951): 8–15, and "English Cane Chairs, Part II," *Connoisseur* (May 1951): 83–91.

2. Glenn Adamson, "The Politics of the Caned Chair," in *American Furniture*, edited by Luke Beckerdite (Hanover, N.H.: University Press of New England for the Chipstone Foundation, 2002), pp. 175–206, at p. 203.

3. Jules David Prown, "Mind in Matter: An Introduction to Material Culture Theory and Method," in *Art as Evidence: Writings on Art and Material Culture* (New Haven, Conn.: Yale University Press, 2001), p. 81; Philip Fisher, *Making and Effacing Art: Modern American Art in a Culture of Museums* (New York: Oxford University Press, 1991), pp. 243–44.

4. Katherine Grier and Mimi Hellman have broken with the existing paradigm and made headway in explaining the phenomenological experience of objects. See Grier, *Culture and Comfort: Parlor Making and Middle Class Identity, 1850–1930* (Washington, D.C.: Smithsonian Books,

1996); Hellman, "Furniture, Sociability, and the Work of Leisure in Eighteenth-Century France," *Eighteenth-Century Studies* 32 (Summer 1999): 415–45; and Hellman, "Interior Motives: Seduction by Decoration in Eighteenth-Century France," in Harold Coda, Andrew Bolton, and Hellman, *Dangerous Liaisons* (New York: Metropolitan Museum of Art, 2004), p. 19.

5. For one of the most recent of the many investigations of this topic, see Angus Trumble, *The Finger* (New York: Farrar, Straus, and Giroux, 2010).

6. Reinier Baarsen et al., *Courts and Colonies: The William and Mary Style in Holland, England and America* (New York: Cooper Hewitt Museum, 1988).

7. Quoted in Michael Ettema, "Nostalgia and American Furniture," *Winterthur Portfolio* 17 (Summer 1982): 141. Hellman, "Furniture, Sociability, and the Work of Leisure," p. 430. For scholars who have commented on the chair's structural weakness, see Symonds, "English Cane Chairs, Part I"; Wallace Nutting, who remarks that they are "apt to grow shaky," in *Furniture Treasury* (1928; reprint, New York: Old America, 1980); and John Kirk, who comments on their "precarious beauty" in *American Furniture: Understanding Styles, Construction and Quality* (New York: Harry Abrams, 2000), p. 65.

8. Hellman, "Furniture, Sociability, and the Work of Leisure," p. 429.

9. For a discussion of period clothing styles, see Linda Baumgarten, *What Clothes Reveal: The Language of Clothing in Colonial and Federal America* (New Haven, Conn.: Yale University Press, 2002).

10. For a fascinating set of earlier chairs whose crests evoke the carving on period gravestones and thus make the sitter look like the transcendent faces on those objects, see Ethan W. Lasser, "Making Things Matter: The Chipstone Galleries at the Milwaukee Art Museum," *Winterthur Portfolio* (forthcoming).

11. Forman, *American Seating Furniture*, p. 306, discusses these chairs.

12. Jonathan Prown, "John Singleton Copley's Furniture and the Art of Invention," in *American Furniture*, edited by Luke Beckerdite (Hanover, N.H.: University Press of New England for the: Chipstone Foundation, 2004), pp. 153–205.

13. Forman, *American Seating Furniture*, p. 237. Baumgarten, *What Clothes Reveal*, pp. 222–36.

14. Randle Holme, *The Academy of Armory, or, A Storehouse of Armory and Blazon* (London, 1688), n.p.

15. Many historians have discussed this condition, including Cary Carson, "The Consumer Revolution in Colonial British America: Why Demand?" in *Of Consuming Interests: The Style of Life in the Eighteenth Century*, edited by Carson, Ronald Hoffman, and Peter J. Albert (Charlottesville: University Press of Virginia, 1994), pp. 483–697.

16. T. H. Breen, *The Marketplace of Revolution: How Consumer Politics Shaped American Independence* (Oxford: Oxford University Press, 2004), pp. 150–54. "The Present melancholy circumstances of the province consider'd, and methods for redress humbly proposed, in a letter from one in the Country to one in Boston" (Boston, 1719), p. 4 (retrieved from Early American Imprints, Series I: Evans, 1639–1800).

17. Adamson, "The Politics of the Caned Chair," p. 204.

18. Breen, *The Marketplace of Revolution*, pp. 156–57.

19. For background on Rollin, see Georges Bertrin, "Charles Rollin," in *The Catholic Encyclopedia*, vol. 13 (New York: Robert Appleton Company, 1912), at www.newadvent.org/cathen/13119b.htm (accessed August 2, 2010).

20. Charles Rollin, "Of Furniture, Dress and Equipage," in *Traité des études* (London, 1726), pp. 30, 39.

21. Ibid., pp. 32–34.

22. Ibid., pp. 30, 31.

Figure 1   Benjamin Henry Latrobe, *United States Capitol, Washington, D.C. Perspective from the Northeast*, 1806. Watercolor and ink on paper. 19¼" x 23¼". (Courtesy, Library of Congress.) The inscription reads: "TO THOMAS JEFFERSON Pres. U.S., B.H. LATROBE, 1806."

Figure 2   Anthony St. John Baker, *The White House and Capitol*, ca. 1827. Watercolor on paper. 7⅝" x 11⅝". (Courtesy, Huntington Library.)

Figure 3   Pierre Charles L'Enfant, *Plan of the City of Washington*, Philadelphia, Pennsylvania, 1792. Engraving. Image, 8¼" x 10¼"; sheet, 13¾" x 16¹⁵⁄₁₆". (Courtesy, Library of Congress.)

Sumpter Priddy and
Ann Steuart

Seating Furniture from the District of Columbia, 1795–1820

▼ IN 1790 THE United States Congress voted to move the nation's capital from Philadelphia to a location nearer the center of the country's rapidly expanding population. President George Washington suggested a site just below the falls of the Potomac River, perched along a stretch of land between the booming towns of Georgetown, Maryland, and Alexandria, Virginia. Shortly thereafter, Congress hired French engineer Pierre L'Enfant to prepare a plan for the new "District of Columbia" and sponsored a national competition seeking designs for two buildings that would dominate the landscape. West Indian native Dr. William Thornton won the prize for the United States Capitol (fig. 1), and Irish-born architect James Hoban won the prize for the President's House (fig. 2). Artisans flooded into the region hoping to secure work, while some of America's most vocal proponents for the arts—including Secretary of State Thomas Jefferson—envisioned ways to furnish the city's new structures in a manner worthy of the young country's high aspirations. The three decades that followed witnessed a period of intensive government patronage for the arts. This article will discuss a number of talented artisans who influenced furniture design in the city, suggest unique local developments that shaped the evolution of their trade, establish a chronology of style as reflected in their products, and explore the diverse forms and ornaments of a previously unrecognized school of furniture that evolved along the banks of the Potomac.

America's new capital city contained three separate jurisdictions, each of which contributed to the furniture story. L'Enfant laid out the plan as a ten-mile square, set on a diagonal that spanned the Potomac River as it ran from northwest to southeast (fig. 3). The bustling community of Georgetown, incorporated in 1751, stretched along the river's hilly northern bank, just above the center of the square. Its economy, initially fueled by tobacco, became increasingly diverse in the intervening years, with mills spreading inland along Rock Creek, which emptied into the Potomac on the south end of town. Piers along Bridge Street attracted ships from Europe, South America, and the Caribbean and helped support a prosperous community of merchants and artisans.

Members of several prominent Maryland and Virginia families moved to Georgetown during the late eighteenth century. Among the most influential were the Carrolls, Bealls, Belts, Masons, and Tayloes. Joining them were powerful émigrés like merchant and Georgetown mayor Robert Peter (1726–1806), who arrived from Scotland in 1745 and established a lineage that was influential for decades. These families helped shape the economic, political, and artistic development of the region. Estimates of Georgetown's population vary slightly according to source, but in 1800, the municipality (incorporated in 1789) had approximately 5,120 inhabitants, of which 1,449 were slaves, and 277, free blacks.[1]

Seven miles south of Georgetown, near the southern tip of the district's ten-mile square, stood Alexandria, Virginia. Founded in 1749 on the south bank of the Potomac, it, too, boasted an active waterfront and a strong economy linked initially to tobacco. Merchant John Carlyle came from the north of England during the 1740s and—seeing opportunity—built warehouses on the waterfront. He then helped plan the town and constructed its first mansion with elaborately carved interiors. Some of northern Virginia's most powerful planters built or purchased homes in Alexandria, including members of the Lee, Custis, and Washington families. Their wealth supported a sizable community of merchants and tradesmen, many from Scotland and England's West Country ports. In 1800 Alexandria had a population of about 4,971, of which 875 were enslaved and 369 were free African Americans.[2]

Congress established the third jurisdiction—"Washington, the District of Columbia"—in 1790, with the intention of locating the seat of government there a decade later. Washington, D.C., was built from the ground up in the rural landscape along the river's north bank, on a parcel of land that stretched southward from Rock Creek to the Potomac River's Eastern Branch, also known as the Anacostia River. L'Enfant envisioned the city in the manner of Europe's grandest, with a series of diagonal boulevards that radiated out from the President's House and the Capitol, thereby providing both elegant vistas and convenient access to nearby rivers and roadways. Despite his vision, Washington's major buildings and infrastructure were woefully unfinished when Congress first convened there in a temporary structure on June 11, 1800. Over the next two decades, development would be indelibly shaped by national politics, by rivalries between Maryland and Virginia, and by the region's largest landowners.[3]

Members of the Carroll family were among the most prominent landowners. Daniel Carroll (1755–1849) owned Duddington, which encompassed several thousand acres atop Jenkins Hill—now known as Capitol Hill—and from there stretched southeast to the Anacostia River. His cousin Charles Carroll of Carrollton, who was the wealthiest man in Maryland, lived in Annapolis, but two of the latter's children had ties to Washington. Daniel and Charles's cousin, Father John Carroll (1735–1815), founded Georgetown University and became the Catholic Church's first American archbishop. Modern scholarship emphasizes the Carroll family's ties to Annapolis and Baltimore, but their early history was also linked strongly to Georgetown.[4]

Known during the period as the Federal City or Washington City, Washington, D.C., had 3,210 free white inhabitants in 1800. When combined with Alexandria and Georgetown, the District of Columbia's total population was just over 13,300. That number represented less than half the population of Baltimore, where a flourishing community of artisans created some of the Chesapeake region's finest neoclassical furnishings. Yet the special circumstances that surrounded Congress's decision to build a new Federal City and to fund it generously, if sporadically, created unprecedented opportunities for government patronage of architecture and the arts and attracted talented artisans from across America.[5]

The District of Columbia's artistic development received tremendous impetus with Thomas Jefferson's election to the presidency in 1800. His fascination and experience with architecture, which was reflected in a lifetime spent refining his home at Monticello and his role in designing Virginia's Capitol in Richmond, had familiarized him with the subtle skills of design and the complexities of building. His service as America's Minister Plenipotentiary to France from 1784 to 1789 had introduced him to some of Europe's finest architecture, strengthened his understanding of ancient classical detail, and reinforced his commitment to the inseparability of architecture and the fine arts.

Jefferson's experiences in France and his brief sojourns in England and Italy placed him in a unique position among Americans dedicated to the arts. While abroad, he developed personal relationships with some of Europe's finest artists and artisans. These included Jean-Antoine Houdon, who came to America in the late 1780s to sculpt America's Revolutionary heroes and, during that visit, produced studies for his renowned full-length sculpture of George Washington, destined for the Rotunda of the Virginia State Capitol. More important to the story at hand, Jefferson inspired a wave of talented artisans to migrate to the region. These craftsmen shaped the Federal City and its artistic legacy in a way that would be felt for decades.[6]

Henry and Joseph Ingle and the Influence of Philadelphia Furniture Styles
During the summer session of the Second Continental Congress in 1783, Jefferson met Henry Ingle (1763–1822) (fig. 4), an apprentice of Philadelphia cabinetmaker and house joiner John Webb. When he completed his term the following year, Ingle traveled to Virginia, where he first settled near Jefferson's home in Albemarle County. Two years later, Ingle moved to Richmond, where he worked with a group of talented and well-connected artisans who were entrusted with erecting Jefferson's revolutionary temple design for the Virginia State Capitol, in its turn the largest building project in America during the 1780s.[7]

Although Ingle entered into a brief partnership with Philadelphia cabinetmaker Elijah Speakman, much of his Richmond career was probably spent working under the direction of British-born joiner Clotworthy Stephenson (d. 1819), who was largely responsible for fabricating the interior woodwork for the Virginia Capitol. Both men subsequently moved to Washington to help build the United States Capitol, the largest structure under construction in America during the 1790s. Stephenson, who was the senior of the two, served as Grand Marshall for the ceremony that laid the cornerstone in 1793 and worked at the Capitol intermittently over the next decade.[8]

At the Virginia Capitol, Ingle also worked closely with carver William Hodgson (1750–1806), whose surviving work includes the Ionic capitals of

Figure 4 Silhouette of Henry Ingle, probably Philadelphia, Pennsylvania, 1790–1800. Paper. Diam. 3⅛". (Courtesy, Historical Society of Washington, D.C.) The frame is original.

Figure 5 Desk-and-bookcase attributed to Henry Ingle with carving attributed to William Hodgson, Richmond, Virginia, 1789. Mahogany and mahogany veneer with yellow pine, tulip poplar, walnut, birch, and cherry. H. 99½", W. 44⅜", D. 21½". (Private collection; photo, Gavin Ashworth.)

Figure 6 Detail of the rosette of the desk-and-bookcase illustrated in fig. 5. (Photo, Gavin Ashworth.)

the pilasters in the Old Senate Chamber and the leaf-carved trusses that support pediments beneath the Capitol dome. Like most professional carvers, Hodgson offered his services to both joiners and cabinetmakers. All of the rosettes and vase-and-flower ornaments on Ingle's finest case pieces originated in Hodgson's shop. The latter's distinctive working style is manifest in the carving on a desk-and-bookcase made for Dabney Minor, an Orange County joiner who also worked at the Virginia Capitol (figs. 5–7). Hodgson's acanthus leaves have a pronounced central vein, a hollow in the middle of each frond, and tips that overlap one another. Other than differences in scale, there is little separating his architectural carving and furniture work. For example, the husks and rosettes Hodgson furnished for the dining room chimneypiece in Woodlands, the home of Amelia County, Virginia, planter Stephen Cocke (fig. 8), are strikingly similar to those on furniture made by Henry Ingle during his Washington career.[9]

Figure 8 Architectural carving attributed to William Hodgson, Woodlands, Amelia County, Virginia, ca. 1790. (Photo, Katherine Wetzel.) Clotworthy Stephenson furnished the plaster ornaments. The architectural components were fabricated and carved in Richmond and shipped to Amelia County.

Ingle left Virginia and returned to Philadelphia in 1791. Three years later, he joined cabinetmaker Jacob Schreiner in a cabinetmaking partnership and a hardware business. Family tradition maintains that Henry worked with his older brother Joseph (1763–1816) in the latter's shop at 273 High Street. Thomas Jefferson, who lived next door while serving as secretary of state in George Washington's administration, purchased furniture from both men during that term, and President Washington hired Ingle for "sundry jobs" at the President's House in 1790.[19]

In the 1790s Philadelphia was abuzz with news of the new Federal City, and, like many Philadelphia artisans, the Ingle brothers must have envisioned the great opportunity that it presented. Joseph moved to Alexandria by 1793, when he advertised locally for an apprentice. Two years later, he acquired a building at 112 South Royal Street, between King and Prince Streets, and set up a cabinetmaking shop (fig. 9). In May 1795 Henry Ingle

Figure 9 112 South Royal Street, Alexandria, Virginia, before 1795. (Photo, Christian Meade.) Joseph Ingle acquired this property in 1795 and maintained a cabinetmaking shop until 1816. His brother Henry worked with him at the site from 1798 to 1801 and possibly earlier.

Figure 10 Candle stand attributed to Henry Ingle, Philadelphia, Pennsylvania, or Alexandria, Virginia, 1790–1800. Mahogany. H. 28½", D. 17¼". (Private collection; photo, Gavin Ashworth.) The label reads "Mahogany candle stand, probably made in Philadelphia . . . by H. Ingle or in his shop. . . . came from Mary Pechin, wife of Henry Ingle."

and Jacob Schreiner announced that they were "declining the Cabinet making business" and offered their inventory for sale. In October of the following year, they dissolved their hardware business: "The Partnership of Schreiner and Ingle, Ironmongers, will by mutual consent expire on the twentieth day of this month."[11]

Whether Henry Ingle worked in Alexandria intermittently over the next several years remains uncertain, but he did not announce his departure from Philadelphia until November 1798. Shortly thereafter, he moved to Alexandria, where he temporarily joined his brother Joseph in the cabinetmaking and undertaking business. In 1799 Henry establishing a separate hardware business half a block away "at the North-west Corner of King and Royal Streets." There he offered a "General Assortment of IRONMONGERY, CUTLERY AND BRASSWARE" as well as "an Assortment of brushes, and a variety of brass wares for buildings and furniture."[12]

A candle stand that dates from the mid-1790s bears a mid-twentieth-century label identifying it as a product of Henry Ingle's shop (fig. 10). Like the desk-and-bookcases that he made in Richmond (fig. 5), the stand resembles contemporaneous Philadelphia work. Parallels are apparent in the shape of the legs and feet and the turnings of the pillar and birdcage. Along with a copy of Joseph Ingle's certificate of membership in the Mechanic Relief Society of Alexandria (fig. 11), the stand remained in the family of Henry and his wife, Mary (Pechin), until the 1970s. [13]

Three different sets of neoclassical chairs descended in families that lived within blocks of Henry and Joseph Ingle's shop (figs. 12, 14, 15). Two other sets have identical backs but lack an early provenance. In light of the chairs'

Figure 11 Joseph Ingle's membership certificate in the Mechanic Relief Society of Alexandria, unknown engraver and printer, Alexandria, Virginia, dated 1811. Copperplate engraving on paper. 8" x 8¾". (Courtesy, Museum of Early Southern Decorative Arts.)

Philadelphia-inspired design and the Ingle brothers' associations with the families who owned them, all this seating can be attributed to the Ingle shops with relative certainty.[14]

Alexandria Mayor Dennis Ramsay (1756–1810), a kinsman of George Washington and a pallbearer at his funeral, owned the set represented by the chair illustrated in figures 12 and 13. Not surprisingly, the Ramsay home originally stood at the northeast corner of King and Fairfax Streets, two and a half blocks from the brothers' shop, and it is logical that he would have owned an Ingle chair. The chair came down in the family until 1960, when descendants donated it to the Smithsonian Institution.[15]

Figure 12 Side chair, Alexandria, Virginia, 1795–1800. Mahogany with tulip poplar. H. 37½", W. 20", D. 17". (Courtesy, National Museum of American History; photo, Museum of Early Southern Decorative Arts.)

Figure 13 Detail of the back of the side chair illustrated in fig. 12.

Figure 14 Side chair, Alexandria, Virginia, 1795–1800. Mahogany with oak. H. 37½", W. 19", D. 17". (Courtesy, Sully Plantation; photo, Museum of Early Southern Decorative Arts.)

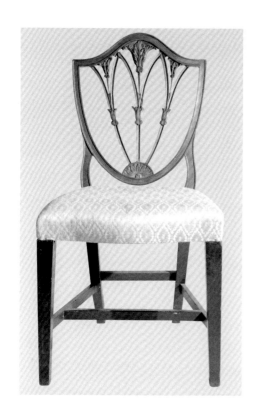

Richard Bland Lee (1761–1827) and his wife, Elizabeth Collins Lee (1768–1858), purchased a similar set of chairs for Sully, which was built in Fairfax County, Virginia, in 1799 (fig. 14). Lee had numerous opportunities to engage the Ingle brothers. He probably met them in Philadelphia through his friend Thomas Jefferson, while serving in Congress between 1789 and 1795. Richard's brother Harry owned property on Oronoco Street, just five blocks from the Ingles' Alexandria shops, and members of the Lee family visited Alexandria frequently for business and pleasure. In 1816 Richard received a two-year appointment from James Madison as "Claims Commissioner" and was responsible for compensating individuals and businesses for property destroyed or damaged in Washington during the War of 1812. In that position Lee was in constant contact with Henry Ingle, who oversaw construction of the Brick Capitol that temporarily housed Congress after the British burned William Thornton's original structure. [16]

The original owner of an armchair from a third set is unknown, but it has a history of descent in the Green family of Alexandria and was probably owned in the early nineteenth century by cabinetmaker William Green (1774–1824) (figs. 15, 16). A native of Sheffield, England, William arrived in Alexandria in 1817. Shortly thereafter, he may have begun working as a journeyman for cabinetmaker John Muir (1770–1815). Muir's business was located at 110 South Royal, next door to the shop where Joseph Ingle practiced his trade from 1795 to 1816. [17]

Figure 15 Armchair, Alexandria, Virginia, or Washington, D.C., 1795–1805. Mahogany with oak and tulip poplar. H. 37½", W. 18⅝", D. 16¼". (Courtesy, Colonial Williamsburg Foundation.) The arms are early additions.

Figure 16 Detail of the carved acanthus leaves on the armchair illustrated in fig. 15.

Green began working independently at 110 South Royal by 1820, when he placed an advertisement thanking local clients for their patronage. Three years later, his son James (b. 1801) joined him in the business, and the following year the younger Green married John Muir's daughter Jane (1803–1880). Although the means by which the chair entered the Green family remain unknown, the object's early leg repairs and arm additions suggest that it may have been taken to William's shop for repair.[18]

The three sets of chairs with Alexandria histories (see figs. 12, 14, 15) have splats based on plate 5 of George Hepplewhite's *Cabinet-Maker and Upholsterer's Guide* (1788) (fig. 17). Although the carving on the chairs shares details with earlier work attributed William Hodgson, there is no documentary evidence that he moved to Alexandria and continued to work for Ingle. If Hodgson did not carve these chairs, his work certainly appears to have influenced the design of the acanthus leaves at the top of the splats.

Figure 17 Design for a side chair illustrated on pl. 5 of George Hepplewhite's *Cabinet-Maker and Upholsterer's Guide* (3rd ed., 1794). (Courtesy, Winterthur Museum.)

Figure 18 Catafalque, possibly by Henry or Joseph Ingle, Alexandria, Virginia, 1790–1800. Walnut. H. 26¾", L. 113½" (with handles), D. 33¾". (Courtesy, Mount Vernon Ladies Association of the Union; photo, Dennis McWaters.)

Ingle commissioned work from Hodgson during the 1780s and might well have taken some of the carver's working drawings when he left Virginia in 1791. At the very least, it is hard to imagine that the men did not influence each other.[19]

Only a small group of objects associated with the Ingles' early Alexandria period survive, but it is clear that they offered a range of options for certain forms. Patrons could obtain chairs with plain or molded legs, seat frames with straight or serpentine front rails, and over-the-rail upholstery or slip seats. For seating with over-the-rail upholstery, the Ingles reinforced the frames with diagonal braces, typically made of poplar and half-dovetailed into the tops of the rails. The braces are positioned close to the leg and usually at a slightly oblique angle. Most of the seat rails on Ingles' chairs are oak, but sporadic use of ash and mahogany has been recorded. The joints on their chairs were secured with glue alone, and the pins occasionally found on some examples represent later refurbishment or repair.[20]

A catafalque illustrated in figure 18 may be associated with one of Joseph and Henry Ingle's most significant commissions, although evidence is insufficient to support more than a tentative attribution. In 1799 George Washington's estate hired them to provide a casket and oversee the former president's funeral. The brothers charged $88 for a "mahogany coffin and silver plate engraved, furnished with lace," provided the catafalque on which the coffin rested during several days of ceremonies, and supplied a horse-drawn hearse to convey the body to Alexandria for a Masonic ceremony before returning it to Mount Vernon for burial. Although unverified oral tradition is all that links the catafalque illustrated in figure 18 to George Washington's funeral, that object's pierced brackets and stretchers are consistent with the Philadelphia style in which the brothers worked, and its molded legs are similar to those on some of the aforementioned Alexandria chairs.[21]

In the June 19, 1800, issue of the *Times and the District of Columbia Advertiser,* Henry Ingle announced his pending move into Washington City, and the following year he purchased a shop on New Jersey Avenue when he entered into a one-year partnership with chair maker and cabinet-maker Enoch Pelton (1770–1829). His new neighborhood was among the most active in the district, with international artisans working at the unfinished Capitol site, legislators engaged in governing, and businessmen trying to capitalize on the benefits of the moment. Though records are sparse, it is clear that Ingle worked at the Capitol intermittently over the years, perhaps with Clotworthy Stephenson, who was active at that site by 1797. In 1808 Ingle was among a group of Capitol artisans who signed a petition to Henry Latrobe, expressing their dedication to the project, despite erratic government funding. When he retired six years later, Ingle was still working from his shop at New Jersey Avenue.[22]

Joseph remained in Alexandria, but records pertaining to his trade are scant. He took an apprentice in 1805 and retired in 1816, just two years before his death. Fragments of a leg and chair banister recovered from a privy behind Joseph's shop appear to date circa 1800, thus warranting considera-

Figure 19 Fragment of a tapered leg with spade foot, possibly Joseph Ingle, Alexandria, Virginia, 1795–1805. Mahogany. Dimensions not recorded. (Courtesy, Alexandria Archaeology Museum; photo, Christian Meade.)

Figure 20 Excavated banister from an urn-back chair, possibly Joseph Ingle, Alexandria, Virginia, 1795–1805. Dimensions not recorded. (Courtesy, Alexandria Archaeology Museum; photo, Christian Meade.)

tion as his work. Both artifacts came from a stratum of ash, thought to have resulted from an 1827 fire that began in James Green's shop on the adjoining property at 110 South Royal. The fire spread eastward toward the river causing great destruction, yet it spared the Ingle property.[23]

The excavated leg has a spade foot that is a separate, one-piece component (fig. 19). Most spade feet are composed of four pieces that are horizontally laminated to the sides of the leg, a procedure that is far more efficient in terms of labor and materials. This difference in construction suggests that the leg is not a discarded fragment from a piece of furniture but rather a showroom prop intended for demonstrating two leg options—one plain and the other terminating in a spade foot. In contrast, the banister appears to have been part of an urn-back chair (fig. 20). The leaves are carved in low relief and have paired shading cuts that diverge from a convex central vein (fig. 21). Although no chair with identical banisters is known, an example originally owned by George Washington's gardener

Figure 21   Detail of the carving on the chair banister illustrated in fig. 20.

Figure 22   Side chair, possibly Joseph Ingle, Alexandria, Virginia, 1795–1800. Mahogany with tulip poplar. H. 37¾", W. 21", D. 19¼". (Courtesy, Gadsby's Tavern Museum, City of Alexandria; photo, Museum of Early Southern Decorative Arts.)

Johan Ehlers suggests that urn-back variants with similar details were popular in Alexandria and the District of Columbia during this period (fig. 22). The back of the Ehlers chair was inspired by the design for a "Bar Back Sofa" in Hepplewhite's *Guide*, a publication frequently consulted by local furniture makers.[24]

Although separating the work of the Ingle brothers is somewhat problematic, chairs from a set originally owned by William Hammond Dorsey

Figure 23 Side chair attributed to Henry Ingle, possibly with Isaac Pelton, Washington, D.C., 1801–1802. Mahogany and oak. H. 37½", W. 21", D. 17⅛". (Courtesy, Maryland Historical Society; photo, Gavin Ashworth.)

Figure 24 Detail of the leg carving on the chair illustrated in fig. 23. (Photo, Gavin Ashworth.)

(1764–1819) of Washington and Baltimore offer clues for identifying Henry's work (fig. 23). Although traditionally attributed to Baltimore, the Dorsey chairs have carved urn backs that are identical to those on the Ramsay, Lee, and Green examples (figs. 12, 14, 15). Dorsey lived in Georgetown before moving to Brookeville in 1810 and almost certainly acquired the chairs shortly after completing the Oaks (now known as Dumbarton Oaks) in 1801. During the period when Dorsey would have commissioned his chairs, Henry Ingle was living above and working from his shop at New Jersey Avenue, a location much closer to the Oaks than Joseph's shop. Dorsey and Henry Ingle also had numerous opportunities to connect through the city's busy social network and also through their shared charitable pursuits—Dorsey was Judge of the Orphan Court for Washington City from 1801 to 1805, and Ingle served as a Trustee for the Poor from 1805 to 1806.[25]

The Dorsey chairs are distinguished by having elaborately carved legs (fig. 24). Each front face has a half-flower at the top and a chain of graduated

Figure 25 Side chair attributed to Henry Ingle, possibly with Isaac Pelton, Washington, D.C., 1801–1802. Mahogany with walnut, cherry, tulip poplar, and mahogany. H. 36½", W. 20¾", D. 19". (Courtesy, Winterthur Museum.) This is the earliest Washington seating form with half-over-the-rail upholstery.

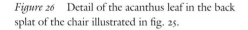

Figure 26 Detail of the acanthus leaf in the back splat of the chair illustrated in fig. 25.

husks that ends just above an astragal-shaped element at the bottom. William Hodgson used tripartite husks with teardrop-shaped stems during the 1780s (fig. 8), thus it is only logical that Henry Ingle incorporated similar designs in his later furniture work. As the Dorsey chairs suggest, Ingle continued to work in the Philadelphia tradition, just as he had in Alexandria, while adapting to the demands of wealthier Washingtonians.[26]

The carving on the Dorsey chairs provides compelling evidence that a larger group of ornate seating furniture was made in Washington. A set of chairs (figs. 25, 26) and at least one card table (fig. 27) that descended in the Harper family of Olney, Montgomery County, Maryland, were clearly carved by the same hand. Stylistically, the chairs are the most fully developed examples from the Washington school. Their back design was derived from plate 36 in Thomas Sheraton's *Cabinet-Maker and Upholsterer's Drawing Book* (fig. 28) and their front legs from plate 2 in Hepplewhite's *Guide*. The design of the Harper chairs differs significantly from that of other seating

Figure 27 Card table attributed to Henry Ingle, Washington, D.C., 1800–1805. Mahogany with tulip poplar, oak, and mahogany. H. 29¼", W. 30¾", D. 15". (Courtesy, Baltimore Museum of Art; gift of Mrs. Harry B. Dillehunt, Jr., in memory of her husband; photo, Museum of Early Southern Decorative Arts.)

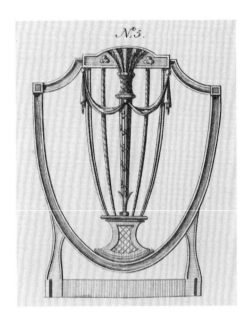

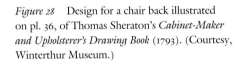

Figure 28 Design for a chair back illustrated on pl. 36, of Thomas Sheraton's *Cabinet-Maker and Upholsterer's Drawing Book* (1793). (Courtesy, Winterthur Museum.)

attributed to Henry Ingle (see figs. 12, 14, 15, 23); however, all these objects have stiles that are shaped and molded in a similar manner and rear legs with virtually identical splay. The acanthus leaves at the base of the Harper chair backs have a pronounced central vein, hollow fronds, and overlapping tips that match those in the large clusters below the crests of the Ramsay, Lee, Green, and Dorsey chairs (figs. 12, 14, 15, 23). On both models, the large central acanthus is flanked on each side by a partial acanthus having three hollow channels that flow upward at the edge of the composition. Similarities also exist between the husks on the center banister of the Harper chairs (fig. 26) and legs of the Dorsey chairs (fig. 24). Despite differences in design, the execution is identical. This is most apparent in the outlining, modeling, and shading of the leaves and modeling of the teardrop-shaped stems.[27]

Previous scholars have asserted that the Harper chairs were originally "owned by Charles Carroll of Carrollton," but they most likely came to his residence when his daughter Katherine "Kitty" Carroll Harper (1778–1861) moved in with him following the death of her husband, Robert Goodloe Harper (1765–1825). The set descended from Mrs. Harper to her great-granddaughter Dorothea Harper Pennington (1896–1995), who sold them to collector Louis Guerineau Myers. The assumption that Charles Carroll commissioned the set has obscured its origin and subsequent history. During the period when these chairs were made, Carroll was focused on helping his children build and furnish new homes rather than personal construction or refurbishment projects.[28]

In 1799 Katherine Carroll met attorney Robert Harper, a United States congressman from South Carolina's 96th district. The following year he moved temporarily to Baltimore to court her and curry favor with her father, who was skeptical of their relationship. During Harper's term, which lasted from 1797 to 1801, he served as chairman of the House of Representative's Ways and Means Committee. In that position he oversaw legislation that raised money for the government—including funds for construction of the Capitol, President's House, and other buildings for the new Federal City. In Washington, Harper interacted with men involved in those Herculean projects, including Henry Ingle. As the son of a cabinetmaker, Harper would have probably appreciated Ingle's skill and political savvy and felt comfortable dealing with him.[29]

Harper succeeded in winning over Charles Carroll, for he married Katherine Carroll on May 7, 1801, and soon thereafter the couple settled in Montgomery County, Maryland. Over the next thirty years, Charles Carroll gave them at least $343,957, which enabled them to build a home and acquire furnishings like the set of side chairs (fig. 25) and the card table (fig. 27). In the final analysis, these objects fit neatly into the chronology of seating furniture associated with Henry Ingle, Harper's life in Washington, D.C., and his association with the Carroll family.[30]

Although the Harper chairs are the finest urn-back examples attributed to Ingle, his shop produced seating with more elaborate carving, including two closely related sets of chairs with backs derived from plate 6 in Hepplewhite's *Guide* (fig. 29). Captain John Singleton of Sumter, South Carolina,

Figure 29 Design for "Chairs" illustrated on pl. 6 of George Hepplewhite's *Cabinet-Maker and Upholsterer's Guide* (3rd ed., 1794). (Courtesy, Winterthur Museum.) The chair on the left was the source for the back of the Harper chairs, and the chair on the right was the source for the half rosette and graduated husks on the Harper chairs and other seating attributed to Henry Ingle.

Figure 30 Side chair attributed to Henry Ingle, Washington, D.C., 1800–1805. Mahogany with tulip poplar and yellow pine. H. 36½", W. 20", D. 18½". (Courtesy, Winterthur Museum.)

Figure 31 Detail of the back of the chair illustrated in fig. 30.

Figure 32 Side chair attributed to Henry Ingle, Washington, D.C., 1800–1805. Mahogany with oak. H. 37¼", W. 20", D. 21". (Private collection; photo, Astorino.)

Figure 33 Detail of the back of the chair illustrated in fig. 32.

Figure 34 Side chair, Washington, D.C., 1800–1810. Mahogany with ash. H. 36½", W. 19⅜", D. 17¼". (Private collection; photo, Museum of Early Southern Decorative Arts.)

Figure 35 Armchair, Washington, D.C., ca. 1800. Mahogany. (*Baltimore Furniture: The Work of Baltimore and Annapolis Cabinetmakers from 1760 to 1810* [Baltimore, Md.: Baltimore Museum of Art, 1947], fig. 56.)

reputedly owned the set represented by the chair illustrated in figures 30 and 31. The sculptural ribbons and drapery, bold central rosette, naturalistic acanthus, and husks with teardrop stems recall William Hodgson's carving for Woodlands (fig. 8) and case furniture made by Ingle in Richmond (figs. 5–7) as well as Ingle's Alexandria chairs (figs. 12, 14, 15).[31]

One of the most common chair designs associated with Henry Ingle has a simpler back with a single carved banister in the middle (fig. 32). The banister has his characteristic half rosette and festoon of graduated husks (fig. 33). Three variations of this chair design are known; all have over-the-rail upholstery and molded legs but differ in the shape of their seats, leg treatment, and stile and banister moldings.[32]

A related set of twelve chairs has a nineteenth-century history of use at the President's House (fig. 34). Representing a simplified variant of the preceding design (fig. 32), the chairs in this set have thinner stock, arched crests, and carving by a less skilled hand. Although clearly not products of Henry Ingle's shop, these objects are characteristic of Washington, D.C., seating from the first decade of the nineteenth century and reflect the growing appeal of this popular regional design. Other chairs from this secondary shop are known; one model is identical to the example illustrated in figure 34, with the exception of having a serpentine crest. As was the case with chairs used in the President's House, seating from Ingle's shop influenced most versions of this particular design.[33]

An armchair illustrated in *Baltimore Furniture: The Work of Baltimore and Annapolis Cabinetmakers from 1760 to 1810* shows how Ingle and other Washington chair makers were updating their products by the beginning of the nineteenth century (fig. 35). The turned arm supports and legs are the most

Figure 36 Sofa attributed to Henry and/or Joseph Ingle, Alexandria, Virginia, or Washington, D.C., 1795–1805. Mahogany and lightwood inlay; secondary woods not recorded. H. 36", W. 79", D. 37¼". (Courtesy, Historical Society of Frederick County, Maryland; photo, Gavin Ashworth.)

Figure 37 Detail of an arm and leg on the sofa illustrated in fig. 36. (Photo, Gavin Ashworth.)

Figure 38 Sofa, Philadelphia, Pennsylvania, 1795–1805. Mahogany with yellow pine, white oak, and white pine. H. 22½", W. 69". (Courtesy, Philadelphia Museum of Art.)

stylistically advanced features. The latter are decorated with fashionable waterleaves that radiate from the center of oval medallions and surround the shank of each leg below its juncture to the seat rail.[34]

The legs and arm supports of this armchair link it to other objects from Ingle shops, including a neoclassical sofa that descended in the Tyler and Belt families of Virginia and Maryland (fig. 36). Like many objects associated with the Ingle brothers, the sofa is a derivation of a Philadelphia prototype. Examples from that city are typically rather small in scale and feature gently swept crests and front legs that transition into baluster-shaped arm supports (fig. 37). The Tyler-Belt sofa shares these details but also has attributes associated with Washington production. In contrast to Philadelphia sofas, which usually have four legs in front and three in the rear (fig. 38), Washington examples typically have four legs at the front and back. Other Washington sofas share the oval medallions on the outer front legs and arms that extend past their supports, ending with a pronounced downward scroll.[35]

The Tyler-Belt sofa has structural details that later became standard on Washington work. Its seat frame is reinforced with two front-to-rear braces. The braces are dovetailed into the tops of the front and rear seat rails and aligned with the middle legs. Screw holes on the inner faces of the legs and

undersides of the braces document the attachment of wooden brackets like those on other sofas in this group. This structural approach contrasts with work from Baltimore and other urban centers to the north, where sofas either lack front-to-rear braces or have braces centered between the legs rather than aligned with them.

Documentary evidence for Henry Ingle's cabinetwork is scarce before 1815, as it is for most Washington artisans associated with the Capitol and President's House. Treasury accounts record payments to him but rarely describe his work. Moreover, destruction of the city's most prominent buildings by the British in 1814 obliterated much of the documentary and physical evidence of his and other contemporary tradesmen's work.

In 1813 two young cabinetmakers, Charles Belt and John D. Hill, announced that they were moving into the building on Capitol Hill "lately occupied as a Cabinet-making shop by Mr. Henry Ingle." By that date, Ingle's interests and business associations had gravitated to the civic and investment arena. His political career began with his election to the city council in 1806 and was propelled by subsequent appointments to various commissions. Ingle's political clout and financial acumen allowed him to participate in partnerships with some of the city's most successful business-men. Able to envision Washington's growing needs, he worked closely with Daniel Carroll of Duddington in several building ventures and with George Blagden (1769–1828) to establish a subscription burial ground that soon gained government support and became the Congressional Cemetery. After Britain invaded and burned Washington, Ingle and his associates formed a public stock company to raise funds and erect a temporary shelter where Congress could meet. The company's Brick Capitol housed the Senate and House of Representatives for four years, during which time Thornton's original was reconstructed. The venture not only brought Henry Ingle increasing prominence but also signaled that his career as an artisan had ended and his role as city father had effectively come into its own.[36]

Stonecarvers and the Introduction of European Neoclassicism

Immigrant stonecarvers had a profound impact on the development of neoclassical style in Washington architecture and furniture. This influence began in 1792, when Robert Adam's Scottish-born protégé Collen William-son was appointed overseer of masons at the President's House, and expanded the following year with the arrival of seven highly skilled stone-cutters culled from his former colleagues at Masonic Lodge 8 in Edinburgh, Scotland. Shortly thereafter George Blagden—a native of Yorkshire, England—left the President's House workforce to oversee all the masons working at the Capitol. For the most demanding work, Blagden recruited a significant force of British workmen.[37]

The stonemasons who built the President's House and Capitol used buff-colored sandstone quarried from the banks of Aquia Creek, forty miles south of Washington. Stonecutters with basic masonry skills cut the stone into precise, rectilinear blocks, so they could be laid with flush joints. Using chisels, files, scrapers, and abrasives, a second group of more accomplished workers fabricated architectural details and moldings in emulation of those of ancient Rome.

The Scottish masons described as "stone-carvers" at the President's House sculpted the elaborate Ionic capitals, naturalistic floral ornaments, and complex geometric friezes in that building. The acanthus rinceaux and griffins on the north door and the delicately modeled floral swags and paterae above provide superb testimony of the talent available within their circle (fig. 39).

Figure 39 Carved ornament over the north entrance of the President's House, attributed to David Cummings, John Davidson, James Dixon, James Dougherty, Henry Edwards, John Hogg, and/or Robert Vincent, Washington D.C., ca. 1797. Carved sandstone. (Courtesy, White House Historical Association.)

Although the carvers are identified by name, they rarely appear in government records. Construction accounts for the President's House are also vague, making it difficult to connect individuals to their specific work or gauge their influence on stone carving in the wider region.[38]

The stone carvers at the President's House are the only tradesmen who can currently be associated with a group of ornate neoclassical tombstones made locally during the 1790s. The most sophisticated of these mark the graves of Sarah (1764–1792) and Eleanor Wren (1746–1798) at Christ Church, Alexandria. Now damaged by time and the elements, the stones attest to their carver's knowledge and mastery of sophisticated classical

Figure 40 Tombstone for Sarah Wren, Christ Church, Alexandria, Virginia, after 1794. Seneca sandstone. H. 31". (Courtesy, Historic Christ Church; photo, Sumpter Priddy and Christian Meade.)

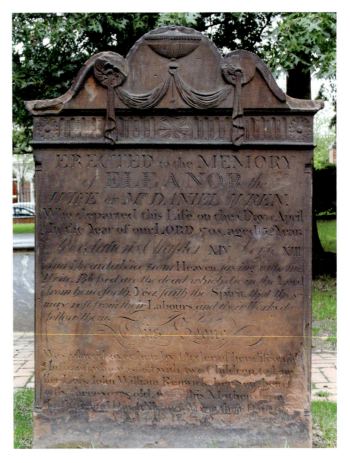

Figure 41 Tombstone for Eleanor Wren, Christ Church, Alexandria, Virginia, after 1798. Seneca sandstone. H. 62½". (Courtesy, Historic Christ Church; photo, Sumpter Priddy and Christian Meade.)

detail (figs. 40, 41). Soon after these stones were carved, similar details appeared on furniture attributed to the Washington school.

In 1801 President-elect Thomas Jefferson expressed concern that America lacked sculptors capable of producing classical statuary worthy of a capital city. After Henry Latrobe was appointed Surveyor of Public Buildings in 1803, the two men formulated a plan to address that problem. Two years later Latrobe requested assistance from Jefferson's friend and former neighbor Philip Mazzei (1730–1816) who was working in Rome as a vintner and merchant:

> The Capitol was begun at a time when the country was entirely destitute of artists, and even of good workmen in the branches of architecture. . . . It is now so far advanced as to make it necessary that we should have as early as possible the assistance of a good sculptor of architectural decorations.[39]

Mazzei had hoped to entice Italy's renowned sculptor Antonio Canova (1757–1822) to come to America, but Napoleon Bonaparte had long since compelled the artist—apparently under significant duress—to produce sculpture for his château at Malmaison as well as portrait busts, full-length figures, and equestrian statues depicting the general for public buildings and spaces. As an alternative, Mazzei hired Canova's associates Giuseppe Franzoni (1779–1815) and Giovanni Andrei (1770–1824). They arrived in America on March 3, 1806, and immediately began working for Latrobe. Franzoni was especially skilled at sculpting figures and sculpted some of Latrobe's most ambitious designs for the Capitol. His work included a full-

Figure 42 Giuseppe Franzoni after a design by Benjamin Henry Latrobe, capital, U.S. Senate vestibule, 1809. Aquia sandstone. (Courtesy, Architect of the Capitol.)

Figure 43 Giovanni Andrei, capital, White House South Portico, ca. 1815. Aquia sandstone. (Courtesy, White House Historical Association.)

Figure 44 Francesco Iardella after a design by Benjamin Henry Latrobe, capital, U.S. Senate Rotunda, 1816. Aquia sandstone. (Courtesy, Architect of the Capitol.)

length representation of Liberty and the Eagle for the south wing of the Capitol, corn capitals (fig. 42) for the Senate vestibule, and a row of caryatid supports for the gallery rail above the old Senate Chamber. The caryatids were destroyed in the Capitol fire in 1814, but sketchy depictions of them are visible in Latrobe's watercolor elevation for that chamber. They are significant because their 1808 date of completion makes them one of the earliest examples recorded in classical America, and because caryatids subsequently appear on early Washington furniture.[40]

After Franzoni's untimely death in 1815, Andrei became the Capitol's chief sculptor (fig. 43). Over the next twenty years, the latter hired several other carvers, including Franzoni's cousin Francesco Iardella (1793–1831), who rendered Latrobe's design for tobacco capitals in 1816 (fig. 44). Three years later, Andrei and Iardella began supervising a group of Italian and Scottish "carvers" whose names appeared on a payroll voucher documenting their work on "furniture for the Presidents House."[41]

William Waters and the Influence of Annapolis Furniture Styles

Georgetown "Cabinet and Chair Maker" William Waters (1766–1859) may have apprenticed with Archibald Chisholm (act. 1770–1796), who emigrated from Scotland in 1772, partnered with Annapolis cabinetmaker John Shaw from 1772 to 1776, and married Waters's sister Elizabeth (1755–1838) in 1777. Where Waters practiced his trade between 1787, when he presumably finished his training, and 1791, when he advertised in Georgetown for an apprentice, remains unknown. By 1793 he had established a shop near the river, where he offered sideboards, dining tables, breakfast tables, and card tables. Waters was the first tradesman in the immediate Washington area who advertised upholstered furniture, including easy chairs, close stool chairs, and bedsteads.[42]

William Waters's ties to his brother-in-law must have been strong, since he left Georgetown briefly in 1793 to partner with Chisholm. In the *Maryland Journal and Baltimore Daily Advertiser*, they reported that they had "contracted to deliver a considerable quantity of Cabinet-Work in a short time" and would "give great encouragement to two or three Journeymen Cabinet and Chair Makers, at their Manufactory in Annapolis." In 1794 Chisholm and Waters disbanded their partnership. Chisholm acquired a small plantation on the banks of the West River and became a planter. Waters returned to Georgetown but did not advertise until December 23, 1796, when he notified the public that he had "several experienced workmen . . . [who] enable him to supply his customers on very short notice." At that time, his inventory included "several Sofas, covered with satin hair cloth and garnished with brass nails and socket castors, mahogany Chairs of different patterns . . . easy chairs . . . and bedsteads."[43]

Waters appears to have anticipated the economic surge imminent with Congress's move from Philadelphia. Among the "ready made furniture" he advertised in September 1799 were a "new billiard table handsomely finished, Mahogany chairs and sofas, Easy chairs, common and cabriole, Mahogany tables of different sorts and sizes, sideboards, desks and drawers, Wash bason stands, &c. with bedsteads of every description." The following year, Waters moved to "Bridge Street, next door to Mr. Elisha Rigg's Store" and diversified his business by providing "board and lodging" for "half a dozen gentlemen." His last advertisement as a cabinetmaker appeared in 1804, when he announced "several beautiful Side Boards large and small, Northumberland Dining Tables in setts, oval and plain Card and Tea Tables, Desks, Drawers and Bedsteads, etc." An addendum to the advertisement signaled his move away from the woodworking trades and toward broader mercantile pursuits involving "Wines, Spirituous Liquors, fresh Teas, Particular Green Coffee, first and second quality Sugars, and a variety of other articles in the grocery line."[44]

In 1810, like many Georgetown tradesmen, Waters moved his shop closer to the seat of government, "near the Seven Buildings" on Pennsylvania Avenue, in Washington City. That year he advertised a "piano and new mahogany furniture," but the wording suggests that he did not make those objects. From 1816 to 1827 Waters held several civic positions including city commissioner, alderman, and city magistrate. He died in Georgetown in 1859, at ninety-two.[45]

The furniture listed in Waters's advertisements indicates that his shop produced a range of sophisticated neoclassical forms. Although no objects can be documented to him, a group of neoclassical sofas from the District of Columbia probably originated in his shop or that of his successor, William Worthington. Waters was the only cabinetmaker in late-eighteenth-century Washington who advertised that form. Three cabriole sofas with over-the-rail upholstery are known. One has plain tapered legs, and two have molded variants. The sofa illustrated in figure 45 descended in the Lipscomb and Quigley families of Georgetown and at one time belonged to Jessie Lipscomb (1797–1875), a wealthy grocer.[46]

The seat frame of the Lipscomb-Quigley sofa has front-to-rear braces and brackets like those on the Ingle example that descended in the Tyler and Belt families (fig. 36). Each corner is reinforced with a diagonal brace that is set into half-dovetails. The front braces are positioned near the leg, but those at the back are set farther out in order to span the rounded corners. To compensate for the inherent weakness of the joints at the rear corners, the maker reinforced them by gluing strips of linen over them. Looking glass makers often used this technique when constructing or repairing frames with heavy mirrors.[47]

Figure 45 Sofa attributed to William Waters or William Worthington, District of Columbia, 1795–1805. Mahogany with tulip poplar and yellow pine. H. 36½", W. 77½", D. 24". (Private collection; photo, Sumpter Priddy.)

Figure 46 Sofa attributed to William Waters or William Worthington, District of Columbia, 1795–1805. Mahogany with tulip poplar and yellow pine. H. 36½", W. 77½", D. 34". (Private collection; photo, Sumpter Priddy.)

Figure 47 Sofa attributed to William Waters or William Worthington, District of Columbia, 1795–1805. Mahogany with tulip poplar and yellow pine. H. 36½", W. 77½", D. 24". (Private collection; photo, Astorino.) The sofa has its original casters, but they are not shown here.

The crest of the Lipscomb-Quigley sofa is lower in relation to the arms than most Baltimore examples of similar form. Sofas made in the District of Columbia also differ from their Baltimore counterparts in having crook'd rear legs. This feature occurs in British sofas and design book illustrations but is rare in American work.

A sofa made for Alexandria physician Peter Wise (1775–1808) is virtually identical to the Lipscomb-Quigley sofa, though with a much deeper seat (fig. 46). Wise family tradition maintains that the sofa was "made to order" for the hefty bachelor, who "weighed 318 pounds when he was 18 years old and was well over 6 feet tall." When Dr. Wise died prematurely at thirty-three years of age, appraisers of his estate assigned it the significant value of $35.[48]

The most fully developed sofa in this group has a history of descent from Georgetown hotelier John Wise (ca. 1740–1815) (figs. 47, 48). He moved to Alexandria during the early 1780s and constructed a tavern on the west side of Royal Street, near the corner of Cameron, in 1785. Three years later he added a three-storey structure on the adjoining lot to create the City Hotel and Tavern. Each of that building's principal dining rooms had chimney-pieces with an overmantel and pediment, some with carved trusses and

Figure 48 Detail of the right arm and leg of the sofa illustrated in fig. 47.

Figure 49 *William Worthington*, Washington, D.C. or Frederick, Maryland, 1820–1825. Oil on canvas. 30" x 25". (Private collection; photo, Philip Beaurline.)

rosettes. Like the sofa, the City Hotel and Tavern attests to their owner's appreciation of sophisticated furniture and architectural style.[49]

Circumstantial evidence suggests that Waters either trained or employed William Worthington Jr. (1775–1839) (fig. 49). Recent research suggests that the latter's father was William Worthington Sr. (1756–1837) of Montgomery County, Maryland, and that his grandparents were John Worthington III and Susannah Hood, of Baltimore County, Maryland. Worthington probably became a journeyman in 1796, the same year Waters announced that he had "several experienced workmen" in his shop. Four years later, Worthington opened a "Cabinet and Chair Manufactory" in Georgetown, describing his production in much the same way that Waters did. The 1800 census of the United States listed Worthington as head of a household that included two older white females and three white males under the age of twenty-five.[50]

Worthington's first shop was on High Street (now Wisconsin Avenue) near Georgetown's finest homes. When Congress moved from Philadelphia in 1800, Worthington announced his relocation "to the City of Washington, near the Great Hotel," midway between the President's House and the Capitol. Later advertisements reveal that he did not close the High Street manufactory but kept it open through 1811, likely as a support facility for his growing business.[51]

Shortly after moving into Washington, Worthington realized that the best areas for businesses like his were along Pennsylvania Avenue in the vicinity of the President's House and along New Jersey Avenue in Henry Ingle's neighborhood. He began building a house and shop at 2105 Pennsylvania Avenue—four blocks from the President's House—and moved there in 1803. Worthington's home was next to the Six Buildings, a new row of fashionable brick town houses. The large scale, convenient location, and architectural sophistication of the Six Buildings attracted prominent tenants, including the Departments of State, War, and Navy. James and Dolley Madison and the War Department occupied other homes on the block before they were destroyed by fire in 1801. The Madisons returned to the neighborhood in 1814 after the British burned the President's House. Like the Monroes, the Madisons later lived at the equally prestigious Seven Buildings, located nearby at the northwest corner of Pennsylvania Avenue and Nineteenth Street N.W. Residents of this prosperous neighborhood became some of Worthington's most important customers.[52]

As his business grew, William Worthington took apprentices from Virginia, Maryland, and the District of Columbia. Seven can be identified by name, including Benjamin Middleton Belt (1785–1828) and John D. Hill (1793–1823), who came from prominent local families. Daniel Carroll of Duddington signed Belt's 1802 indenture, but the former's role in Worthington's business, if any, remains unknown.[53]

Worthington's public service, which included militia duty and membership on the city council, also kept him in the public eye. With William Waters shifting his business to mercantile pursuits after 1804 and Henry Ingle retiring from the trade in 1812, Worthington rose to the forefront of Washington's cabinetmaking community. On June 15, 1814, he received his first presidential commission when he repaired a picture frame. Although he billed only a dollar, the job apparently opened doors.[54]

In 1815 "George Boyd, Esquire, Agent for the President's Furniture," received authorization to commission Worthington for work on behalf of the Madisons. The cabinetmaker's statement detailed a large delivery on March 13 and several smaller ones running into the middle of June. Among the forms listed were a "secretary desk," a large dining table, a writing table, two other tables, "two settees covered in linen," a "couch on castors," six chairs, a "large family bedstead complete," five low beds, and a "common size bedstead." The chairs were only $1.50 each, which suggest they were not upholstered. By contrast, the settees cost $45 each, and the couch was priced at $32. Worthington also provided a variety of services including "fixing blinds in windows," putting a shelf on a mantelpiece, and repairing a looking glass. Worthington's total charges to the government were $428, but Mrs. Madison assumed payment for the couch, which she took home to Montpelier in Orange County, Virginia. The term "couch" referred to a stylish French form that encouraged women to recline when seated. Today that form is often described as a recamier.[55]

The Monroe Presidency and the Influence of French Neoclassicism
Worthington also received the patronage of James Madison's successor, James Monroe (1758–1831). Monroe's aesthetic sensibilities began to coalesce after his 1786 marriage to Elizabeth Kortwright (1768–1830), daughter of a prosperous New York merchant. In 1796 Monroe received a two-year appointment as Minister Plenipotentiary to France. Shortly after arriving, the Monroes enrolled their daughter, Elizabeth (1787–1836), in the school of Mme Jeanne-Louise-Henriette Campan at St-Germain-en-Laye. There, Eliza forged a close friendship with Hortense Beauharnais, whose mother, Joséphine, had recently married Napoléon Bonaparte.[56]

The Monroes returned to America in 1799, the same year that Napoléon mounted a military campaign in Egypt. During the general's absence, his wife, Joséphine, purchased the Château de Malmaison on the outskirts of Paris and hired Charles Percier (1764–1838) and Pierre-François-Léonard Fontaine (1762–1853) to transform its interiors. The firm engaged that city's most talented artists and artisans to drape, paint, gild and sculpt furnishings for an unprecedented classical interior with exotic Egyptian details, then presented their sumptuous designs in *Recueil de décorations intérieures* (1801). The expenses incurred by Napoléon's extensive military campaign and Joséphine's extravagant tastes threatened to bankrupt France's treasury and forced Napoléon to approach the United States about purchasing the Louisiana Territory. After negotiating the purchase in France in 1803, Monroe served as Minister Plenipotentiary to Great Britain from 1804 to 1807. Although his new station was London, the Monroes spent much of their time in France and attended Napoléon's coronation in Notre-Dame Cathedral on December 2, 1804.[57]

In the midst of these world-changing events, Eliza Monroe and Hortense Beauharnais went about their business as friends. Though undocumented, Eliza probably saw Empress Joséphine's private round bedchamber, which was dominated by a monumental bedstead designed by Percier and Fontaine (fig. 50). The underlying structure, though comparatively simple, had gilded swans perched atop stands on either side of the headboard and a cornucopia at either end of the footboard. A bold canopy, topped by a gilded Roman eagle, towered overhead, with red and white silk hangings embroidered in gold. Objects of this type had a profound influence on the interior decor of the Monroes' house in Washington.[58]

During James's presidency, the Monroes spoke French in private, employed a French chef, and decorated the President's House with French furnishings. The firm Russell and LaFarge—America's consular agents at the French port of Le Havre—commissioned furnishings from the finest workrooms of Paris. Among the objects they shipped to Washington in 1818

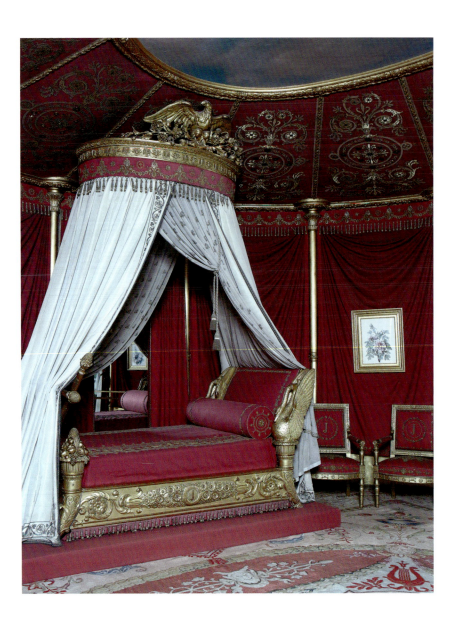

Figure 50 French bedstead attributed to Jacob Desmalter and Co. after a design by Charles Percier and Pierre-François-Léonard Fontaine, Château de Malmaison, Rueil-Malmaison, France, 1799–1803. (Courtesy, Réunion des Musées Nationaux; photo, Art Resource, NY.)

were a thirty-eight-piece suite of gilded beech seating furniture by Pierre Bellangé, silver by Jean-Baptiste-Claude Odiot, painted and gilded porcelain by Honoré and Dagoty, figural bronze clocks by Denière et Mateline, and lighting devices and mantel ornaments from Pierre-Phillipe Thomire. The Monroes also purchased goods and services from French émigré artisans including Charles Alexandre, who did much of the upholstery and paperhanging for the Monroes in the President's House, and Louis Labille, who provided the same services for their private residence in Washington and their country home, Montpelier.[59]

Some of the most significant French influence on the President's House appears to have come from Baron René de Perdreauville. Born into an aristocratic Parisian family, he fled France following Napoléon's abdication. In 1815 de Perdreauville immigrated to America with his wife, Marie-Victoire-Adèle Le Masurier, and their children. It is likely that the Monroes knew him when they lived in France. Three years after his arrival in this country, the couple hired de Perdreauville to oversee an upholstery workroom and ancillary facilities including a storeroom for wood and a forge for making specialized hardware. His workmen also painted window cornices, upholstered seating, fabricated draperies, and made upholstered French armchairs, described as *fauteuil*.[60]

In 1818 Monroe issued a pamphlet titled *Message from the President of the United States upon the Subject of the Furniture Necessary for the President's House,* in which he criticized government allocations for furnishings as "altogether inadequate." His goals were to increase congressional appropriations for furnishings and to reappoint George Boyd as agent for their acquisition and care. With Boyd answerable to Congress, Monroe could furnish the President's House as he saw fit while shielding himself from public scrutiny. Editorials in a number of newspapers condemned "the expensive manner in which Congress have thought proper to furnish the President's house," but placed little blame on Monroe.[61]

After a brief respite to alleviate criticism, work resumed at the President's House. At this stage of the project, the Monroes and their French advisers turned to local artisans to supplement the elaborate furnishings ordered from abroad. Of the half dozen cabinetmakers who contributed to the project, William Worthington was clearly their favorite. None of Worthington's presidential furniture from this period has been identified, but his invoices to Boyd describe specific forms and, in some instances, individual details.[62]

On August 4, 1818, William Worthington submitted a bill that included "1 mahogany French bedstead, fluted posts" valued at $45 and another example for the "northeast room" valued at $22. The first was destined for the room occupied by the president's daughter, Eliza Monroe Hay, and the second, for a nearby guest room. Two days later, Washington turner Joseph Fagains charged Boyd $2 for "turning 8 pieces for bedsteads." The "pieces" were undoubtedly finials that surmounted each post. The following spring, Worthington's former apprentice Benjamin Belt submitted an invoice for "2 Crowns for bedsteads" at $22 each and "2 Urns for do at $5 each." The "urns," which may have been carved, would have capped each "crown."[63]

Charles Alexandre's bill of January 29, 1819, describes his work for the northeast room—"Making a window drapery, and crown bed, putting up the same for 12.00"—and includes a charge for "iron work for the crown . . . 1.00." Two months later, he submitted another invoice for upholstery in Eliza's room, which included window dressings and bed hangings that were twice as expensive as those provided earlier: "two pairs of window curtains, &c. $25.00; making the trimmings of a crown bed, &c. . . . $25.00; 9 yards of cambrick . . . $2.70; three dozen rings . . . 75[¢]; 1 clothes pin . . . 50[¢]; 32 yards of red and yellow fringe at $1.50."[64]

A French bedstead made in Washington, D.C., matches descriptions of the example Worthington made for Eliza Monroe (figs. 51–53). Instead of balusters based on Renaissance forms, the maker used Doric columns with stop fluting for the corners and a simpler version of that order for the colonnades of the headboard. Of all the classical orders used by eighteenth- and early-nineteenth-century Chesapeake builders and turners, Doric was the most popular.[65]

Figure 52 Detail of the carved rail on the French bedstead illustrated in fig. 51.

Figure 53 Detail of the carved post on the French bedstead illustrated in fig. 51.

Beneath the capitals are swags separated by jabots (fig. 53), a decorative detail used by regional stone carvers since the 1790s and by makers of comparable "composition ornaments" on neoclassical chimneypieces, cornices, doorways, and other architectural fixtures installed throughout the city. A mantelpiece on the second floor of the Bank of Alexandria has slender columns with similar swag-and-jabot decoration and was likely made by Irish-born ornament maker George Andrews (d. 1816) (figs. 54, 55). At Jefferson's request, Andrews moved from New York to Washington to work at the President's House. It is possible that one of the carvers who made molds for Andrews carved parts of Eliza Monroe's bedstead and that the ornaments on architectural fixtures in her bedroom echoed those on the furnishings.[66]

Figure 54 Chimneypiece in a second-floor room in the Bank of Alexandria, 133 North Fairfax, Alexandria, Virginia, 1807. (Courtesy, Northern Virginia Regional Parks Authority; photo, Christian Meade.) The composition ornament is attributed to George Andrews. The President's House probably had similar chimneypieces.

Figure 55 Detail of the composition ornament on the chimneypiece illustrated in fig. 54.

Although missing from the bedstead, the crown was a separate unit suspended at least four feet above the tops of the posts. Sheraton published designs for several bedsteads with crowns, a form he called a "French Bedstead" or a "French State Bed." His engravings suggest that the crown on Eliza's bed had a rectangular frame surmounted by a domed or peaked top. The curtains would have been attached around the lower edge of the crown, allowing them to drape over the iron rods and ends of the bed. The rods, which were listed in Charles Alexandre's invoice, were probably bowed or serpentine, with a broad flange pierced with a hole on each end. Iron pins extending up from the tops of the posts fitted into the holes. With a finial placed on top of each post, a larger finial capping the crown, and elaborate curtains below, the bedstead would have resembled an exotic tent.[67]

Alexandre's bill for work in Eliza's bedroom also included a $4.00 charge for "2 stands for the eagles." An "Inventory of the Furniture in the President's House" taken on March 24, 1825, listed "1 Elegant mahogany bedstead, gilt eagle mounted" among the furnishings in the "fifth room," which was unequivocally hers. Adjacent entries listed "1 Hair mattress, feather bed, bolster, and pillows . . . 1 Pair sheets, one pair blankets, Marseilles quilt [and] . . . 1 set chintz dome bed curtains." The "2 Sets [of] chintz window curtains" listed separately almost certainly matched the fabric on the bed.[68]

Designs in Thomas Sheraton's *Cabinet-Maker and Upholsterer's Drawing Book* (1791) and *Cabinet-Maker's Dictionary* (1803) are possible sources of inspiration for the basic form and certain specific details on Eliza's bed. The "Canopy Bed" illustrated on plate 6 in the 1804 edition of the *Drawing Book* has a wall-mounted crown capped by an eagle (figs. 56, 57) and resembles the example that Percier and Fontaine designed for Empress Joséphine. In contrast to the swans that flanked her bed, Sheraton used a dove perched

Figure 56 "Canopy Bed" illustrated on pl. 6 of Thomas Sheraton's *Cabinet-Maker and Upholsterer's Drawing Book* (1804). (Courtesy, Winterthur Museum.)

Figure 57 Detail of the plate illustrated in fig. 56. (Courtesy, Winterthur Museum.)

atop a stand, its wings outspread and beak clasping drapery. Given the fact that no comparable published image from the period is known, plate 6 may well have influenced Worthington's design.[69]

Another Washington artist with intimate knowledge of French state beds was Italian sculptor Giuseppe Valaperta. According to Latrobe, Valaperta "was engaged before the fall of Napoleon in the decoration . . . at Malmaison." The sculptor's personal effects, inventoried in 1817, included a profile of Joséphine Bonaparte taken from life at her palace. Given the similarities between her state bed and Eliza's crown bed, it is possible that Valaperta may have been involved in the latter object's design.[70]

Worthington or the Monroes probably commissioned a local carver to furnish the eagles for Eliza's bed. Their options included specialists accustomed to producing ornaments for furniture and architecture as well as stone carvers and sculptors accustomed to working in wood (see figs. 58, 59). A voucher submitted by Giovanni Andrei requested payment for "Four Carvers" who had worked on "Furniture for the Presidents House" in August and September 1819. Four of these men are identified by name: Francesco Fortini, Owen Horgan, John Woods, and one J. Elyson. Their work, which took a cumulative 207½ days, must have been important, since it required oversight by Andrei and Francesco Iardella. If the eagles on Eliza Hays's bedstead originated within that circle of craftsmen, they would have been its crowning glory.[71]

Figure 58   Keystone, Bank of Alexandria, Alexandria, Virginia, 1807. Aquia sandstone. (Courtesy, Northern Virginia Regional Parks Authority; photo, Christian Meade.)

Figure 59   Giuseppi Valaperta, eagle in the Hall of Statues, U.S. Capitol, 1815. Aquia sandstone. (Courtesy, Architect of the Capitol.)

Competing Craftsmen, Competing Styles
Worthington's principal competitor appears to have been William King Jr. (1771–1854), a Pennsylvania native who trained with Annapolis cabinetmaker John Shaw, established a shop in Georgetown in 1795, and worked there for more than fifty years. Like Worthington, King had strong ties to James Monroe. In May 1818 Monroe wrote Commissioner of Public Buildings and agent for the President's House furniture Samuel Lane:

> The chairs, for the East room, and tables and any other articles, for that room and the mahogany benches, small tables and chairs for the hall will be made by Mr. Worthington and Mr. King. I have reason to think that King has a good model for the chairs, and that it may be better for him to make them and for Worthington to make the other articles, or as many as can, in time. But arrange this in a delicate manner between them, as I had spoken to Mr. Worthington first.

In December 1818 King received payment for a handsome suite of French-inspired seating comprising twenty-four armchairs valued at $33 each

Figure 60 Armchair attributed to William King Jr., Georgetown, D.C., 1818. Mahogany with ash and maple. H. 40⅞", W. 25½", D. 25⅛". (Courtesy, Collection of Ash Lawn Highland; photo, Hirschl & Adler Galleries, New York.)

Figure 61 Sofa attributed to William King Jr., Georgetown, D.C., 1815–1825. Mahogany with walnut and yellow pine; brass casters. H. 32⅞", W. 89¼", D. 25¼". (Courtesy, Colonial Williamsburg Foundation.)

Figure 62 Side chair attributed to William King Jr., Georgetown, D.C., 1815–1825. Mahogany with tulip poplar and white pine. H. 32⅝", W. 17⅞", D. 16". (Courtesy, Colonial Williamsburg Foundation.) Saber legs are rare on Washington seating.

(fig. 60) and four sofas at $49.50 each. Lane's copy of the invoice noted that the total had been reduced because the upholstery and final varnish were "not done." A number of the chairs are known, but the sofas have not been identified. The sofas, which matched the chairs in almost every detail, appear in a Mathew Brady photograph of the President's House interiors taken in 1865, but it is not known if they survive.[72]

King made a Grecian sofa and eight matching chairs for Georgetown businessman Clement Smith (1776–1839) and his wife, Margaret (1783–1862) (figs. 61, 62). A closely related sofa without carving descended in King's family. The sofas are distinguished by having unusually heavy seat rails, which support a separate wooden frame for upholstery. The frame has four front-to-back braces. This feature does not appear on earlier Washington seating.[73]

Figure 63 Side chair attributed to William Worthington, Washington, D.C., 1805–1815. Mahogany with ash and yellow pine. H. 37½," W. 18½", D. 17¼". (Private collection; photo, Astorino.)

Figure 64 Detail of the carved crest of the chair illustrated in fig. 63.

The Smith family sofa and chairs were carved by the same hand, although the grapevine on the chairs is on an oval field with a plain ground, whereas the decoration on the sofa is on a rectangular field with a punched background. Aside from the President's House seating, these are the only chairs that survive from King's shop.

Figure 65 Side chair attributed to William Worthington, Washington, D.C., 1805–1815. Mahogany with ash, yellow pine, cherry, and mahogany. H. 36¼", W. 18½", D. 17¼". (Private collection; photo, Astorino.)

Figure 66 Detail of the carved crest of the side chair illustrated in fig. 65.

William Worthington's chairs present a sharp stylistic counterpoint to King's work (figs. 63–67). Nine examples from three different sets were based on the left-hand chair on plate 9 in Hepplewhite's *Guide* (1788) (fig. 68). The chair in the engraving has reeded stiles surmounted by carved blocks, a splat with five delicate columns, each having a four-petal flower in the center, a

Figure 67 Side chair attributed to William Worthington, Washington, D.C., 1805–1815. Mahogany with yellow pine, ash, cherry, and mahogany. H. 33", W. 18½", D. 17¼". (Private collection; photo, Astorino.) This chair is from a set that descended in the family of Dr. Reverdy Ghiselin (1765–1823) and his wife, Margaret (1783–1850), who lived near Nottingham in Prince George's County, Maryland.

Figure 68 Designs for chairs illustrated on pl. 9 of George Hepplewhite's *Cabinet-Maker and Upholsterer's Guide* (1794). (Courtesy, Winterthur Museum.)

Figure 69 Side chair attributed to William Worthington, Washington, D.C., 1805–1815. Mahogany and mahogany veneer with oak. H. 35¾", W. 19¾", D. 16⅜". (Private collection; photo, Museum of Early Southern Decorative Arts.) This chair is one of a pair.

drapery panel, quarter fans, and a molded crest rail capped by a baldachin. All Worthington chairs of this type represent variations of Hepplewhite's design yet also have carved details similar to those on the bedstead illustrated in figure 51. The small blocks that flank the crest of each chair are likewise miniature versions of those at the top of the bedposts (fig. 53), and all these objects have related drapery-and-jabot carving. The bowknots with ribbons occur only on the chairs.[74]

Worthington's chairs display subtle variation from set to set, but their construction is consistent. Common features include mortise-and-tenon joints originally secured with glue alone; square, vertically grained glue blocks where the side and rear rails meet the back posts; double-laminated front rails (on serpentine and compass-shaped examples); two dovetailed front-to-rear braces; and front legs with open mortises at the top and a screw countersunk from the back to hold them in place. The braces are straight on the lower edge and slightly concave at the top (fig. 65).

A chair that descended in the Earle family of Melfield in Queen Anne's County, Maryland, has a compass seat and turned legs (fig. 69) that are identical to those on the example illustrated in figure 65. Although the Earle chair never had front-to-rear seat braces, all other aspects of its construction are consistent with seating from Worthington's shop. Like many of the pieces illustrated here, the chair reflects a style that is commonly associated with Philadelphia and Baltimore but can now be linked to the District of Columbia as well. Other Washington, D.C., compass-seat chairs having identical backs but different leg designs are also recorded.

Two groups of sofas (figs. 70–75) provide further evidence that the aforementioned chairs (figs. 63–67) are from Worthington's shop. The sofas are constructed like the earlier cabriole forms (figs. 45–48) and have similar decorative details including carved paterae and inlaid guilloches. These shared features and the probable date ranges for the sofas support the theory that Worthington trained with William Waters.

The first of these sofas (fig. 70) is one of three examples with a projecting central crest, four legs at the front and rear, turned and reeded arm supports,

Figure 70 Sofa attributed to William Worthington, Washington, D.C., 1800–1810. Mahogany and mahogany veneer with mahogany, white pine, and chestnut. H. 38¼", W. 81", D. 30½". (Courtesy, James Madison's Montpelier.)

and scrolled arms. Although some of these features occur on work attributed to the Ingle shops (figs. 36, 37), Worthington's sofas are longer, higher at the back, and have plaques on the crest. This example, the simplest variant of the group, has neither inlay nor carving but retains a significant portion of its original upholstery, including two original bolsters. Another sofa in this group descended in the Mason family of Georgetown and may have been commissioned by General John Mason V (1766–1849) and his wife,

Figure 71 Sofa attributed to William Worthington, Washington, D.C., 1800–1810. Mahogany, satinwood, rosewood veneer and lightwood and darkwood inlays. H. 38¼", W. 82½", D. 30½". (*American Antiques from Israel Sack Collection*, 10 vols. [Washington, D.C.: Highland House, 1982], 2: 1334.)

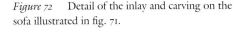

Figure 72 Detail of the inlay and carving on the sofa illustrated in fig. 71.

Figure 73 Sofa attributed to William Worthington, Washington, D.C., 1800–1810. Mahogany and satinwood veneers with mahogany, white pine, and chestnut. H. 38¼", W. 81", D. 30½". (Private collection; photo, Marc Anderson.)

Anna (1776–1856) (figs. 71, 72). He served as president of the Bank of Columbia, which held funds for the Commissioner of Public Buildings. The final sofa in this group has carved paterae on the outer front legs and a baldachin identical to those on Worthington's most elegant side chairs (figs. 73–75).[75]

In the District of Columbia, where political courtship played no less a role than social courtship, the sofa was especially popular. In 1800 Margaret Bayard Smith (1778–1844) of Philadelphia arrived in Washington with her husband, Samuel (1772–1845), editor of the newly founded *National Intelligencer*. Over the next four decades, she composed a series of letters that

Figure 74 A view of the back of the sofa illustrated in fig. 73. (Private collection; photo, Marc Anderson.)

Figure 75 Detail of the inlaid and carved leg on the sofa illustrated in fig. 73.

recorded the social and political life of the city. Of material objects, she was particularly observant of upholstered furniture—sofas, couches, and fauteuil—and the activities that took place on or around them.

In August 1809 Margaret Smith visited President and Mrs. Madison (1768–1849) at Montpelier. According to Smith, the first lady's bedchamber had a large bed, a sofa, and fauteuil, all of which "bespoke comfort." On a subsequent visit with her daughter Anna, Smith described a couch that may have been the example Worthington made in 1815:

> [Mrs. Madison's bedchamber is] . . . furnished with every convenience and much elegance. Before a large sopha, lay her work. Couches, easy-chairs &c invited us to ease and comfortable indulgence. . . . She drew [pulled] Anna on the sopha beside her and gave her half a dozen pretty books to look over, while drawing a French arm chair, or fauteuil . . . close by her.[76]

The sofa Worthington made for Major George Peter (1779–1861) and his wife, Ann (1791–1814), would have been appropriate for the finest public or private setting (figs. 76–79). The couple purchased unspecified furniture from the cabinetmaker on four separate occasions between 1810 and 1811, with charges totaling $312.50. Presumably, the sofa was among those furnishings and intended for use in the Peters' Georgetown house or Montgomery County, Maryland, plantation, Montanverd.[77]

The carving on the center panel of the crest features a classical kylix and vines with leaves and flowers (fig. 78). Although these naturalistic elements recall those on the rails of the French bedstead attributed to Worthington

Figure 76 Sofa attributed to William Worthington, Washington, D.C., 1810–1811. Mahogany with tulip poplar. H. 39", W. 77⅞", D. 25⅝". (Courtesy, Pearre-Peter family; photo, Gavin Ashworth.)

Figure 77 Detail of the carved patera on the right front leg of the sofa illustrated in fig. 76. (Photo, Gavin Ashworth.)

Figure 78 Detail of the carved central panel in the crest of the sofa illustrated in fig. 76. (Photo, Gavin Ashworth.)

Figure 79 Detail of the carved side panel in the crest of the sofa illustrated in fig. 76. (Photo, Gavin Ashworth.)

(fig. 52), they appear to have been carved by a different hand. The drapery on the flanking panels (fig. 79) has even earlier antecedents, as indicated by the tombstone carved for Eleanor Wrenn (fig. 80). The work of Scottish stone carvers informed regional furniture designs from the 1790s well into the 1810s.

The Peter family owned the land where Seneca stone, like that used for Eleanor's tombstone, was quarried. This material was prized as a supplement for Aquia stone, which was extracted from government quarries and parsed out for specific public building projects. George Blagden, who supervised the masons and stone carvers at the Capitol, was charged with securing Seneca stone for government contracts. With connections to Washington's most aristocratic families and elite artisans, he may have influenced the Peter family's aesthetic choices and their patronage of artisans.[78]

The Peter sofa is the earliest Washington example with a scroll back, a design first published in *The London Cabinet Book of Prices* (1802). New York cabinetmaker Duncan Phyfe has been credited with producing the earliest American examples of this form circa 1803. Although a northern prototype could have inspired the design of the Peter sofa, the possibility exists that it

could be contemporaneous with or earlier than those attributed to Phyfe and represents a separate evolutionary line from the same European sources that inspired him. It is demonstrable that the arms, legs, carved details, and construction of the Peter sofa are virtually identical to those on Ingle sofas (figs. 36, 37) dating from the late 1790s. British émigré craftsmen who were familiar with the latest furniture designs could have introduced the scroll-back design to Washington shortly thereafter. Given the fact that design books typically illustrated furniture forms and decorative details that were already in production, scroll backs probably predate the *London Cabinet Book of Prices* by at least a couple of years.[79]

A Campeachy, or "Spanish" chair (fig. 81) has swag and tassel ornaments (fig. 82) that appear to be by the hand responsible for carving the Peter family sofa. This is the earliest example of that form in the District of

Figure 80 Detail of the double drapery carved on the Eleanor Wren tombstone illustrated in fig. 41.

Figure 81 Campeachy chair attributed to William Worthington, Washington, D.C., 1815–1820. Mahogany with tulip popular and yellow pine. H. 37½", W. 21", D. 31½". (Courtesy, Peter Patout; photo, Ellen McDermott, New York.)

Figure 82 Detail of the carved crest rail on the chair illustrated in fig. 81.

Figure 83 Detail of the carved rosette on the chair illustrated in fig. 81.

Figure 84 Detail of a rosette on Sarah Wren's tombstone illustrated in fig. 40.

Figure 85 Campeachy chair attributed to William Worthington, Washington, D.C., 1810–1820. Mahogany with yellow pine. H. 40½", W. 21⅝", D. 29½". (Courtesy, Winterthur Museum; photo, Laszlo Bodo.) Worthington's Campeachy chairs have a bowed brace that is either dovetailed or mortised into the inner edges of the back frame.

Columbia, although as Diane Ehrenpreis's article in this volume suggests, Campeachy chairs from New Orleans probably arrived in Washington during the early years of Jefferson's term as president (1801–1809). All of Worthington's interpretations have reeding on the back, seat, arms, and arm supports. The chair illustrated in figure 81 is further distinguished by having rosettes at either end of the front seat rail (fig. 83). Although rosettes of this type are relatively generic neoclassical details, the examples on this Campeachy chair closely resemble those on Sarah Wren's tombstone (figs. 41, 84) and a Washington chair (fig. 30).[80]

Two other Campeachy chairs are attributed to Worthington's shop (figs. 85, 86). Neither is carved, yet their gracefully swept frames attest to his skill as a designer. Although the stock used for these chairs is thicker than that commonly seen on examples from the Caribbean and Gulf of Mexico, Worthington's workmen made the back and seat appear lighter by cutting a

Figure 86 Campeachy chair attributed to William Worthington, Washington, D.C., 1810–1820. Mahogany with yellow pine. H. 38½", W. 24", D. 33⅛". (Courtesy, Collection of Mrs. George M. Kaufman.)

Figure 87 Side chair, possibly Benjamin Belt or Gustavus Beall, Washington, D.C., 1814–1817. Mahogany with mahogany and white pine. H. 33", W. 19", D. 21½". (Courtesy, New Hampshire Historical Society.)

broad rabbet on the inner edge and covering it with brass-nailed leather upholstery. The downward flow and scrolled terminals of the arms also distinguish Worthington's chairs from Louisiana, Central American, and Caribbean examples, which typically have flat, horizontally scrolled arms.[81]

Just as couches allowed women like Margaret Smith to "recline . . . at ease," Campeachy chairs performed the same function for men. Indeed, the casual position encouraged by the latter form was a rejection of eighteenth-century rational mores that encouraged an upright posture with the feet placed squarely on the floor. The great classicist Thomas Jefferson occasionally used the term "siesta chair" to describe one of the chairs at Monticello, suggesting his acceptance of new romantic sensibilities.[82]

Stylistic Independence, Stylistic Innovation
While serving as New Hampshire congressman between 1814 and 1817 Daniel Webster (1782–1852) purchased a set of two armchairs and eight side chairs (fig. 87) with crests that are stylistically related to those on the carved Campeachy chair (figs. 81, 82) and the Peter family sofa (figs. 77–79). Although Webster's chairs have other features associated with Worthington, including the leafy patera in the middle of the back and two front-to-back seat braces, their somewhat awkward ogee legs and less competent carving suggest that they are from another shop.[83]

Regardless of aesthetics, Webster's chairs show how Washington cabinetmakers moved away from English pattern books to designs current in America during the late 1810s and early 1820s. This shift may have been precipitated by the War of 1812, which created anti-British sentiment among the local populace. The curule banisters in the back, round seats, and tapered ogee legs are similar to those on seating made by Duncan Phyfe and other New York cabinetmakers circa 1810, and two of the details appear on plate 6 of *The New York Book of Prices for Manufacturing Cabinet and Chair Work* (1816) (fig. 88). Webster's chairs may be from the shop of Gustavus Beall, who trained in Washington and worked as a journeyman in New York in 1811 and 1812 before returning to Washington. A carved breakfast table (fig. 89) is the only piece of furniture documented to Beall, and its design and ornament have decided New York overtones. Beall was also one of the few Washington artisans who advertised carved seating furniture.[84]

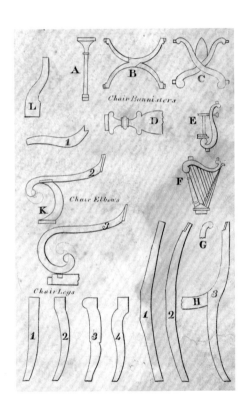

Figure 88 Designs for chair components on pl. 6 in New York Society of Cabinet Makers, *The New York Book of Prices for Manufacturing Cabinet and Chair Work*, 1816. (Courtesy, Museum of Early Southern Decorative Arts.)

Figure 89 Gustavus Beall, table, Georgetown, D.C., ca. 1815. Mahogany and mahogany veneer with oak and white pine. H. 28½", W. 42⅜" (open), D. 31¾". (Courtesy, Museum of Early Southern Decorative Arts.)

The drapery motifs carved on the Peter sofa (fig. 76), Campeachy chair (fig. 81) and Webster chairs (fig. 87) have Washington antecedents in stone that predate Phyfe's use of drapery swags on seating furniture by nearly five years. However, it is likely that all these designs emanated from Scotland, where many of the Federal City's leading artisans trained and where Phyfe and several of his New York contemporaries were born. The goal in raising this issue is not to question New York's economic or artistic dominance but to suggest caution in assuming that the course of American civilization inevitably flowed from North to South.

A Waning Career and an Enduring Legacy

In June 1818 William Worthington, Benjamin Belt, Gustavus Beall, and H. V. Hill submitted proposals to build 192 desks and their accompanying chairs for the House of Representatives. Among their competitors were New York cabinetmakers Honoré Lannuier and Thomas Constantine, the latter of whom secured the commission but lost money in the process. Worthington subsequently received commissions from other government departments. In 1819 United States Treasurer Thomas Tudor Tucker paid Worthington $166 for work for the navy. The furniture the cabinetmaker provided was probably for captains' quarters.[85]

The 1820 United States Census of Manufactures—taken on the heels of the devastating bank panic that swept America the year before—recorded that Worthington's shop had three workmen and produced $7,500 worth of furniture. It is unclear whether that modest sum reflected loss of business from the bank panic or signaled the beginning of Worthington's retreat from the furniture-making business. The next reference to him as a cabinetmaker is in 1825, when he made Abigail Adams a variety of case pieces, a table, and a bed. In October and November of the same year, Worthington constructed furniture for John Quincy Adams's Secretary of War James Barbour. Four years later, he worked briefly in Annapolis with George Shaw, the youngest son of Annapolis cabinetmaker John Shaw, although George had previously set up shop in Georgetown but soon returned to Annapolis. No furniture from the partnership is known. Worthington died in Georgetown on June 7, 1843, and was buried in Oak Hill Cemetery. His obituary, which appeared in the *Daily Madisonian*, was brief and did not allude to his importance as either a craftsman or a civic leader. His wife, Harriet, continued to live over the shop in the Six Buildings until her death in 1862.[86]

Although the material legacy of Worthington's career is substantial, his influence on furniture styles in the District of Columbia was manifest for years after his retirement in the work and careers of apprentices like John D. Hill and Benjamin Belt. Although his apprenticeship is undocumented, Hill's brother Henry V. (1791–1850) may also have trained with Worthington. The younger Hill moved into Henry Ingle's New Jersey Avenue shop in 1813 and was commissioned to make prototypes for a chair and desk for the House of Representatives five years later. The prototypes established the standard for the bidding process that Thomas Constantine subsequently won. On April 2, 1820, Henry Hill billed President Monroe's furnishings fund $52.50 for fourteen inexpensive ($3.50 each) cherry chairs. Bills submitted to the Adams administration on April 20, 1825, listed another dozen chairs at exactly the same price as well as a "Spanish Chair" valued at $15. Hill's last two presidential commissions, in 1825 and 1831 respectively, were comparatively small and did not involve seating.[87]

Hill's work received accolades in the *Daily National Intelligencer*. One article described a seating form commissioned by the Department of State as having been "made in the form of those Spanish Chairs introduced here by Mr. Jefferson." Hill added a number of ingenious contraptions to his Spanish chair, including leather "regulated in its degree of tension by a roller with rack and pinion" and a writing desk on a pivoting arm, "which may be drawn in front of the person who sits in the chair." A later article noted that a library case made by Hill for storing and displaying maps was "a contrivance of Mr. Jefferson." The description of the case indicates that Hill attempted to improve Jefferson's design by adding a pulley system to produce "a new and very convenient mode of arranging" the maps.[88]

Seating for a New Nation

A suite of twenty-four caryatid armchairs (fig. 90) and four matching settees used by the Monroe family at the President's House appear to be Washington products. These objects reflect numerous influences that converged in the city during the early nineteenth century and provide insights into the furniture trade of that period. Derived from plate 55 in George Smith's (act. 1786–1828) *Designs for Household Furnishings* (1804), the armchairs are made entirely of soft maple and ash, woods that grow on both sides of the Atlantic (fig. 91). Although their ambitious design might prompt speculation that the chairs were made in London, where the Monroe family lived intermittently during James's tenure as minister to Britain, or in Paris, where the family spent significant time before returning to America, evidence points to the contrary. When compared with the carved and gilded furnishings that

Figure 90 Armchair, probably Washington, D.C., 1815–1820. Maple and ash. H. 33¹⁄₁₆", W. 23⁵⁄₈", D. 18". (Courtesy, James Monroe Museum and Memorial Library; photo, Gavin Ashworth.) Maple was favored for American painted chairs in the 1810–1840 period. Unlike most European antique maple furniture from Europe, the Monroe chairs are not riddled with insect damage.

James and Elizabeth purchased abroad, the chairs appear awkward in proportion and provincial in execution. Any possibility of a European origin is further undercut by the fact that the chairs do not appear on any of the ships' manifests or packing lists that America's consular representatives or European customs agents compiled when the Monroe family left Europe or arrived back on American shores. Nor do they correspond with any pieces enumerated on the subsequent lists associated with French orders shipped to Washington between 1817 and 1819 with the specific intent of refurnishing the President's House.[89]

A number of sculptors in the District of Columbia had the skills necessary to produce the caryatid supports (fig. 92), including Carlo Franzoni, whose brother Giuseppe had carved the now destroyed caryatids for Latrobe's Senate Gallery a decade before. Others capable of the work included Giovanni Andrei and Franceso Iardella, the chief sculptors at the Capitol, their assistant Giuseppe Valaperta, and, potentially, Francesco

Figure 91   Designs for "Drawing Room Chairs in Profile" illustrated on pl. 55 of George Smith's *Designs for Household Furniture* (1808). (Courtesy, Winterthur Museum.)

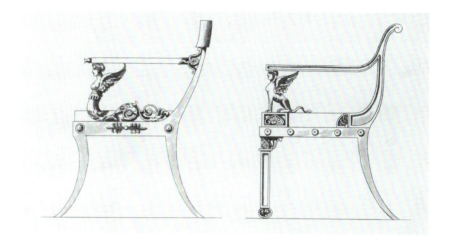

Figure 92   Detail of a caryatid on the armchair illustrated in fig. 90. (Photo, Gavin Ashworth.)

Figure 93 John Philip Fondé, side chair, Philadelphia, Pennsylvania, 1816. Ash, white pine, and white oak. H. 31¾", W. 18", D. 21". (Courtesy, Baltimore Museum of Art.)

Fortini, who worked beneath Andrei and Iardella on the Monroe furniture at the President's House. Although the caryatids on the Monroe chairs are less naturalistic than their architectural counterparts in the nation's Capitol, the carvers and sculptors may have adjusted the modeling and finish of the work to accommodate their patrons' budget or time constraints.[90]

Washington had numerous artisans capable of making and decorating the chair frames. These included chairmaker Henry Roe Burden (1771–1819) and ornamental painter John Philip Fondé (1794–1831). The men previously worked in Philadelphia, where Fondé decorated a set of ten chairs (fig. 93) in 1816 for Major David Lenox (1754–1828) and his wife, Tacy (d. 1834). Burden left Philadelphia in 1815 and moved to Washington, where he set up shop on Pennsylvania Avenue and went into partnership with Joseph Cassin, offering an assortment of painted furniture, including "cane, rush, and wood seat chairs, cribs, and settees."[91]

Burden had moved to Bridge Street (now M Street) in Georgetown before January 1818, when Fondé announced his business "adjoining H. R. Burden and Company's chair manufactory." In his new location, Fondé described himself as a sign and ornamental painter and offered to hire "chair painters, gilders, and japanners." On December 1, 1819, he received $37 from the House of Representatives for "Numbering doors, painting Tables, Signs for Committee Rooms, Post Office, Clerk's Office, etc." and providing gold leaf for a clock.[92]

Although there is insufficient evidence to attribute the Monroe chairs' design, construction, carving, and ornamental decoration to specific craftsmen, this furniture encapsulates the story of early neoclassical seating from the District of Columbia. The collaboration of statesmen who understood the convergence of taste and power, with renowned designers, local furniture makers, and émigré sculptors generated distinctive furnishings and interior ornaments that were essential complements to the city's new national architecture and served as important vehicles for shaping domestic and foreign impressions of the capital, and of America. Together, these men seized the opportunities of the moment to develop a distinctive style worthy of America's new seat of government and one that helped visiting diplomats to see and understand that the seemingly young country was no longer a wilderness but, rather, sufficiently mature to engage constructively on the larger world stage.

ACKNOWLEDGMENTS   The authors are grateful to Jenna Huffman, Laura Libert, and Elyse Poinsett for their diligence and extensive research in bringing this article to fruition. Other colleagues who have made valuable contributions over the years: Gary Albert, William Allen, William Allman, Lu Bartlett, Luke Beckerdite, Susan Borchardt, Megan Budinger, Leslie Buhler, William Bushong, Heidi Campbell-Shoaf, Lisa Mason Cheney, Tara Chicarda, Wendy Cooper, Douglas Copeley, Morgan Delaney, Julie Dennis, Alexandra Deutsch, Michael Dunn, William Voss Elder, Farar Elliott, Eleanor Gadsden, Lynn Hastings, Achsah Henderson, Astrid Hendrikson, Carolyn Holmes, Frank Horton,

Conover Hunt, Ronald Hurst, Ken Kato, Wendy Kail, Peter Kenny, Alexandra Kirtley, Robert Leath, Mark Letzer, Kristin Lloyd, Sasha Lourie, June Lucas, Osborne Mackey, Barbara Magid, Kelly McCartney, Milly McGehee, Keith McKay, Christian Meade, Melissa C. Naulin, Susan Newton, Peter Patout, Peter and Mary Pearre, Jeffrey Plank, Grant Quertermous, Joan Quinn, Paul Reber, Martha Rowe, Albert Sack, Susan Schoelwer, Susan Shames, Diane Skvarla, Bill Thomas, Matthew Thurlow, Jennifer Van Horn, Martha Vick, Ron Vukelich, and Gregory Weidman.

1. Kathleen M. Lesko, Valerie Melissa Babb, and Carroll R. Gibbs, *Black Georgetown Remembered: A History of the Georgetown Black Community from the Founding of the Town of George to the Present Historic District* (Washington, D.C.: Georgetown University Press, 1991), pp. 2–3.

2. T. Michael Miller, *Artisans and Merchants of Alexandria, Virginia, 1780–1820*, 2 vols. (Westminster, Md.: Heritage Books, 1991), 1: xix.

3. For histories of Washington, D.C., see Kenneth R. Bowling, *Creating the Federal City, 1774–1800: Potomac Fever* (Washington, D.C.: American Institute of Architects, 1988); Thomas Froncek, *The City of Washington: An Illustrated History* (New York: Wings, 1992); and Keith E. Melder and Melinda Young Stuart, *City of Magnificent Intentions: A History of Washington, District of Columbia* (Washington, D.C.: Intac, 1997).

4. Their cousin Daniel Carroll (1730–1796) of Rock Creek owned thousands of acres inland from Georgetown and served as one of three Commissioners for the Federal City.

5. In 1800 Baltimore had a population of approximately 26,500 (Population of the 33 Urban Places: 1800, United States Census Bureau, 1998-06-15, at www.census.gov/population/www/documentation/twps0027/tab03.txt [accessed December 13, 2008]).

6. William Howard Adams, *The Eye of Thomas Jefferson* (Charlottesville: University of Virginia Press, 1976), p. 108.

7. Sumpter Priddy and Martha Vick, "The Work of Clotworthy Stephenson, William Hodgson, and Henry Ingle in Richmond, Virginia, 1787–1797," in *American Furniture*, edited by Luke Beckerdite (Hanover, N.H.: University Press of New England for the Chipstone Foundation, 1994), pp. 206–33.

8. For more on Ingle's Richmond career, see ibid. Ingle appears to have met General Washington (Virginia Campbell Moore, "Reminiscences of Washington as Recalled by a Descendent of the Ingle Family," *Records of the Columbia Historical Society, Washington, D.C.* 3 [1900]: 96–114). In 1801 Stephenson became involved with the Washington Building Company (Wilhelmus Bogart Bryan, *A History of the National Capitol*, 2 vols. [New York: McMillan and Co., 1916], 1: 433, and William C. Allen, *History of the United States Capitol* [Washington, D.C.: Architect of the Capitol, 2001], p. 37).

9. The authors thank furniture scholar and carver Robert M. McCullough Jr. for sharing his observations on Hodgson's work. The desk-and-bookcase is inscribed "Dabney Manor" and dated "Jan. 24th, 1789." Hodgson carved swags composed of husks for Richmond Randolph Lodge Number 19 (Priddy and Vick, "The Work of Stephenson, Hodgson, and Ingle," p. 211).

10. Jefferson lived in Thomas Leiper's House at 274 High Street. He did not identify the pieces in his Memorandum Book of expenses. A candle stand related to the example that descended in the Ingle family (fig. 10) is in the Monticello collection and may represent Ingle's work. Ingle's accounts with Jefferson are briefly discussed in Susan Stein, *The Worlds of Thomas Jefferson at Monticello* (New York: Harry N. Abrams, 1993), pp. 248, 268, 282, 306. In the April 11, 1794, issue of the *Philadelphia Gazette and Universal Daily Advertiser*, Henry Ingle advertised on behalf of the city's "Master Cabinet Makers," seeking to hire "Thirty to Forty JOURNEYMEN CABINET-MAKERS, to whom the best prices will be given." Whether these workmen were needed for projects in Philadelphia or Washington is unclear. Ingle's work for Washington in Philadelphia is documented in an abstracted version of Tobias Lear's accounts in Stephen Decatur Jr., *Private Affairs of George Washington* (Boston: Houghton Mifflin, 1933), p. 170.

11. James McCormack's indenture to Joseph Ingle, August 28, 1793, [Alexandria Co., Va.], Hustings Court Order Book, 1791–1796, p. 146. Joseph purchased his Alexandria property on May 14, 1795 (Richard J. Muzzroli, "General Notes," Preliminary Working Drawing of Archaeological Work Done on Shaft No. 3KSW-3 Located in the Rear of 112 So. Royal St. Alexandria, Va. 1970, site report, Alexandria Archaeology, Alexandria, Va., 1970, p. 3K5-2).

Ingle and Shreiner dissolved their partnership on May 19, 1795 (*Philadelphia Gazette and Universal Daily Advertiser*, October 15, 1796).

12. *Philadelphia Gazette*, November 16, 1798. Henry Ingle advertised his hardware business in the *Columbian Mirror and Alexandria Gazette*, September 7, 1799.

13. For a Philadelphia prototype, see William McPherson Hornor Jr., *Blue Book: Philadelphia Furniture, William Penn to George Washington* (1935; reprint, Washington, D.C.: Highland House Publishers, 1977), p. 244, pls. 396–97. Henry's profile portrait and a number of family papers were presented by an unidentified donor to the Washington Historical Society ca. 1900 (Henry Ingle Family Papers 1829–1898, Historical Society of Washington, D.C., 1983.145).

14. For the chairs with identical backs, see Museum of Early Southern Decorative Arts (hereafter MESDA), file S-10998 and S-9892. Both have tapered legs, and the chair in file S-9892 has spade feet in the front.

15. Ramsay's father, William Ramsay (1716–1785), was a lifelong friend of Washington, a minister to Alexandria's Scottish community, and the town's first mayor. Dennis Ramsay's mother, Ann McCarty Bell, was Washington's cousin. See National Society of the Colonial Dames of America, *Letters to Washington and Accompanying Papers* (Boston: Houghton Mifflin and Co., 1898–1902), p. 368 n. 1.

16. For more on the Lee chairs, see MESDA research file S-6972. Allen, *History of the United States Capitol*, p. 112.

17. Oscar Fitzgerald, *The Green Family of Cabinetmakers: An Alexandria Institution, 1817–1887; An Exhibition of 19th Century Furniture* (Alexandria, Va.: Lyceum, 1986). For a discussion of the Green chair, see Ronald Hurst and Jonathan Prown, *Southern Furniture, 1680–1830: The Colonial Williamsburg Collection* (New York: Harry N. Abrams, 1987), pp. 129–31.

18. *Alexandria Gazette*, March 13, 1820. The alteration is discussed in Hurst and Prown, *Southern Furniture*, p. 129. For more on the Green family, see Fitzgerald, *The Green Family of Cabinetmakers*.

19. Hepplewhite and other period furniture makers used the term "urn back." A merchant named William Hodgson lived in Alexandria during the 1790s, thus complicating research on the carver (Miller, *Artisans and Merchants*, 1: 208–9). The authors thank Robert M. McCullough Jr. for pointing out parallels between the two groups of work.

20. Pins on Ingle furniture are the result of repair or tightening.

21. "Henry and Joseph Ingle to the Estate of George Washington," January 15, 1800, *The Papers of George Washington*, found in Anderson Galleries, *Catalogue of the Library of the Late Bishop Joseph Fletcher Hurst*, New York, 1904, p. 25. Two years later, the Ingle brothers provided the same services for Mrs. Washington's burial. The Alexandria Masonic Lodge 22 acquired the catafalque after Washington's funeral, presumably from member Joseph Ingle. In 1802 the lodge erected a new building in which the members set up a museum and exhibited their prized possessions, including many associated with President Washington's Masonic funeral. The catafalque remained there until an 1870 fire destroyed the building. It was reputedly saved but never returned (Charles H. Callahan, "Alexandria Washington Lodge No. 22," in *The Lodge of Washington and His Masonic Neighbors* [Alexandria, Va.: G. E. French, 1876], p. 28).

22. Ingle acquired the property from Thomas Law (1756–1834), who married Elizabeth Parke Custis ("Thomas Law Papers, 1791–1834," MS 2386, Maryland Historical Society, Baltimore). For information on the hardware store, see *Centennial History of Washington, D.C.*, edited by Harvey W. Crew et al. (Dayton, Ohio: United Brethren Publishing House, 1892), p. 406. The 1808 embargo and diminished tax revenue caused the erratic funding (William C. Allen, *History of the United States Capitol: A Chronicle of Design, Construction, and Politics* [Washington, D.C.: U.S. Government Printing Office, 2001], p. 37). The workers' petition is in National Archives, RG 233, 195/D9. Beginning in 1807, Ingle sold hardware and other supplies to the navy and the Navy Yard. Navy Yard references are in *Treasurer's Accounts, 10th Congress, 1st Session*, National Archives, Washington, D.C. For Henry Ingle, see *Times and District of Columbia Daily Advertiser*, June 19, 1800; *National Intelligencer*, October 10, 1801; and *National Intelligencer*, November 22, 1802.

23. For Joseph Ingle's work on the courthouse in Alexandria County, see Levy Court Minute book, 1807–1827, October 27, 1801. For the coffin Joseph made for Benjamin Shreve in 1802, see Alexandria City Wills, 1800–1804, p. 253. For Thomas Hennekin's apprenticeship to Joseph on September 21, 1805, see Alexandria County Orphans Court Records, 1801–1805, p. 307. Joseph advertised his house and lot for sale or lease in the June 21, 1815, issue of the *Alexandria Gazette, Commercial and Political*. Muzzroli, "General Notes," p. 3K5-2.

24. The chair was donated to Gadsby's Tavern Museum in the 1950s by Ehlers' great-great-granddaughter, Cora Duffey, and transferred to the City of Alexandria when it assumed jurisdiction over the site.

25. For information on Dorsey's Georgetown home, see Walter Berns, *Making Patriots* (Chicago, Il.: University of Chicago Press, 2001), p. 52. Dorsey's move to Brookeville, Maryland, is described in Joshua Dorsey Warfield, *The Founders of Anne Arundel and Howard Counties, Maryland* (Baltimore, Md.: Kohn and Pollock, 1905). For William Hammond Dorsey's appointment to Orphan's Court, see William Henry Dennis, "Orphans' Court and Register of Wills, District of Columbia," *Records of the Columbia Historical Society, Washington, D.C.* 3 (1900): 212.

26. The chairs are attributed to Baltimore in publications from the 1920s onward.

27. The five-part inlay consists of a wide central band of lightwood, flanked above and below by simple dark wood stringing and, on the outer edges, lightwood stringing.

28. The chairs descended from the Harpers to their son and daughter-in-law, Charles Carroll Harper, and from Charlotte Harper to daughter Emily Louisa Harper and her husband, William Clapham Pennington, to their daughter Dorothea Harper Pennington Nelson. Mrs. Nelson's chair was pictured in *Baltimore Furniture: The Work of Baltimore and Annapolis Cabinetmakers from 1760 to 1810* (Baltimore, Md.: Baltimore Museum of Art, 1947), p. 95, fig. 58. York, Pennsylvania, antique dealer Joe Kindig Jr. acquired the chairs from the Louis Myers estate, then sold two to Winterthur Museum and one to the Maryland Historical Society.

29. *Baltimore Furniture*, p. 95.

30. Edward C. Papenfuse, "English Aristocrat in an American Setting," in *"Anywhere so long there by freedom": Charles Carroll of Carrollton, His Family and His Maryland*, edited by Ann C. Van Devanter (Baltimore, Md.: Baltimore Museum of Art, 1975), p. 56. Charles Carroll's will stipulated that his grandson Charles Carroll of Doughoregan receive all of his household furnishings, including portraits, silver, and furniture. That the Harper chairs left the home and descended through daughter Kitty's line verifies that the elder Carroll never owned the chairs. See William Voss Elder III, "Furniture, Silver, Memorabilia, and Other Household Objects Relating to the Carroll Family," in ibid., p. 285. While studying the "Carroll" chair at Winterthur in 1957, furniture historian John Pearce wrote James D. Breckenridge, curator at the Baltimore Museum of Art: "It would then seem possible that the furniture had been made originally for Robert Goodloe Harper." Breckenridge responded: "The statement usually made is simply that these chairs once belonged to Charles Carroll of Carrollton; the catalogue's claim that he was the original owner seems only an inference." In a later letter Breckenridge added: "Other pieces in the same style, as close as to seem part of the same set, such as the pair of tables . . . do not seem to have ever had any Carroll association" (Pearce to Breckenridge, October 13 and 15, 1957, Winterthur accession file 57.770.1,2).

31. Decorative arts scholar Charles Montgomery noted that "the hollow seat and molded legs of [the Singleton chair]" were "not normally found on Baltimore chairs" and compared it with the Harper chair to reinforce that observation (Charles F. Montgomery, *American Furniture: The Federal Period* [New York: Viking Press, 1966], pp. 152–53). A related set of chairs appears in American Art Association Anderson Galleries, *Sale Catalogue of the Roland V. Vaughn Private Collection*, New York, November 14, 1931, lot 122. The chairs in that sale are in the Metropolitan Museum of Art.

32. Richard Hancock Bryant of Bethesda and Potomac, Maryland, purchased the chair either at a Washington, D.C., house sale or a local auction (Weschlers or Sloans) between 1950 and 1985 (Christopher Bryant to Sumpter Priddy, August 26, 2010). The other chairs referenced in this paragraph are in Washington, D.C., collections.

33. The chair is one from a set of twelve. When MESDA recorded the chairs in 1980, the owners reported that their ancestors had acquired the seating in "1850 at a sale at the White House" (MESDA research file S-10853). A second chair with identical carving and a serpentine crest rail sold at Adam A. Weschler Auctioneers, Washington, D.C., May 16, 1992, lot 290.

34. *Baltimore Furniture*, p. 93.

35. The sofa was donated to the Frederick County Historical Society by Cecelia Belt (1872–1958). Her husband, Dr. William Bradley Tyler Belt (1871–1942), was the son of Thomas Hanson Belt Jr. of Baltimore (1820–1880) and his second wife, Maria Tyler (1832–1909) of Frederick County, Maryland. Maria was the daughter of Dr. William Tyler (1784–1872) and his wife, Maria.

36. For the partnership, see *Daily National Intelligencer*, March 30, 1813. Ingle's civic service began in 1805, when he joined merchant James Hodgson and architect James Hoban on the

board of directors for the city's Merchant Fairs (*National Intelligencer*, April 26, 1805). In 1806 Ingle was elected to the city council and became Trustee of the Poor, serving with Peter Lennox, Clerk of the Works at the President's House. The following year Ingle served as registrar for the new Protestant Episcopal Church, constructed on land formerly belonging to Daniel Carroll of Duddington. Vestrymen included mason George Blagden and lumber merchant Griffith Coombe. Blagden and Coombe helped erect the Brick Capitol on a lot that Ingle and his partners owned. Wilhelmus Bogart Bryan, *A History of the National Capitol from Its Foundation through the Period of the Adoption of the Organic Act* (New York: MacMillan, 1916), p. 637.

37. Collen Williamson worked with Robert Adam (1728–1792) on Moy House in Marayshire, Scotland, in the early 1760s. Williamson's designs for the house were chosen over Adam's (National Monuments Record of Scotland, site no. 75141). Williamson was a relative of Georgetown tavern owner Roger Suter. The commissioners of the city held their meetings at Suter's Tavern. William C. Allen, *History of Slave Laborers in the Construction of the United States Capitol* (Washington, D.C.: Architect of the Capitol, 2005), p. 4. Lee H. Nelson, *White House Stone Carving, Builders and Restorers* (Washington, D.C.: National Park Service, 1992). A native of Attercliffe, Yorkshire, England, Blagden became an alderman of the city, a director of the Bank of Washington, and, with Henry Ingle, a founder of Congressional Cemetery. Blagden's first three years were spent partially in business with George Richardson (1762–1807), who dissolved their partnership in 1797 (*Columbia Mirror* and *Alexandria Gazette*, July 21, 1797). George Richardson appears to have been born in Pennsylvania.

38. The stone "carvers" mentioned in the President's House accounts during the 1790s were David Cummings, John Davidson, James Dixon, James Dougherty, Henry Edwards, John Hogg, and Robert Vincent (Robert James Kapsch, "The Labor History of the Construction and Reconstruction of the White House, 1793–1817" [Ph.D. diss., University of Maryland, 1993], pp. 374–377, 383, 403). George Blagden went on leave from the Capitol to work at the President's House in 1797—the year in which artisans completed this façade. This suggests that he may have been involved with the latter. All subsequent attributions to sculptors working on the Capitol come from Allen, *History of the United States Capitol*, pp. 49–124.

39. Joseph Downs, "The Capitol," *Metropolitan Museum of Art Bulletin* 1, no. 5 (January 1943): 172.

40. For Canova's relationship with Napoléon, see Christopher M. S. Johns, *Antonio Canova and the Politics of Patronage in Revolutionary and Napoleonic Europe* (Berkeley: University of California Press, 1998), pp. 88–123. For Mazzei, see Phillip Mazzei, Samuel Eugene Scalia, and Margherita Marchione, *My Life and Wanderings* (New York: American Institute of Italian Studies, 1980), p. 391; *The Italian American Experience: An Encyclopedia*, edited by Salvatore J. LaGumina, Frank J. Cavaioli, Salvatore Primeggia, and Joseph A. Varacalli (New York: Routledge, 1999), p. 33; and Irma B. Jaffe, *The Italian Presence in American Art, 1760–1860* (New York: Fordham University Press, 1989), p. 133. Andrei had trained Franzoni, and the two men married sisters. Furthermore, Franzoni's father, Francesco Antonio Franzoni (1734–1818), had numerous ties to Canova. After training in the Renaissance center of Carrara, Francesco moved to Rome, where he served Pope Pius VI as chief restorer of the Vatican's ancient sculpture and monuments. From that hallowed position he inspired the young Canova, who later credited him as a dominant figure in his development, and knew his family well. Mazzei—having visited Canova's studio—hired his friends Andrei and Franzoni on behalf of the American government. Among the sculptures that the elder Franzoni restored for the Vatican was a first-century Roman marble chariot and horse, now visible at the Museo Pio-Clementino. This provided a prototype for Carlo Franzoni's *The Car of History*, which the younger Franzoni sculpted over the entry to the Old House of Representatives, now Statuary Hall. For images, see Allen, *History of the United States Capitol*, p. 121.

41. Andrei carved Corinthian capitals for the House chamber and Latrobe's design for magnolia capitals for the Senate Gallery, destroyed in the 1814 fire. Andrei also hired Giuseppi Franzoni's younger brother Carlo (1786–1819), who sculpted *Liberty and Young America* in plaster for the Supreme Court, then focused on his heralded *Car of History*— arguably the finest neoclassical sculpture in America. See Charles E. Fairman, *Art and Artists of the Capitol of the United States of America* (Washington, D.C.: Government Printing Office, 1919), pp. 41–42; and Architect of the Capitol, *Art in the United States Capitol* (Washington, D.C.: Government Printing Office, 1978), p. 367. Iardella also carved a cherub-encrusted sarcophagus to mark the site of seventeenth-century Drayton family tombs at Magnolia Plantation, outside Charleston, South Carolina. Representative William Drayton (1776–1846) commissioned the sculptor

shortly after he was elected congressman in 1825. The sarcophagus, which was shipped from Washington sometime before Iardella's death in 1831, has not been published.

42. For more on Chisholm and Shaw, see William Voss Elder III and Lu Bartlett, "Cabinet-making in Shaw's Annapolis," in *John Shaw: Cabinetmaker of Annapolis*, edited by Elder and Bartlett (Baltimore, Md.: Baltimore Museum of Art, 1983), p. 31. For advertisements by Waters, see *Maryland Journal*, October 25, 1791; *Maryland Journal and Baltimore Daily Advertiser*, June 14, 1793; *Centinel of Liberty and Georgetown Advertiser*, December 23, 1796, and September 24, 1799; and the *Washington Federalist*, June 14, 1802.

43. *Maryland Journal*, June 14, 1793. *Maryland Gazette*, September 25, 1794; and *Centinel of Liberty and Georgetown Advertiser*, December 23, 1796.

44. *Centinel of Liberty and Georgetown Advertiser*, September 24, 1799, and July 15, 1800.

45. Notices of William Waters's elections to various civic posts were announced in *National Intelligencer*, August 17, 1810; *Daily National Advertiser,* June 27, 1816, and November 19, 1818; and *City Washington Gazette*, April 12, 1819.

46. The sofa was acquired at the 2008 estate auction of Virginia Louisa Quigley (1912–2007). Her parents—James Birl Compton (1873–1964) of Culpeper Country, Virginia, and Annie Louisa Cunningham (1875–1968)—lived with Quigley's maternal grandparents, Jessie Genevieve Lipscomb (1839–1923) and William Archibald Cunningham (1835–1915). Cunningham emigrated from Scotland to Georgetown, while Lipscomb was a local resident. In the previous generation, Quigley's great-grandfather Jessie Lipscomb (1797–1875) was a wealthy grocer and may have been the original owner of the sofa. The authors thank Pennsylvania antique dealer Kelly Kinzle for information on the Quigleys and the sofa.

47. Seat braces on sofas made in other regions are typically dovetailed into the front and rear rails in the open spaces flanking the legs.

48. Peter Wise was the son of Peter and Ann (Bolling) Wise of Petersburg and not related to Alexandria hotelier John Wise. Alexandria, Virginia, Alexandria Wills, Book C., p. 19. The sofa descended from Dr. Wise's brother George (1778–1856) to granddaughter Florence Wise Darst (1875–1948). Sumpter Priddy studied and photographed the piece in the mid-1980s, when it was still in family hands.

49. Wise's City Hotel was sold in 1795 to John Gadsby and is now known as Gadsby's Tavern.

50. Several of Worthington's apprentices had the surname Waters, including cousins Somer-sett (1813) and Walter (1815). Both apprentices were distant relations to William Walters. Harry Wright Newman, *Anne Arundel Gentry* (Annapolis, Md.: published by the author, 1933), pp. 320–22, discusses Worthington but confused the cabinetmaker with his father, William Sr. That error has been repeated in most subsequent publications that mention the Worthington family. The authors thank Astrid Henrikson of Charlottesville, Virginia, for genealogical research on the Worthingtons. In 1829 William Jr. moved temporarily from Georgetown to Annapolis to assist John Shaw's son George, after the young man took over his father's business. Elder and Bartlett, eds., *John Shaw*, p. 24. Kinship is suggested by several events. In April 1761 Worthington's first cousin once removed Ann Worthington (b.1738) married Weymouth Shaw (b. 1734) of Anne Arundel County; they named their son John (1763–1847). Worthington's aunt Ruth Worthington (1742–1786) married Dr. John Shaw (d. 1786) of Annapolis—though clearly not the cabinetmaker. See Henry C. Peden, *Marylanders to Carolina: Migration of Marylanders to North Carolina and South Carolina Prior to 1800* (Westminster, Md.: Heritage Books, 2006), p. 141. 1800 United States Federal Census, Washington, District of Columbia.

51. The Great Hotel, also known as the Lottery, was partially erected by Samuel Blodgett circa 1793 and situated on the crest of what was considered the F Street ridge; it was located at the northeast corner of Eighth and E Streets. *Washington Federalist*, December 19, 1800. In the December 28, 1811, issue of the *National Intelligencer*, Worthington reported that he had moved from High Street to his "shop adjoining the Six Buildings."

52. In the October 10, 1803, issue of the *National Intelligencer,* John M'Elwee announced that he had convex mirrors, girandoles, and other elegant accessories for sale at "Mr. William Worthington's Pennsylvania Avenue." Worthington's advertisements from that location appeared in the *National Intelligencer* on October 9, 1809, and December 28, 1811. Worthington's house was on lot 21, square 74, and became the seventh in that row. The Madisons and the War Department rented space in a building on the south side of the Six Buildings until November 8, 1800, when it burned. See Office of the Historian, U.S. Department of State, "One of the 'Six Buildings,' Washington, September 1800–May 1801." See also James M. Goode, *Capital Losses: A Cultural History of Washington's Destroyed Buildings* (Washington, D.C.: Smithsonian Institution Press, 1979), pp. 140–41.

53. District of Columbia, Record of Apprentices' Indentures, 1801–1811. Newspaper references transcribed in MESDA's craftsman files identified the following Worthington apprentices: William Jones (June 1802), John Plant (May 1808), Alpheus Hyatt (April 1810), William L. Wilkinson (June 1810), Lee M. Speake (1813), Michael Lowe Jr. (June 1815), Rufus Belt (1816), and John Hayre (September 1820). Worthington's household must have changed considerably in 1802, when he married Harriet Anderson (1781–1862) of Frederick County, Maryland (*Hornet*, December 28, 1802). The couple subsequently had three daughters (District of Columbia, Record of Apprentices' Indentures, 1801–1811, October 30, 1802, p. 43).

54. Worthington served in First Company, 3rd Battalion, 1st Legion of the Washington, D.C., Militia. Christian Hines's *Early Recollections of Washington City* (1866), in John Clagett Proctor, *Washington Past and Present: A History*, 4 vols. (New York: Lewis Historical Publishing Company, 1930), 1: 361. For Worthington's election to the council, see William V. Cox, *Celebration of the One Hundredth Anniversary of the Establishment of the Seat of Government in the District of Columbia* (Washington, D.C.: Joint Committee on Printing, 1900), p. 300.

55. Record Group 215, Miscellaneous Treasury Accounts, July 10, 1815, National Archives: "Received payment from George Boyd, Esq. agent for the Presidents furniture fund William Worthington." For the "Report on the appraisal of the President's Furnishings," see Esther Singleton, *The Story of the White House*, 2 vols. (New York: McClure Company, 1907) 1: 104. Worthington helped appraise the furnishings.

56. Mme Jeanne-Louise-Henriette Campan's school was located near the gates of Napoléon and Joséphine's Château de Malmaison (see below). Madame Campan, *Memoirs of the Court of Marie Antoinette*, 2 vols. (Philadelphia: Parry and McMillan, 1854). See also Sumpter Priddy III and Joan Quinn, "A Monroe Punch Bowl and American Lithographers in Paris, 1814–1824," in *Ceramics in America*, edited by Robert Hunter (Easthampton, Mass.: Antique Collectors' Club for the Chipstone Foundation, 2008), pp. 186–202.

57. For biographical information on James and Elizabeth Monroe, see Harry Ammon, *James Monroe: The Quest for National Identity* (New York: McGraw-Hill, 1971); Harlow Unger, *The Last Founding Father: James Monroe and a Nation's Call to Greatness* (New York: Da Capo Press, 2009); and Lee Langston Harrison, *A Presidential Legacy: The Monroe Collection* (Fredericksburg, Va.: James Monroe Museum, 1997).

58. Percier and Fontaine supplied Jacob Desmalter and Co. with full-scale drawings from which their workshop executed the furniture. Joséphine's bedstead owed its stylistic origins to royal traditions and to the canopy of state that surmounted the thrones of Europe's most powerful kings and queens. The tradition began in ancient times, with a crimson cloth that graced the wall behind royal chairs, then continued upward, and draped forward, to form an elementary canopy. The comparatively simple convention—a *baldachino* as it was known in Italy, *baldachin* in France, and baldequin in England—evolved over time into an elaborately carved and upholstered structure that towered over thrones, high altars, and, eventually, bedsteads for Europe's wealthiest or most powerful individuals.

59. The suite had upholstery by Laveissière in fabric purchased by LaFarge at Cartier fils. William Seale, *The President's House* (Washington, D.C.: White House Historical Association and the National Geographic Society, 1986), pp. 153–54. *Alexandria Times*, September 11, 1799. Labille moved from Paris to Philadelphia after the French Revolution, then relocated to Alexandria before finally settling in Washington. The authors thank Grant Quertermous, assistant curator at James Madison's Montpelier, for this information.

60. Rafe Blaufarb, *Bonapartists in the Borderlands: French Exiles and Refugees on the Gulf Coast, 1815–1835* (Tuscaloosa: University of Alabama Press, 2006), p. 41. René-Elisabeth-David de Perdreauville was born at Versailles in 1776. He was a French aristocrat and military officer. Details of his life are found in the journal *Union des Coeurs: A la Gloire du G.:A: de L'U, 75 ans à la rue Massot: Journées commémoratives 8 et 9 novembre 2003* (Paris, 2003), p. 27. Seale, *The President's House*, p. 148. Undated accounts from the spring of 1818, submitted to William Lee for reimbursement on May 1, 1818, "Documents in Relation to Furniture, &c. for the Presidents House," President's House, Miscellaneous Treasury Accounts, Record Group 215, National Archives.

61. *Message from the President of the United States upon the Subject of the Furniture Necessary for the President's House, &c.* (1818). *Carolina Centinel*, May 20, 1818.

62. Worthington made a third crown bedstead for Commodore and Mrs. Stephen Decatur. The bed was valued at $12 in the bill Worthington submitted on January 8, 1820, to "The estate of Commodore Stephen Decatur, Decd." (Seale, *The President's House*, p. 153.) Eleanor P. Gadsden to Sumpter Priddy III, May 21, 1998.

63. President's House, Miscellaneous Treasury Accounts, Records Group 215, National Archives.

64. Ibid.

65. For a Virginia crib with a Doric colonnade, see *George Washington's Mount Vernon*, edited by Wendell Garrett (New York: Monacelli Press, 1998), p. 69.

66. Mark Reinberger, *Utility and Beauty: Robert Wellford and Composition Ornament in America* (Newark: University of Delaware Press, 2004), pp. 89–90. When Andrews's original ornaments were destroyed in the 1814 fire, he was brought back to replicate them. Later renovations destroyed most of his work. Undertaker Richard Conway oversaw construction of the Bank of Alexandria. Ingle's Richmond carver, William Hodgson, carved molds for composition as well as furniture. Hodgson's 1806 estate sale included "1 nest of drawers with a quantity of composition" and "60 composition molds" that realized $60 when sold ("Account of Sales made this day of the estate of William Hodgson, dec'd," February 21, 1807, Richmond Hustings Deed Book 5, 1807–1810, pp. 10–11).

67. See Thomas Sheraton, *Cabinet Encyclopedia* (London, 1804), pl. 6, for a bedstead design with a rectangular crown and a peaked roof; and Thomas Sheraton, *Cabinet-Maker and Upholsterer's Drawing Book in Four Parts*, 3rd ed. (1802), pl. 45, for a "French State Bed" with a rectangular crown having domed sides.

68. *Letters from the Commissioner of the Public Buildings Transmitting an Inventory of the Furniture in the President's House, December 7, 1825* (Washington, D.C.: Gales & Seaton, 1825), p. 6. The authors thank Betty Monkman for this reference.

69. Every "French" or crown bed designed by Percier and Fontaine and published in *Recueil de décorations intérieures comprenant tout ce qui a rapport à l'ameublement* (Paris, 1812) has an offset crown and was intended to be placed against a wall. Several New York French beds have an eagle head carved atop each front post (Peter M. Kenny, Frances F. Bretter, and Ulrich Leben, *Honoré Lannuier: Cabinet Maker from Paris; The Life and Work of a French Ébéniste in Federal New York* [New York: Metropolitan Museum of Art, 1998], p. 102, pl. 49).

70. Valaperta advertised his skills as a portraitist in *Federal Gazette and Baltimore Daily Advertiser*, September 29, 1815. The Latrobe letter is quoted in Ihna T. Frary, *They Built the Capitol* (Richmond, Va.: Garrett and Massie, 1940), pp. 125–26. The sale of Valaperta's possessions took place on April 11, 1818 (*Daily National Intelligencer*, April 7, 1818). The artist's profiles of Thomas Jefferson, James Madison, and James Monroe are at the New-York Historical Society. Eliza may also have been involved in the design of her bedstead. On his invoice for the crown and finials, Belt certified: "the above articles were by Miss Munroe order and that the price is as stated as agreed to by Mr. Benjn. M. Belt." The invoice was consigned "C. Alexandre Upholsterer" and accepted by signature from Samuel Lane, agent for the President's House Furniture Fund. Belt was paid on March 6, 1819. Benjamin Belt to the President's House, February 12, 1819, President's House, Miscellaneous Treasury Accounts, Record Group 215, Monroe Document Group 43754, National Archives.

71. Presidents House, Miscellaneous Treasury Accounts, Monroe, Document Group 43754, National Archives, RG 215; "Pay Roll," [voucher] dated "August and September 1819," submitted by Giovanni Andrei and witnessed by Francis Iardella. Francis Fortini charged $2 per day for 104 days; Owen Horgan charged $1.50 per day for 37½ days; and John Woods charged $1.50 per day for 66 days. Andrei submitted the bill for $207.50, presumably shorting the men for a significant portion of their pay.

72. *The Mortality Books of William King, Sr., 1795–1832* and *The Mortality Books of William King Jr., 1833–1863*, Historical Society of Washington, D.C., acc. no. 2000.144. James Monroe to Samuel Lane, May 30, 1818, as cited in *A Comprehensive Catalog of the Correspondence and Papers of James Monroe*, edited by Daniel Preston (Westport, Conn.: Greenwood Press, 2001), p. 729. Three of the chairs King made for the Monroes are in the White House, two are in the Daughters of the American Revolution Museum, Washington, D.C., one is in the Lincoln's Collection at Ford's Theatre, and one is at James Monroe's Ash Lawn/Highlands. See Anne Castrodale Golovin, "William King Jr., Georgetown Furniture Maker," *Antiques* 109, no. 5 (May 1977): 1032–37; and Golovin, "Cabinetmakers and Chairmakers of Washington, D.C., 1791–1840," *Antiques* 107, no. 5 (May 1975): 898–922. See also Betty Monkman, *The White House* (Washington, D.C.: White House Historical Association, 2000).

73. The Smith set is further discussed in Hurst and Prown, *Southern Furniture*, pp. 155–60.

74. The chair illustrated in figure 63 is one of five examples from a set owned by Dr. Reverdy Ghiselin (1765–1823) and his wife, Margaret (1783–1850). For other examples, see Patricia E. Kane, *300 Years of American Furniture* (Boston: New York Graphic, 1976), no. 150; *American*

Antiques from Israel Sack Collection, 10 vols. (Washington, D.C.: Highland House, 1981), 1: 258, no. 644; and Christie's, *Important American Furniture, Silver, Furniture, Folk Art and Decorative Arts*, New York, June 22, 1994, lot 241.

75. Collector Charles K. Davis owned the Mason sofa when it was published in "Masterpieces of Early American Furniture in Private Collection," *Antiques* 38, no. 5 (March 1940). See also *American Antiques from Israel Sack Collection* (1974; reprint, Washington, D.C.: Highland House Publishers, 1982), 5: 1334; and Albert Sack, *Fine Points of Furniture* (New York: Crown Publishers, 1950), p. 228. The Masons built an elegant home on Analostan Island, located in the Potomac River a quarter mile from Georgetown's waterfront (Mary E. Curry, "Theodore Roosevelt Island: A Broken Link to Early Washington, D.C. History," *Records of the Columbia Historical Society of Washington, D.C.* 71–72 [1972]: 14–33). For the Bank of Columbia, see Bob Arnebeck, *Through a Fiery Trial* (New York: Madison Books, 1991), pp. 589–90.

76. Margaret Bayard Smith, *The First Forty Years of Washington Society: In the Family Letters of Margaret Bayard Smith* (New York: Frederick Ungar Publishing Co., 1965), pp. 67, 234; see also pp. 67, 95, 133, 164, 201. In 1825 Smith advised Treasury Secretary William H. Crawford to "dispense with the chair" in his office and substitute a sofa (ibid., p. 201).

77. The sofa descended to their son Dr. Armistead Peter (1840–1902), who married first cousin Martha Custis Kennon (1843–1886) of Tudor Place, Georgetown. The house, designed by Capitol architect William Thornton, was completed in 1809 for Maj. Peter's brother and sister-in-law, Thomas Peter and Martha Custis Peter. George and Thomas were sons of Scottish émigré Robert Peter (1726–1806), Georgetown's first mayor. George Peter's canceled checks to Worthington are dated March 16, 1810 ($75); May 29, 1810 ($100); March 12, 1811 ($61); and March 7, 1812 ($76.50.) A November 15, 1815, receipt from Worthington to "Maj. Geo. Peter" listed "1 large wardrobe @ $65." (Maj. George Peter Manuscript Collection, Tudor Place). The sofa was described in a later inventory as "one Scroll back sofa the back Elegantly carved" and valued at $100—the highest amount assigned to any object in the house (untitled inventory, Maj. George Peter Papers, MS 4, box 3, folder 1, Tudor Place). The authors thank Leslie Buhler and Wendy Kail for these references.

78. For a map of the Seneca quarry and a brief history, see Mike High, "Notes on Seneca Quarry & Stonecutting Mill," in *The C & O Canal Companion* (Baltimore, Md.: Johns Hopkins University Press, 2000). For an account of Blagden's duties, see Les Stanford, *Washington Burning: How a Frenchman's Vision for Our Nation's Capital Survived the Congress, the Founding Fathers and the Invading British Army* (New York: Crown Publishing, 2008), p. 188.

79. For related New York sofas, see Berry B. Tracy, *Federal Furniture and Decorative Arts at Boscobel* (New York: Harry Abrams, 1981), p. 33, fig. 4; and Nancy McClelland, *Duncan Phyfe and the English Regency, 1795–1830* (New York: Dover Publications, 1980), pp. 249–50. The Akin sofa's central kylix also bears a certain affinity to the reeded urn that crowns Eleanor Wren's 1798 grave marker.

80. According to the current owner, the Campeachy chair probably arrived in Woodville during the 1940s through a marriage of the Bergeron and Catchings families from Louisiana (Peter Patout to Sumpter Priddy, November 27, 2007).

81. Campeachy chairs from the Caribbean and Mississippi Valley generally have a crest rail with tenons that extend into through-mortises cut into the adjoining stiles. Chairs produced in Latin cultures rarely have dovetailed braces akin to those on Worthington's Campeachy chairs. Aside from the crest and front rail, most rely solely on stretchers for stability. Campeachy chairs usually have seat leather wrapped around delicate stiles and nailed along the outside edge, rather than anchored inside the stiles.

82. Boyd, *The First Forty Years of Washington Society*, p. 67.

83. Donna-Belle Garvan, Curator, New Hampshire Historical Society, first suggested a Southern origin for the Webster chairs (Donna-Belle Garvan to Frank L. Horton, May 20, 1981, correspondence files, MESDA). Webster left the chairs in New Hampshire when he moved to Massachusetts. He served as Massachusetts 1st District Congressman from 1823 to 1827. The authors thank Wesley G. Bella, Director of Collections and Exhibitions, New Hampshire Historical Society, for this information.

84. Gustavus (1790–1866) and Thomas H. (1786–1830) Beall were born in Maryland. For their New York dates and locations, see *Elliot's Improved New-York Double Directory* (New York: William Elliot, 1811), and *Longworth's American Almanac, New-York Register, and City Directory* (New York: David Longworth, 1812), MESDA.

85. On June 8, 1818, Worthington "received [$440.50] . . . from Samuel Lane for the President's House," President's House, Miscellaneous Treasury Accounts, Record Group 215,

National Archives. The cabinetmaker delivered the president's furniture on August 4 of that year but was not paid until December 31, 1818 (Commissioner of Public Buildings to William Worthington Jr., President's House, Miscellaneous Treasury Accounts, Record Group 215, National Archives). *City of Washington Gazette*, June 22, 1818. For Constantine's chairs and desks, see Matthew A. Thurlow, "Aesthetics, Politics, and Power in Early-Nineteenth-Century Washington: Thomas Constantine & Co.'s Furniture for the United States Capitol, 1818–1819," in *American Furniture*, edited by Luke Beckerdite (Easthampton, Mass.: Antique Collectors' Club for the Chipstone Foundation, 2006), pp. 184–228. On November 25, 1817, Worthington made " 10 [book] cases . . . at 20 dollars each" for the President's House (Thomas T. Tucker, *Letter from the Treasurer of the United States, Transmitting the Annual Account of His Office to the 30th of June, 1820* [Washington, D.C.: Gales and Seaton, 1820]); *War and Navy Accounts from 1st October, 1819, to 30th September 1820* (Washington, D.C.: Gales & Seaton, 1820), pp. 167–69. Worthington purchased mahogany from Philadelphia cabinetmaker Thomas Whitaker in June 1820 (Deborah Ducoff-Barone, "Philadelphia Furniture Makers, 1816–1830," *Antiques* 145, no. 5 [May 1994]: 755). In 1819 Worthington had one order for mahogany, turning, and sawing for the President's House totaling $50.20 (President's House, Miscellaneous Treasury Accounts, Record Group 215, National Archives).

86. United States Census of Manufactures, Washington, D.C., 1820. "Mrs. Adams Bought of William Worthington for the Presidents House, Washington City, March 26, 1825," President's House, Miscellaneous Treasury Accounts, Record Group 215, National Archives; Account, James Barbour to William Worthington, October 13 and November 24, 1825, box 1, Papers of the Barbour Family, MS 1486, University of Virginia, Charlottesville; Elder and Bartlett, eds. *John Shaw*, p. 24. *Daily Madisonian*, February 6, 1843. Wesley E. Pippenger, *Oak Hill Cemetery, Georgetown, D.C.: Monument Inscriptions and Burial Data (Part One)* (Georgetown, D.C.: Oak Hill Cemetery, 2006), p. 728.

87. John D. Hill apprenticed to Worthington in 1814. The Hill brothers' mother, Mary Carroll Hill (1744–1796), was Charles Carroll's second cousin. Henry V. Hill was executor of John D. Hill's estate (*Daily National Intelligencer*, April 25, 1820). Henry moved into Ingle's former shop in partnership with Charles R. Belt. The latter left the business shortly thereafter and set up shop on his own. For additional furniture made by Hill, see "Henry Hill to the President's House, April 2, 1820"; "United States Presidents House to H. V. Hill, April 2, 1825"; "Henry Hill to the President of the United States, April 20, 1825"; "President of the United States to H. V. Hill, July 1, 1825"; and "President of the U. States to H. V. Hill, Sept. 24, 1831"; President's House, Miscellaneous Treasury Accounts, Record Group 215, National Archives.

88. *Daily National Intelligencer*, July 28, 1827, and October 21, 1828.

89. The suite was published in Esther Singleton, *Furniture of Our Forefathers* (Garden City, N.Y.: Doubleday, Page and Co., 1913), p. 565; and Lee Langston Harrison, *A Presidential Legacy: The Monroe Collection* (Fredericksburg, Va.: James Monroe Museum, 1997), p. 224. George Smith, *A Collection of Designs for Household Furniture and Interior Decorations* (1804; reprint, New York: Praeger Publishers, 1971), pl. 10. The authors thank Megan Budinger, Curator and Assistant Director, James Monroe Library, for information on the caryatid chairs.

90. The caryatids are discussed in Allen, *History of the United States Capitol*, p. 90.

91. Burden and Cassin advertised their partnership between October 1815 and May 1818 (Golovin, "Cabinetmakers and Chairmakers of Washington, D.C.," pp. 909–10).

92. Alexandra Alevizatos Kirtley, "The Painted Furniture of Philadelphia: A Reappraisal," *Antiques* 169, no. 5 (May 2006): 134–45. For fancy chairs, see Sumpter Priddy, *American Fancy: Exuberance in the Arts, 1790–1840* (Milwaukee, Wis.: Milwaukee Art Museum and the Chipstone Foundation, 2004), pp. 135–58. Kirtley, "The Painted Furniture of Philadelphia," pp. 142–44. Fondé remained in Washington until 1830, lived briefly in Baltimore, and died en route to New Orleans.

Figure 1   Side chair attributed to John Gaines III, Portsmouth, New Hampshire, 1735–1743. Maple. H. 40¼", W. 20½", D. 17". (Private collection; photo, Gavin Ashworth.) The blocked, rush seat and the retaining strips are restored.

Robert F. Trent,
Erik Gronning, and
Alan Andersen

The Gaines
Attributions and
Baroque Seating in
Northeastern New
England

▼ A L M O S T E V E R Y prominent New England auction house
has offered seating attributed to the Gaines chair makers of Ipswich,
Massachusetts, and Portsmouth, New Hampshire. During the last twenty
years, attributions for some chairs have shifted to "Boston, North Shore, or
southern New Hampshire." This broad-brush approach reflects recent publications that assert Boston origins for certain seating forms. This article
assesses the background of Gaines attributions and the traits of a securely
documented set of four side chairs made by John Gaines III of Portsmouth.
Chairs attributed to Boston, Salem, Ipswich, Newbury, and Portsmouth
that were not made by either of the two Gaines shop traditions are also discussed, so that future scholars will not confuse them with Gaines work.
Even with the publication of these various shop traditions, much remains
to be discovered about eastern Massachusetts and New Hampshire seating
of the 1720–1760 period.[1]

Origins of the Gaines Attributions
Three members of the Gaines family are involved in attributions pertaining to this study: John Gaines Jr. (1677–1748) of Ipswich, Massachusetts;
John II's younger son, Thomas Gaines (1712–1761), who stayed in Ipswich
and worked with his father; and John II's older son, John Gaines III
(1704–1743), who moved from Ipswich to Portsmouth, New Hampshire,
about 1724 and established his own shop. John Gaines III's son George
(1736–1809) was a woodworker, but was too young at the time of his father's
death to have been trained by him.[2]

   The only securely documented "Gaines" seating from either Ipswich or
Portsmouth are four surviving chairs from a set made by John Gaines III
for his personal use (fig. 1). The chairs descended in the Brewster family of
Portsmouth and were well known by the late 1870s. All four remained in the
family until 1998, when the chairs sold at auction. Important traits of this
set are their stylized pierced, carved crests (fig. 2) and their solid, carved,
oversize Spanish feet with a central groove on the middle toe. Of less obvi-
ous concern are the turnings of the front and rear stretchers as well as the
splat profiles and the captured rush seats.[3]

   An armchair with identical features (fig. 3) can also be attributed to John
Gaines III's Portsmouth shop. It entered the antiques marketplace during
the 1920s and was subsequently acquired by Mitchell Taradash, a prominent
collector. With its outward flaring molded arms and bold scrolled grips, this
example has been celebrated as the finest surviving Gaines armchair.[4]

Figure 2   Detail of the crest of the chair illustrated in fig. 1. (Photo, Luke Beckerdite.)

Figure 3   Armchair attributed to John Gaines III, Portsmouth, New Hampshire, 1735–1743. Maple. H. 42³⁄₁₆", W. 25½", D. 16³⁄₈" (seat). (Private collection; photo, Winterthur Library, Decorative Arts Photographic Collection.) This photograph was taken ca. 1930. At that time, the rush on the blocked seat frame and some of the arched retaining strips were missing.

By the beginning of the twentieth century, several features associated with the Gaines armchair and side chairs were considered highly desirable by American furniture collectors. Even though the Gaines name was not yet assigned to these seating forms, unscrupulous dealers began making fakes similar to the armchair, often by altering period examples. This practice continued well into the 1970s if not later.[5]

The crest design favored by John Gaines III (fig. 2) differs from the C-scroll-and-foliate type seen on most turned New England banister backs (see fig. 45) as well as those on stylistically later seating with cabriole legs (see fig. 68). His archetypal crest has a triple-swept cove molding that ends in volutes at each end. Underneath this molding is stylized, carved leafage framed by piercings. Flanking the foliage are secondary carved moldings that merge into complementarily molded rear posts.

The crests of Gaines chairs were carved in much the same way as those on contemporaneous British (figs. 4, 5) and New England seating. Elements of the design were laid out using a pattern likely made of paper, pasteboard, or some other material that was thin and easily registered with wrought finish nails or other fasteners. Evidence for attachment is rare because most carvers affixed their patterns in areas where wood was designated for later removal. On Gaines chairs, the crest cutouts would have been logical sites.

Figure 4 Cane chair, London, England, 1710–1720. Beech. H. 53⅝", W. 18¼", D. 18⅜". (Courtesy, Cape Anne Museum; photo, Andrew Davis.) High-backed London cane chairs with scrolled crests may have influenced the design of Gaines chairs. This example may have been owned in Essex County, Massachusetts, during the eighteenth century.

Figure 5   Detail of the crest of the chair illustrated in fig. 4. (Photo, Andrew Davis.) Although the design of the crest is metropolitan in origin, the carving is perfunctory in execution.

Figure 6   Paper pattern of a reproduction Gaines crest glued to a crest blank. (Courtesy, Andersen & Stauffer; photo, Andrew Davis.)

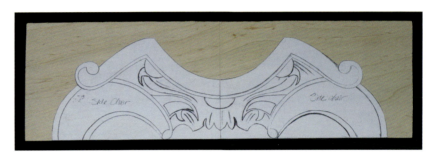

Figure 7   Reproduction Gaines crest with the apertures sawn out. (Courtesy, Andersen & Stauffer; photo, Andrew Davis.)

Figure 8   Reproduction Gaines crest partially carved. (Courtesy, Andersen & Stauffer; photo, Andrew Davis.)

Figure 9   Reproduction Gaines crest at a later stage of carving. (Courtesy, Andersen & Stauffer; photo, Andrew Davis.)

What is not clear is how much information period patterns transferred to the piece being worked. Most carvers who produced the same designs over and over required little guidance to outline, model, and shade their work.[6]

Today, replicating the crests for a set of Gaines chairs begins with photography of an original specimen and the production of full-scale drawings, the latter of which can be photocopied and glued to each crest blank to insure uniformity (fig. 6). Mortises for the post or stile tenons are cut before the carving begins. If a mistake is made, the time required to carve the crest is not lost. The next step is to saw out the interior apertures with a coping saw (fig. 7). It has been speculated that the apertures were roughly excavated with vertical gouge cuts, but such an approach seems too risky. The gouging theory emerged because of counter-chamfering found on the reverse surfaces of carved crests with piercing. Some have thought that this chamfering was intended to clean up tears from blasting through the crest blank with gouges, but the chamfers were more likely intended to lighten the appearance of the carving.

The following step is to rough out the triple-swept cove molding with gouges (fig. 8). In fact, almost all the modeling of the crest can be executed with as few as six to ten different diameters of gouges. Vertical strikes outline the pellets of the volutes and the outlines of leaves, while most of the rest of the carving involves holding the gouges at low angles. Smoothing the surfaces of some forms is accomplished with flat chisels. The final flourishes are made with V-shaped parting tools, used to indicate the veins in the leafage (fig. 9). Another final adjustment is fairing the moldings into those of the rear posts, which is fine-tuned after the chair is assembled.

The arms of Gaines chairs (figs. 10, 11) rise at the juncture with the front posts, then flare out sharply to terminate in molded scrolls with protruding volutes. These features, above all others, have contributed to John Gaines III's reputation as a masterful designer and carver, but it is unlikely that they are an original conceit. Similar terminals are seen on English armchairs, which may, in turn, have been based on Venetian prototypes renowned for their extravagant forms and detailing.[7]

Figure 10   Detail of an armchair attributed to John Gaines III, showing an overhead view of the arm. (Courtesy, Winterthur Museum, bequest of H. F. du Pont; photo, Laszlo Bodo.)

Figure 11   Detail of an armchair attributed to John Gaines III, showing a side view of the arm. (Courtesy, Winterthur Museum, bequest of H. F. du Pont; photo, Laszlo Bodo.)

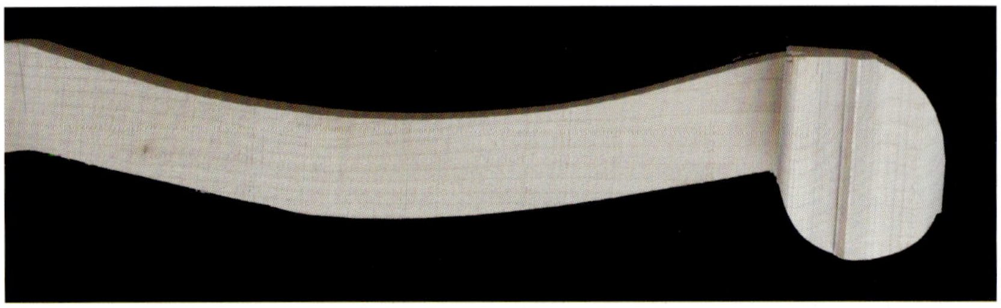

Figure 12   Sawn blank for a reproduction Gaines arm. (Courtesy, Andersen & Stauffer; photo, Andrew Davis.)

Figure 13   Roughed-out molding for a reproduction Gaines arm. (Courtesy, Andersen & Stauffer; photo, Andrew Davis.)

Figure 14   Carved grip for a reproduction Gaines arm. (Courtesy, Andersen & Stauffer; photo, Andrew Davis.)

Most of the work required to produce scrolled arms like those on Gaines chairs involves sawing, rather than carving (fig. 12). The basic shape is established by patterns, one for the overall plan and perhaps two for the side elevation of the arm. The rough outline of the protruding volutes could have been sawn or established with gouges and chisels, but evidence of the former would have been removed during the finish carving.

After the arm is sawn to shape, the chamfers on the underside are cut with a spokeshave, and the molded upper surfaces are roughed out with gouges. Some makers may have used a rounded bench scraper to smooth these molded surfaces, almost in the manner of using a scratch-stock iron (figs. 13, 14). Other makers of Portsmouth chairs seem to have used scratch stocks in this location. In carving the protruding volutes, the first task is locating the central elements, which stand out in high relief. These are rendered with vertical cuts made with a relatively small gouge. The carver then has to decide if he will begin at the outside of each scroll and work in, or the reverse.

The oversize Spanish feet of Gaines chairs conform to a fairly strict pattern and are made entirely from the stock of the front posts (figs. 15, 16). This was a wasteful procedure, since it required cross-sectional dimensions greater than those needed elsewhere. This technique differs from that used for most metropolitan seating, wherein Spanish feet were constructed by gluing pieces of wood to the posts to provide stock for the protruding toes. Gaines feet are also distinguished by being severely recessed, on all four

Figure 15 Sawn foot for a reproduction Gaines chair. (Courtesy, Andersen & Stauffer; photo, Andrew Davis.)

Figure 16 Carved foot for a reproduction Gaines chair. (Courtesy, Andersen & Stauffer; photo, Andrew Davis.)

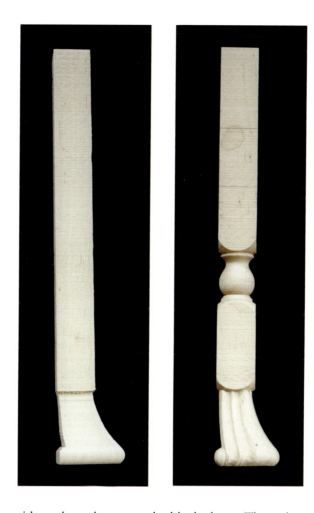

sides, where they meet the block above. The arris creating the recess was turned in sequence with the urns on each post. The feet protrude much farther than those on most contemporaneous English and Boston chairs, but not enough to prevent the stock from being centered on the lathe. Only a single profile pattern is required to lay out the foot, which is sawn from the front and the side to produce all four elevations. The two inner faces of the foot are cleaned up with a flat chisel, and most of the saw kerfs on the outer faces are removed during carving. The carving is restricted to two flutes on the outer sides of the feet and a deep, flat-bottomed groove on the leading edge of the toes. Almost all this work is done with gouges. Most inaccuracies regarding Gaines attributions are based on the feet. However, as Portsmouth chairs by other makers reveal, the foot design associated with John Gaines III was not exclusive to his shop (see fig. 36).

The turnings on Gaines chairs are fairly sophisticated in form and arrangement. Some armchairs have front stretchers with exaggerated balusters separated by a thin torus molding with flanking scotias; however, large-diameter turnings are not exclusive to Gaines chairs. The rear stretchers of Gaines chairs often display barrel-like, extended knops at the centers, although some chairs have smaller, sharper knops in the same location.

The vasiform splats, or banisters, of earlier Gaines chairs are a variant of the yen-yen or "Chinese-baluster-vase-on-a-pedestal" form. Another version of this design, in which the pedestal is set on top of the vase, appears on other Portsmouth chairs of roughly the same period, like those illustrated in figures 25 and 29. Both splat designs have metropolitan precedents, although the lack of filleting in the Gaines examples makes them appear less architectural.

Figure 17 Detail of a Gaines chair from the Brewster set (see fig. 1), showing the restored, blocked rush seat and arched retaining strips based on those of the armchair illustrated in fig. 2. (Courtesy, Winterthur Museum, purchased with funds provided by an anonymous donor and Mr. and Mrs. Theodore Alfond; photo, Jim Schneck.)

Figure 18 Detail of a Gaines chair from the Brewster set (see fig. 1), showing the small shaved bracket supporting the restored rushed seat frame.

The seats of most Gaines chairs also differ from those on comparable New England examples, which have rush bottoms suspended from roughly shaved rails. Craftsmen in the Gaines tradition typically used rectangular seat rails with conventional mortise-and-tenon joints and made separate frames with exposed blocks at the corners to accommodate the rush (fig. 17). Armchair seat frames are supported by four small brackets nailed to the rear posts; side chair seat frames rest on ledges cut into the front posts and brackets nailed to the rear posts (fig. 18). Retaining strips that are nailed on top of the seat rails keep the frames in place. These strips, which have a simple arched profile, are often missing. On many Gaines chairs, the original rushed frames have been replaced with textile- or leather-covered slip seats or over-the-rail upholstery (see figs. 25, 27).[8]

A final feature of Portsmouth Gaines chairs is their extremely coarse finish. The joinery is about on a par with metropolitan work, but the rear surfaces of the posts and splats are often very roughly planed and not smoothed with shaves or scrapers (fig. 19). These defects contradict the heroic folklore celebrating John Gaines III as a meticulous craftsman. Aside from what can be gleaned from surviving examples, little is known about the seating made in John Gaines III's shop. Scattered account book references indicate that he traded sets of chairs described as "black" or "banister [back]" with various Portsmouth artisans and merchants like Sir William Pepperell. Undoubtedly, such chairs represented the bulk seating Gaines made for export and most probably had plain crests and turned feet. By the same token, the archetypal chair typically associated with John Gaines III probably represented commissioned work for local consumption.

Figure 19 Rear view of the chair illustrated in fig. 1, showing the rough dressing of the frame. (Photo, Luke Beckerdite.)

Boston Prototypes for Portsmouth Gaines Chairs

Low-backed Boston leather chairs with molded crests have been cited as possible antecedents for the Gaines crest. These forms are, however, extremely rare today and somewhat implausible as prototypes. It is more likely that closer Boston (see fig. 22) or London (figs. 4, 5) models existed. Certainly, the compositional device of a great molded scroll with a central breakout was current in many London high-backed cane chairs. Paradoxically, the tallest London cane chairs ever made, dating 1710 to 1720, coincided with the emergence of designs, like the Gaines chairs, that mimicked the more compact proportions of Chinese seating.[9]

A standard type of Boston chair with a vasiform banister has often been mistakenly associated with the Gaines chair makers of Portsmouth (fig. 20).

Figure 20   Side chair, Boston, Massachusetts, 1735–1750. Maple. H. 42¼", W. 17¾", D. 18⅝". (Courtesy, Winterthur Museum, bequest of H. F. du Pont; photo, George Fistrovich.)

Figure 21   Side chair, Boston, Massachusetts, 1720–1735. Walnut and maple. H. 41½", W. 19½", D. 20". (Chipstone Foundation; photo, Gavin Ashworth.)

The Boston examples have features associated with John Gaines III, but most deviate in two important respects: the toes of their Spanish feet are applied; and the retaining strips of the seat frames are flat, with quarter-round edges. The Boston chair illustrated in figure 20 has been altered in the same manner as many Gaines chairs: the inner edges of the retaining strips have been trimmed back to accommodate a replaced, upholstered, loose seat. As the rough rear surfaces of Gaines chairs suggest, craftsmen in those shops may have been following Boston precedent in the way they finished their products. Boston chairs like the example illustrated in figure 20 relate directly to a specific model of leather chair produced in that city (fig. 21).[10]

Figure 22 Armchair, possibly Boston, Massachusetts, or Portsmouth, New Hampshire, 1730–1750. Maple. H. 42", W. 26", D. 25". (Private collection; photo, Gavin Ashworth.)

Both the vasiform and leather-backed variants of this type of Boston chair have a design defect also seen on other seating from this period. When making such chairs, the shoulders of the joints between the seat rails and rear posts should be sawn at an angle so the rear heels and the back of the crest rail are plumb, which is the case in most metropolitan seating. On several Boston chairs, the heels extend back farther than the crest, giving those objects the appearance of leaning forward. Although this feature has been cited as diagnostic in attributions to John Gaines III, it was probably influenced by contemporary Boston work.

An armchair, possibly made in Boston, may represent another potential prototype for Portsmouth Gaines chairs (fig. 22). This beautifully conceived and executed chair, with a tight, highly detailed crest, appears at first glance to be a Gaines chair. On sustained examination, its turnings and carving differ substantially. The toes are applied, and the arms do not

Figure 23 Side chair, possibly Portsmouth, New Hampshire, 1730–1750. Maple. H. 42¼", W. 19", D. 18¼". (Chipstone Foundation; photo, Gavin Ashworth).

have the exaggerated volutes seen in Gaines chairs. Furthermore, the carving of the crest does not seem to relate to leafage executed by John Gaines III or by his possible carving subcontractor, Joseph Davis of Portsmouth.[11]

Another chair whose origin is more ambiguous has a unique variant of the double-peaked, molded crest design (fig. 23) and a blocked, rushed seat frame—a detail not commonly seen on Gaines chairs. The turnings share some features with Gaines chairs but depart in other respects. This could be another Boston prototype or, more likely, a Portsmouth outlier from the main Gaines shop tradition.[12]

Portsmouth Chairs in the Gaines Style

In her catalogue of early American furniture at the Metropolitan Museum of Art, furniture historian Frances Gruber Safford attributed the chair illustrated in figure 24 to John Gaines III, largely based on its having feet similar to those associated with his shop. She also argued that it originally had heavily scrolled arms, and that its present arms were probably installed in Portsmouth later in the eighteenth century. In actuality, this chair could have been made by one of several Portsmouth craftsmen. The carving on the crest differs significantly from that on seating more convincingly associated with Gaines, and the turnings have no relation to those associated with his shop tradition. Other than the feet, the only detail suggesting a connection

Figure 24   Armchair, Portsmouth, New Hampshire, 1725–1760. Maple, poplar, and ash. H. 44½", W. 26½", D. 22½". (Courtesy, Metropolitan Museum of Art, gift of Mrs. Russell Sage; photo, Gavin Ashworth / Art Resource, NY.)

between this chair and the Gaines shop is the gouge work inside the large C-scrolls of the crest. This occurs on Gaines chairs but is too generic to be meaningful. Similar gouge work occurs on the crests of banister-back chairs from Salem, Massachusetts.[13]

Several Portsmouth chairs with vasiform banisters that were not made in the shop of John Gaines III are cited in *Portsmouth Furniture: Masterworks of the New Hampshire Seacoast*. One variant (fig. 25) has many of the same features as a Gaines chair but differs in having rear posts with a less sinuous ogee profile, a narrower banister augmented with small spurs, Spanish feet with laminated toes, and more finished rear surfaces (fig. 26). Nevertheless, the similarities between this chair and Gaines seating suggest that its maker

Figure 25 Side chair, Portsmouth, New Hampshire, 1735–1750. Maple. H. 40¼", W. 20⅝", D. 16½". (Private collection; photo, Andrew Davis.) An apprentice or journeyman from John Gaines III's shop may have made this chair.

Figure 26 Detail of a foot on the chair illustrated in fig. 25, showing the pieced-out toes. (Private collection; photo, Andrew Davis.)

Figure 27 Side chair, Portsmouth, New Hampshire, 1740–1760. Maple. H. 30⅞", W. 20¾", D. 16". (Private collection; photo, Andrew Davis.) An apprentice or journeyman from John Gaines III's shop may have made this chair. The upholstery is modern. Originally, the chair had a blocked rush seat held by retaining strips.

may have worked in Gaines's shop or, at the very least, been influenced by comparable London or Boston prototypes. Another Portsmouth chair displays even stronger affinities with John Gaines III's work (fig. 27); however, its cut-card leafage and lower back suggest that it might date after Gaines's death in 1743. Gaines could have been producing chairs inspired by so-called Queen Anne designs only from the mid-1720s until his death, a relatively short time for him to have made the approximately thirty-five examples attributed to him.[14]

A more severe model of Portsmouth chair may have been based on London seating in the "Chinese scholars' taste" (figs. 28, 29). On these chairs, the heels are set too far forward, giving the seating a sway-backed appear-

Figure 28 Armchair and two side chairs, Portsmouth, New Hampshire, 1740–1760. Maple. Dimensions not recorded. (Private collection; photo, Leigh Keno Antiques.)

ance (fig. 29) that differs from the front-leaning aspect of most Gaines products. Some contemporary Boston examples display similar design defects, reinforcing the theory that they influenced Portsmouth work. The frames on the chairs illustrated in figures 28 and 29 appear narrow when viewed from the side, and their banisters are thin and did not require chamfers to lighten and sharpen their appearance. Because "India-backed" seating was fashionable in London from 1715 to 1730, these chairs may have been as esteemed as the more visually ostentatious examples associated with the Gaines shops.[15]

Figure 29 Side chair, Portsmouth, New Hampshire, 1740–1760. Maple. H. 41⅜", W. 21⅜", D. 18½". (Courtesy, Strawbery Banke Museum, anonymous loan; photo, Andrew Davis.) The feet are restored. The turnings on the side and rear stretchers are rare in Boston seating but common in Portsmouth work.

Figure 30 Armchair, Portsmouth, New Hampshire, 1740–1775. Maple. H. 44⅝", W. 25½", D. 22¾". (Courtesy, Old Sturbridge Village; photo, Andrew Davis.) The bottoms of the feet are restored about 1".

Other Portsmouth Seating

Several groups of chairs demonstrate that the market for seating in Portsmouth was much more diverse than previously thought. One group of banister backs with a distinctive sunburst, or fan, crest has long been associated with that town. Many of these chairs have simple scrolled arms with a drooping front volute. This same arm appears on other Portsmouth seating, most notably chairs with either scalloped crests or oak leaf crests.[16]

Four chairs with arched crests flanked by spurs and robust, detailed turnings probably date 1740–1775. These chairs are heavier in weight than later variants and display two different kinds of Spanish feet. An armchair with elaborate baluster-shaped turnings has a Spanish foot without laminated toes and undercut ankles (fig. 30). The foot carving consists of four flutes cut with a relatively steep-sided gouge. The scroll arms have moldings on

Figure 31 Armchair, Portsmouth, New Hampshire, 1740–1770. Maple. H. 46¾", W. 24¾", D. 21½". (Private collection; photo, Andrew Davis.) The bottoms of the feet are restored about 1½".

the upper sides and drooping front terminals with softly modeled volutes on the sides. The carved fan on the crest surrounds a half-round reserve with cross-hatching and three pointed leaves. A more elaborate version of this crest design can be seen on the armchair illustrated in figure 31. Although its feet have suffered losses, they appear to have been carved like those on the preceding example (fig. 30). A third armchair (fig. 32) and a related side chair (fig. 33) are somewhat simpler in detail but display a more sculptural version of the Spanish foot, also cut entirely from the stock of the front

posts. The ankles of the feet are undercut, and the toes extend well beyond
the squares of the posts above. Their dramatic sweep is similar to that of the
more fully developed carved feet associated with John Gaines III.[17]

Another important genre of Portsmouth seating is represented by an
armchair that belonged to Sir William Pepperell (1696–1759) of Kittery,
Maine (fig. 34). The back features an extremely rare variant of the so-called
split spindle—a bilaterally symmetrical, baluster-shaped turning with no
relationship to the turned columns on the rear posts—and plump finials

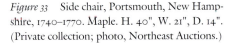

Figure 33 Side chair, Portsmouth, New Hampshire, 1740–1770. Maple. H. 40", W. 21", D. 14". (Private collection; photo, Northeast Auctions.)

Figure 34 Armchair, Portsmouth, New Hampshire, 1730–1760. Maple and ash. H. 45¾", W. 25", D. 20". (Courtesy, Strawbery Banke Museum, gift of Sally Sangser and Nancy Borden in memory of their brother Henry Chandler Homer; photo, Andrew Davis.) The feet are missing.

with large buttons at the top. The arms have a pronounced drooping grip, like those of the fan-crested examples (figs. 30–32), but they are excessively long and extend well beyond the front posts. The front stretcher is not diagnostic as far as origin is concerned, but the form and "bipartite" arrangement of the turned elements on the side stretchers are more typical of Portsmouth work than that associated with other New England chair-making traditions. Although the Pepperell armchair's feet are missing, their form can be extrapolated from another example by the same maker (fig. 35). The arms of the latter are more normal in length, and the profile of the columnar section of the banisters echoes the turnings on the rear posts. The carving on the crests of both chairs is crude, with shading cuts that barely follow the flow of the design (see fig. 78 in appendix).[18]

Figure 35 Armchair, Portsmouth, New Hampshire, 1730–1760. Maple and ash. Dimensions not recorded. (Private collection; photo, Sotheby's.)

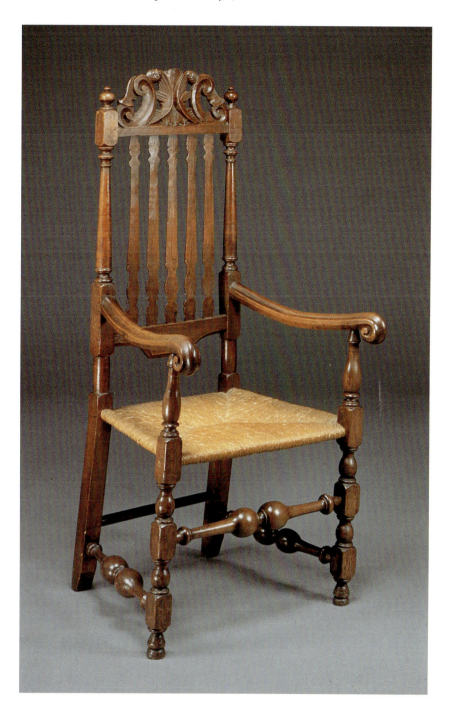

Other chairs from the same shop have superior carving (fig. 36), similar turnings, and elegant Spanish feet cut from the solid. The crests of these chairs (see fig. 79 in appendix) are unusual in having leaves that drop from the volutes of a C-scroll in the center and rise from intersecting scrollwork on either side. The descending leaves bear a strong resemblance to carving attributed to Joseph Davis of Portsmouth. The close relationship between

Figure 36 Side chair, Portsmouth, New Hampshire, 1730–1760. Poplar, maple, and ash. H. 47½", W. 21", D. 16½". (Courtesy, Metropolitan Museum of Art, gift of Mrs. Screven Lorillard; photo, Gavin Ashworth / Art Resource, NY.)

the feet on this chair and those on seating by John Gaines III suggests that the latter may have subcontracted carving to Davis.[19]

Two simple banister-back chairs with turned feet (figs. 37, 38) share traits with other Portsmouth seating, particularly the crests with prominent spurs at the sides (figs. 30–33). Hundreds of chairs of this type, usually painted black, were exported from Portsmouth between 1725 and the Revolution. Little is known about comparably simple slat-back chairs, which were presumably also made in considerable numbers.

Figure 37 Side chair, Portsmouth, New Hampshire, 1750–1775. Maple and ash. H. 48½", W. 18½", D. 20". (Courtesy, Witch House Museum, Department of Parks and Recreation, City of Salem, Massachusetts; photo, Andrew Davis.)

Figure 38 Side chair, Portsmouth, New Hampshire, 1750–1775. Maple and ash. H. 45½", W. 18½", D. 19". (Courtesy, Witch House Museum, Department of Parks and Recreation, City of Salem, Massachusetts; photo, Andrew Davis.)

The Gaines Shops and Chair Making in Ipswich

With all the attention devoted to Portsmouth Gaines chairs, few scholars have speculated about what John Gaines II and Thomas Gaines were making in Ipswich, Massachusetts. One might get the impression from previous discussions of John Gaines III that he moved to Portsmouth in 1724 because he was an enterprising young man, whereas his father and brother remained in Ipswich because they were comfortable in a provincial backwater. This view of the Gaines artisans and of the town of Ipswich itself is anachronistic. Ipswich paid the second-highest town tax in Massachusetts until the 1740s. Like every port in Essex County, including rivals Marblehead, Salem, Beverly, Manchester, Gloucester, and Newbury, Ipswich had an active harbor, at the mouth of the Ipswich River, where it flows into

Figure 39 Overmantel panel, Ipswich, Massachusetts, 1740–1760. Pine. 18¼" x 55". (Courtesy, Ipswich Museum, gift of George W. Caldwell; photo, Andrew Davis.)

Figure 40 Side chair, Ipswich, Massachusetts, 1740–1760. Maple and ash. H. 52½", W. 18¾", D. 13½". (Private collection; photo, Sotheby's.)

Plum Island Sound. Merchants in all these Essex County towns were determined to break the hegemony of Boston merchants.[20]

The painted overmantel panel illustrated in figure 39 depicts the cove between the Great Neck and the Little Neck, where Ipswich's cod-fishing industry was concentrated. In the foreground are oceangoing schooners, and in the background are salted fish flakes drying on a hill and warehouses on piers for securing quintals of dried cod. The same facilities probably were used for other mercantile activities as well. Shipping manifests indicate that local cabinetmakers and chair makers exported crates of furniture from the town. Crated furniture may have been brought down the river in lighters (one is shown in the painting) or in flat-bottomed hay barges known as "gundalows," before being transferred to the holds of oceangoing vessels.[21]

An account book maintained by John Gaines II and Thomas Gaines covering the years 1707 to 1762 has been a primary source for most of the publications pertaining to those craftsmen since the mid-1950s. The book reputedly descended in the Appleton family along with a side chair (fig. 40). This chair is unquestionably from the same shop as the examples illustrated in figure 41. All have lightweight frames, relatively debased turnings, and rudimentary carved crests. Although some scholars have suggested that the carving on these chairs is related to that on Portsmouth examples from the shop of John Gaines III, side-by-side comparisons indicate that is not the case. The Ipswich chairs are distinctive localized interpretations of Boston banister-back chairs with highly stylized crests. While it is possible that John Gaines II made the chair that descended with his account book and the example illustrated in figure 40, that scenario seems unlikely. The joinery and carving of those objects is less skillful than that associated with the Portsmouth shop of John III, who had previously trained and worked with his father.[22]

Figure 41 Side chairs, Ipswich, Massachusetts, 1740–1760. Maple and ash. H. 46", W. 18⅝", D. 15½". (Courtesy, Ipswich Museum; photo, Andrew Davis.) The carving of the triangular reserve on the stay rails is slightly different.

The history of the side chair illustrated in figure 42 is less clear, but it may also be an Ipswich example. It has a dramatic scrolled crest with leaves rising from and dropping below the ogee sections, a straight-sided banister reminiscent of those on some Boston and London chairs, a seat with over-the-rail upholstery, and square-sectioned cabriole legs with leaf cuffs, flat scalloped stretchers, and Spanish feet. While several of these features occur in Boston seating, they have never been found united in one chair. The crest carving and rough rear surfaces of the frame resemble Portsmouth work, but the similarities are not sufficient to support any conclusions.[23]

Figure 42   Side chair, possibly John Gaines II or Thomas Gaines I, probably Ipswich, Massachusetts, 1730–1760. Maple. H. 42½", W. 18½", D. 15". (Courtesy, Ipswich Museum; photo, Gavin Ashworth.) It is possible that the maker and carver of this chair were not the same person.

The quandary of where and by whom this extraordinary chair was made is deepened by the existence of plausible prototypes, most notably a set of London cane seating owned by Portsmouth merchant Tobias Lear III (1706–1751) (fig. 43). The Lear chairs provide exact precedents for the shape and beading of the flat stretchers, the cylindrical turnings on the lower portions of the back posts, and the sharp knop and elaborate stops of the rear stretcher. The elaborate crest and cuffs of the chair illustrated in figure 42 may be an individual conceit, since they deviate from the design of the Lear chairs and are conceptually more ambitious than those on contemporary Boston examples. Chairs with similar straight-sided, ogee banisters, or "India backs" were fashionable in England and her colonies. Thomas Gaines used that term to describe a set of chairs he made in 1759.[24]

Figure 43   Side chair, London, England, 1725–1740. Beech. H. 42½", W. 20 ⅛", D. 19". (Courtesy, Strawbery Banke Museum, gift of Mary Storer Decatur; photo, Andrew Davis.) The feet are missing.

Figure 44 Armchair, Boston, Massachusetts, 1710–1740. Maple and ash. H. 53", W. 24¼", D. 24¾". (Private collection; photo, Andrew Davis.) The design of this chair has exact parallels in Boston leather chairs.

Figure 45 Detail of the crest of the armchair illustrated in fig. 44. (Photo, Andrew Davis.)

Boston Banister-Back Chairs

The diffusion model for banister-back chair design in New England has traditionally centered on Boston, despite the fact that little has been published on Boston examples of that form. A plausible argument for attributing several banister-back chairs to Boston can be made by comparing them with leather chairs from that city. Furniture historian Benno M. Forman asserted that both types of seating were made in the same shops, and early banister-back examples with accomplished joinery, turning, and carving suggest that he was correct (fig. 44).[25]

The crest rail carving on the chair illustrated in figure 44 conforms to a familiar pattern (fig. 45), featuring vertically oriented foliage flanked by large, opposing C-scrolls with loosely wound volutes and connecting leafage. Cutouts lighten and accentuate the design, but in terms of overall workmanship, the modeling and shading are relatively stereotyped. Crests of this general type influenced Essex County and Portsmouth seating more than the turnings on Boston chair frames. In other New England ports, chair makers developed their own variations on Boston crest designs to distinguish their work from that of metropolitan competitors. Some Boston chair makers purchased carved crests, arms, and turned components from specialists, whereas others did most, or all, of their work in-house. Chair makers in other ports did the same, although the use of piecework in manufacture must have been more common in Boston. The distribution of Boston banister-back chairs of this caliber was relatively wide. An armchair (fig. 46) from the shop that made the example illustrated in figure 44

Figure 46 Armchair, Boston, Massachusetts, 1720–1740. Maple and ash. Dimensions not recorded. (Private collection; photo, Northeast Auctions.) This chair and the example illustrated in fig. 44 have rectangular side and rear stretchers, whereas most chairs from other New England ports have turned examples. The use of rectangular side and rear stretchers on Boston banister-back chairs supports Benno Forman's theory that they were made side by side with leather chairs.

belonged to William Pepperell. His chair differs in that the front stretcher is turned rather than carved.[26]

A Boston side chair with a crest similar to those on the armchairs is distinguished by having front posts with turned tops and baluster-and-ball feet (fig. 47). It also has rectangular side and rear stretchers. Later banister-back chairs from Boston probably had turned stretchers, and more work is needed to separate them from other eastern Massachusetts examples.[27]

Figure 47 Side chair, Boston, Massachusetts, 1720–1740. Maple and ash. H. 49", W. 18¾", D. 16⅜". (Private collection; photo, Gavin Ashworth.)

Salem Banister-Back Chairs

Histories associated with a distinctive group of banister-back chairs, traditionally ascribed to the North Shore, support a more specific attribution to Salem. Although only three men were referred to as "chair-makers" in a 1762 list of craftsmen in that town, there is no reason to assume that artisans described as "shop joiners" did not also make chairs. In urban areas, banister-backed chairs and other seating forms were often assembled from components purchased from specialists, which could include turners, joiners, and carvers.[28]

Most banister-back chairs were probably made in sets or multiples of six. Horizontal components were produced in large numbers well ahead of assembly, partly because it was cost-effective and partly because construction depended on inserting dry turned components into wet, or at least somewhat green, posts. Whether plain or carved, crests also had to dry before assembly. Presumably, carvers made crests or stretchers of the same pattern sequentially and in large numbers, since that process would have been much more efficient than shifting from one pattern to another. As was the case with specialist turners, carvers made components to order for some chair makers, while offering standard piecework that others could modify to fit their frames. Under the latter scenario, identical stretchers, turned rails, or carving could appear on seating by different makers. Because posts needed to be green at the time of assembly, they were made last. To accommodate the demand for turned and joined seating, regional sawmills must have maintained substantial stocks of poplar, which was the preferred wood for posts that were intended to receive paint. The soft, even grain of poplar made it ideal for sawing, turning, and mortising. As these assembly procedures suggest, chairs may have been assembled with parts made by several tradesmen over an extended period of time.[29]

An early armchair that descended in the Devereux family of Marblehead, Massachusetts, exhibits many traits associated with Salem seating (fig. 48). The stretchers are the most distinctive components, having bilaterally symmetrical balusters with large bulbous elements that transition abruptly into sharply tapered columns like those on some Boston cane chairs. In Salem, the use of molded and split, turned banisters was coeval. The moldings on the banisters of the Devereux chair are reminiscent of those associated with joiners John Symonds (d. 1671) and his son James (1633–1714), who were active in Salem during the seventeenth century. Later members of their family, including Thomas Symonds (d. 1758) and his son Benjamin (1714–1779), were involved in the furniture-making trades and might have made chairs like the Devereux example or at least furnished parts for them.[30]

Although the crests of most Salem chairs conform to a familiar pattern, which consists of vertically oriented leafage in the center and opposing scrolls on either side, several different hands are discernible. The carver of the Devereux chair shaded his leaves with a conventional, small gouge (fig. 49) rather than a more steep-sided veiner or V-shaped parting tool, which were preferred by some of his contemporaries. On the leaves connecting the outer scroll volutes, he made the shading cuts perpendicular to the flow. In

Figure 48 Armchair, Salem, Massachusetts, 1725–1750. Maple, poplar, and ash. H. 48⅝", W. 26⅛", D. 19". (Private collection; photo, Gavin Ashworth.) The feet are restored. The arms of Salem banister-back chairs display marked variation. On this example, the arms have a pronounced outward twist at the wrists and large scrolled terminals. There may be some stylistic relationship between these arms and those of Portsmouth seating.

Figure 49 Detail of the crest of the armchair illustrated in fig. 48. (Photo, Luke Beckerdite.)

Figure 50 Detail showing the gouge cuts on the upper surfaces of the end volutes of the crest of the armchair illustrated in fig. 48. (Photo, Luke Beckerdite.)

Figure 51 Armchair, Salem, Massachusetts, 1725–1750. Maple, poplar, and ash. H. 49¾", W. 22⅜". (Courtesy, Museum of the City of New York; photo, Gavin Ashworth.) The arms of this chair are relatively straight and have small terminals.

later rococo carving, perpendicular fluting was often done to represent the back of a leaf, but on this chair it appears to be an individual idiosyncrasy. The same can be said of the peculiar fluting on the top edges of the outer leaves, although this detail does appear on some Boston crests (fig. 50).

The Devereux armchair and a contemporaneous example from the same shop illustrate the range of options available to Salem consumers: turned or molded banisters; stretchers with a variety of details and arrangements; arms with different sweeps, moldings, and terminals; and crests by different carvers. Although the crest designs of the armchair illustrated in figure 51 and the Devereux example are similar, the former has flatter C-scrolls and paired shading cuts that diverge in an awkward manner (fig. 52).[31]

A side chair with strong affinities to the Devereux armchair (fig. 48) has a crest by yet another carver, a plain stay rail with a molded lower edge,

Figure 52   Detail of the crest of the armchair illustrated in fig. 51. (Photo, Gavin Ashworth.)

Figure 53   Side chair, Salem, Massachusetts, 1725–1750. Maple, poplar, and ash. H. 48⅝", W. 18⅜", D. 16½". (Courtesy, Historic New England, gift of Dorothy S. F. M. Codman.)

Figure 54 Side chair, Salem, Massachusetts, 1725–1760. Maple, poplar, and ash. H. 48⅜", W. 18", D. 16¾". (Private collection; photo, Gavin Ashworth.). The feet are restored.

and seat blocks at the juncture with the front posts (fig. 53). The distinctive turnings on the front posts may have been derived from English caned chairs, as they have known precedents in contemporary Boston seating. A second side chair (fig. 54) is more closely allied to the armchair illustrated in figure 51. Both seating forms have similar rear posts, spindles, and stay rails, and their carved crests appear to be by the same hand. The painted decoration on the side chair is similar to that on London cane chairs (fig. 55) and may be original. Not all Salem banister-back side chairs are as elaborate as the examples illustrated in figures 53 and 54. Indeed, some local

Figure 55 Side chair, London, England,
1720–1740. Beech. H. 45¾", W. 18½", D. 18".
(Private collection; photo, Jim Schneck.)

Figure 56 Side chair, Salem, Massachusetts, 1735–1760. Maple, poplar, and ash. H. 47⅞", W. 18", D. 16½". (Courtesy, Cape Ann Museum, gift of Alfred Mayor; photo, Andrew Davis.) This chair and its mate descended in the Dennison family of the Annisquam section of Gloucester, Massachusetts.

artisans appear to have used relatively plain stretchers (fig. 56), crests (fig. 57), and stay rails to keep prices in check and compete with Boston chair makers and other regional rivals. Later banister-back chairs that differ little from their earlier counterparts attest to the success of Salem chair makers in satisfying consumer demand. The armchair illustrated in figure 58 has features introduced during the 1710s that remained fashionable into the 1760s.[32]

Figure 57 Side chair, Salem, Massachusetts, 1740–1770. Maple, poplar, and ash. H. 47", W. 18", D. 18". (Private collection; photo, Gavin Ashworth.) The feet are restored.

Another school of banister-back chairs may be from Salem, but its attribution is a bit more tenuous. Most examples have eccentric details in conjunction with straight-molded banisters, severely tapering columnar turnings, and Spanish feet carved from the solid with a turned molding at the ankle. Some of the other turnings on these chairs are unusual by New England standards, including the simplified columns on the rear posts, which resemble those of English cane chairs. An armchair that was modified in the nineteenth

Figure 58   Armchair, Salem, Massachusetts,
1740–1770. Maple, poplar, and ash. H. 49",
W. 24¾", D. 19". (Courtesy, Glebe House,
purchased with funds provided by Lispinard
Seabury Crocker; photo, Tom Schwenke.)

Figure 59 Armchair, southern Essex County, Massachusetts, 1740–1770. Woods not recorded. H. 50½". (Private collection; photo, Sotheby's.) The black-and-gold paint and incised decoration are nineteenth-century embellishments.

Figure 60 Side chair, southern Essex County, Massachusetts, 1740–1770. Maple. H. 47½", W. 19", D. 16". (Courtesy, Winterthur Museum, bequest of H. F. du Pont; photo, Jim Schneck.)

century with Eastlake incising and yellow highlights displays a flat crest with a plumed flourish and volutes on the ends (fig. 59). No immediate New England precedent for this design is known, unless it represents an abstracted version of the crests on some Boston cane chairs. A side chair (fig. 60) has many of the same attributes, although the top of the crest is simplified into what looks like a pedestal. The maker used the blocked, rushed form of seat. Another armchair (fig. 61) has an unprecedented triple-swept, molded crest with a tight, narrow version of what American furniture scholars call a "saddle." Again, no immediate local precedent for this exaggerated feature is known, but it may reflect a stylish, mannered London precedent. The armchair illustrated in figure 61 also has a straight, molded stay rail, yet another tie to the main Salem tradition.[33]

Newbury Banister-Back Chairs
Furniture scholar John D. Vander Sande has identified a group of banister-back chairs made in Newbury, a major Essex County port to the north of

Figure 61 Armchair, southern Essex County, Massachusetts, 1740–1770. (Wallace Nutting, *Furniture Treasury,* 2 vols. [Framingham, Mass.: Old America Company, 1928], 2:2089.)

Figure 62 Armchair, Newbury, Massachusetts, 1730–1760. Maple, poplar, and ash. H. 49¾", W. 23¼", D. 19¾". (Private collection; photo, Gavin Ashworth.)

Salem, on the other side of Ipswich and the Cape Ann Peninsula. Newbury had two ports, the original one on the shallow Parker River and a later one on the larger Merrimac River. Both these ports supported facilities much like those in the overmantel painting of Ipswich harbor (fig. 39).

Most of the turnings on Newbury banister backs conform to Boston patterns. The armchair illustrated in figure 62 displays some of these metropolitan features, most apparent in the bilaterally symmetrical balusters of the stretchers. A second armchair (fig. 63) has more idiosyncratic turnings as well as uncarved arms that are reminiscent of work from nearby Portsmouth. The feet on the armchair illustrated in figure 62 are carved from the solid, with a distinct, curved undercut to the two rear surfaces.

What sets these Newbury chairs apart from other local regions is their carving, which appears to have been done by the chair maker rather than by a specialist. His earlier crests (figs. 86, 87 in appendix) have stylized central leaves that rise only slightly higher than the finials and rear surfaces that are

Figure 63   Armchair, Newbury, Massachusetts, 1740–1770. Woods not recorded. H. 47½", W. 23", D. 16½". (Courtesy, Friends of Historic Kingston and the Fred J. Johnston Museum, bequest of Fred J. Johnston; photo, Douglas Baz.) The feet are restored.

Figure 64   Side chair, Newbury, Massachusetts, 1740–1770. Maple, poplar, and ash. H. 46", W. 19½", D. 16½". (Courtesy, Historical Society of Old Newbury, gift of Margaret FitzGerald and Iola Benedict; photo, Gavin Ashworth.)

counter-chamfered with a small-diameter gouge (fig. 87 in appendix). Most carvers used a larger tool for that type of work and made their cuts with considerably less precision and regimentation.

Later crests by this Newbury maker are varied in design and execution. Some have leaves that are spiky and stylized (fig. 64), some have leaves that are more naturalistically modeled and shaded (fig. 65), and some have nothing more than a scalloped upper edge to evoke the shape of carved variants (fig. 66).[34]

Figure 65 Side chair, Newbury, Massachusetts, 1740–1770, Maple, poplar, and ash. H. 46⅝", W. 19½", D. 15½". (Private collection; photo, Gavin Ashworth.)

Figure 66 Side chair, Newbury, Massachusetts, 1740–1770. Maple, poplar, and ash. H. 45½", W. 19", D. 15¼". (Private collection; photo, Gavin Ashworth.)

Boston Banister-Back Seating in the Manner of Boston Cane Chairs

The chair illustrated in figure 67 is one of three Boston examples with "crook'd," or ogee, banisters bearing original caners' marks. The molded stiles and crests on these chairs and other seating in the so-called "I" group are based on imported London seating. English furniture scholar Adam Bowett has documented a set of London chairs with similar stiles and crests that appears to date 1715–1717; thus, Boston versions were probably being made by the early 1720s.[35]

Several joined chairs inspired by Boston caned seating are known. The chair illustrated in figure 68 has a molded back and turned stretchers derived from cane chairs, combined with a vasiform banister and squared, incised cabriole legs with Spanish feet. Although scholars have been reluctant to date Boston seating with vasiform banisters much before the late 1720s, this chair could date circa 1725. A heavier armchair, presumably made between 1735 and 1745, has the same banister profile, combined with details taken

Figure 69 Armchair, Boston, Massachusetts,
1730–1750. Maple. H. 48½", W. 25⅝", D. 23½".
(Private collection; photo, Laszlo Bodo.) The feet
are partially restored.

from leather chairs (fig. 69). The relationship of this type of seating to
Gaines chairs is unclear. The problem resides in determining if both the
Boston chair makers and John Gaines III relied on imported English pro-
totypes, as opposed to an older, diffusionist model that asserts Boston ori-
gins for all eastern Massachusetts seating. In any case, the existence of
Boston seating sharing some traits with Gaines chairs renders the idea that
John Gaines III invented his designs doubtful.

Figure 70 Side chair, possibly Essex County, Massachusetts, 1740–1770. Maple, poplar, and ash. H. 47¼", W. 18½", D. 17". (Private collection; photo, Andrew Davis.)

Figure 71 Side chair, probably northern Essex County, Massachusetts, 1740–1770. Maple and ash. H. 49½", W. 18", D. 16⅝". (Courtesy, Currier Gallery of Art; photo, Andrew Davis.) This chair is one of four identical examples that reputedly belonged to Meschach Weare of Hampton Falls, New Hampshire.

The history of Massachusetts and New Hampshire banister-back seating from the first half of the eighteenth century is only beginning to come into focus. Numerous Essex County chairs with varied carving and frame treatments suggest that much more research is needed (figs. 70, 71). It is hoped that this article will inspire other scholars to do fieldwork, document stair balusters as a basis for identifying regional chair turnings, and publish monographs on local chair-making traditions. Only then will we begin to understand the complexities of seating styles in New England.

ACKNOWLEDGMENTS   For assistance with this article, the authors thank Kimberly Alexander, Patrick Alley, Mark Anderson, Gavin Ashworth, Doug Baz, Luke Beckerdite, Ronald Bourgeault, Derin Bray, Rev. Rebecca Brown, Jean Burks, Katherine Chaison, Wendy Cooper, Andrew Davis, Jeanne Gable, James L. Garvin, Bethany Groff, Mrs. Constance Godfrey, Norman and Mary Gronning, Joseph W. Hammond, Brock Jobe, Jane Kellar, Tom Kelleher, Judith Kelz, Leigh Keno, Mr. and Mrs. Donald Koleman, Richard Kyllo, Jim Lahar, Ethan Lasser, Jim Leonard, Arthur Liverant, Cindy Macky, Giacomo Mirabella, Susan Nelson, Susan Newton, Martha Oaks, Elizabeth Peterson, Jonathan Prown, Adrienne Sage, Nancy Sazama, Irving and Anita Schorsch, Andrew Spahr, Tom Stauffer, Elizabeth Tibbetts, Jonathan and Paige Trace, Harry Mack Truax II, John and Marie Vander Sande, Tara Vose, Kemble Widmer, Jay Williamson, and Mr. and Mrs. Martin Wunsch.

1. For more on early Boston seating, see Benno M. Forman, *American Seating Furniture, 1630–1730* (New York: W. W. Norton, 1988); Roger Gonzales and Daniel Putnam Brown Jr., "Boston and New York Leather Chairs: A Reappraisal," in *American Furniture*, edited by Luke Beckerdite (Hanover, N.H.: University Press of New England for the Chipstone Foundation, 1996), pp. 175–94; Joan Barzilay Freund and Leigh Keno, "The Making and Marketing of Boston Seating Furniture in the Late Baroque Style," in *American Furniture*, edited by Luke Beckerdite (Hanover, N.H.: University Press of New England for the Chipstone Foundation, 1998), pp. 1–40; and Glenn Adamson, "The Politics of the Caned Chair," in *American Furniture*, edited by Luke Beckerdite (Hanover, N.H.: University Press of New England for the Chipstone Foundation, 2002), pp. 174–206.

2. The most recent evaluation of the Gaines attributions is in *Portsmouth Furniture: Masterworks from the New Hampshire Seacoast*, edited by Brock Jobe (Boston: Society for the Preservation of New England Antiquities, 1993), pp. 47, 48, 295–300.

3. The set of four chairs remained in the Brewster family until they were sold at auction (Northeast Auctions, New Hampshire Auction, Manchester, New Hampshire, November 7–8, 1998, lots 1097, 1098). One chair is in the Winterthur Museum, one is in the Strawbery Banke Museum, and two are in a private collection.

4. For the history of the armchair illustrated in fig. 3, see Jobe, ed., *Portsmouth Furniture*, pp. 295–97.

5. For a heavily restored "Gaines" chair, see Frances Gruber Safford, *American Furniture in the Metropolitan Museum of Art*, vol. 1, *Early Colonial Period: The Seventeenth-Century and William and Mary Styles* (New York: Metropolitan Museum of Art, 2007), pp. 358–60, no. 137. Luke Beckerdite and Alan Miller, "Furniture Fakes from the Chipstone Collection," in *American Furniture*, edited by Luke Beckerdite (Hanover, N.H.: University Press of New England for the Chipstone Foundation, 2002), pp. 65–67.

6. The use of nails to attach carving patterns is discussed in Luke Beckerdite, "Carving Practices in Eighteenth-Century Boston," in *New England Furniture: Essays in Memory of Benno Forman*, edited by Brock Jobe (Boston: Society for the Preservation of New England Antiquities, 1987), pp. 132–33.

7. For an overall view of the armchair, see Nancy E. Richards and Nancy Goyne Evans, *New England Furniture at Winterthur: Queen Anne and Chippendale Periods* (Winterthur, Del.: Winterthur Museum, 1997), pp. 33–35, no. 18. For illustrations of English chairs with protruding volutes on the grips, see Adam Bowett, *English Furniture, 1660–1714, from Charles II to Queen Anne* (Woodbridge, Eng.: Antique Collectors' Club, 2002), pls. 8:8, 8:18, 8:22, 8:28, 8:57. For northern Italian chairs with exaggerated arms, see G. Morazzoni, *Il mobile veneziano del 1700*, 2 vols. (Milan: Görlich-Editore, 1958), 1: pls. 18b, 21, 34a, 41, 43, 2: pl. 283.

8. A few Gaines chairs have conventionally woven seats. The armchair illustrated in fig. 3 is the only surviving example with most of its original retaining strips.

9. A Boston low-backed chair with triple-swept crest is illustrated in Forman, *American Seating Furniture*, pp. 306–8. For London seating of the 1710–1720 period, see Bowett, *English*

Furniture, 1660–1714, pp. 230–73; and Adam Bowett, *Early Georgian Furniture, 1715–1740* (Woodbridge, Eng.: Antique Collectors' Club, 2009), pp. 144–96.

10. The Boston chair illustrated in fig. 20 was attributed to "Boston, northeastern Massachusetts, or coastal New Hampshire" in Richards and Evans, *New England Furniture at Winterthur*, pp. 8–9, no. 2. Formerly, these chairs were attributed to Newport, Rhode Island, on the basis of an example at the Newport Historical Society that belonged to William Ellery of Newport. For a reattribution to Boston, see Erik K. Gronning and Dennis Carr, "Rhode Island Gateleg Tables," *Antiques* 165, no. 5 (May 2004): 122–27.

11. Objects attributed to Davis are discussed in Brock Jobe, "An Introduction to Portsmouth Furniture of the Mid-Eighteenth Century," in Jobe, ed., *Essays in Memory of Benno Forman*, pp. 166–78; and Jobe, ed., *Portsmouth Furniture*, pp. 46, 47, 128–33, 234–36.

12. This chair is illustrated in Oswaldo Rodriguez Roque, *American Furniture at Chipstone* (Madison: University of Wisconsin Press, 1984), pp. 110–11, no. 46, where it was attributed to John Gaines III. Luke Beckerdite has proposed that the carving on this object is by the same hand that was responsible for the ornament on a dressing table and altar table attributed to Joseph Davis (see n. 11 above.) A chair in the Art Institute of Chicago has an atypical "Gaines" crest rail and elaborate carving (Judith A. Barter, Kimberly Rhodes, and Seth Thayer, *American Arts at the Art Institute of Chicago: From Colonial Times to World War I* [New York: Hudson Hill Press, for the Art Institute of Chicago, 1998], p. 62, no. 11).

13. Safford, *Early Colonial Period*, pp. 81–82, no. 29. Several "Gaines" chairs with carved crests are heavily restored (see Richards and Evans, *New England Furniture at Winterthur*, pp. 33–34, no. 18). Some examples that have recently appeared in the marketplace are almost certainly early-twentieth-century fakes.

14. Jobe, ed., *Portsmouth Furniture*, pp. 48–49, 218–20, 285–91, 301–5. Sotheby's, *Important Americana*, New York, January 21, 2006, lot 402. Northeast Auctions, *The Dinah and Stephen Lefkowitz Folk Art Collection*, Portsmouth, N.H., August 3, 2007, lot 750. The assessment of thirty-five chairs is determined from the number published in previous literature and new discoveries made by the authors.

15. The set of chairs illustrated in fig. 28 was illustrated in Wallace Nutting, *Furniture Treasury*, 2 vols. (New York: Macmillan Co., 1928), 2: nos. 2103, 2104. For India-backed seating in England, see Bowett, *Early Georgian Furniture*, pp. 156–60; and Adam Bowett, "The India-backed Chair, 1715–40," *Apollo* 491 (January 2003): 3–9.

16. For variants, see Jobe, ed., *Portsmouth Furniture*, pp. 48–49, 285–91.

17. The authors thank Derin Bray for calling the Shelburne armchair to their attention. Other closely related chairs have been published in F. W. Fussenich advertisement, *Antiques* 16, no. 6 (December 1929): 467; *Anderson Galleries, Collection of the Late Thomas B. Clarke*, December 2–5, 1931, lot 626; Rosella V. Becker advertisement, *Antiques* 57, no. 4 (April 1950): 293; Tillou Gallery advertisement, *Antiques* 88, no. 6 (December 1965): 799; Millard F. Rogers Jr., "Living with Antiques: Millbach, the Ohio Home of Mr. and Mrs. Harry S. Bugbee," *Antiques* 150, no. 3 (September 1966): 351; Tillou Gallery advertisement, *Antiques* 108, no. 1 (January 1975): 85; Patricia E. Kane, *300 Years of American Seating Furniture: Chairs and Beds from the Mabel Brady Garvan and Other Collections at Yale University* (Boston: New York Graphic Society, 1975), pp. 69–70, nos. 48, 49; Sotheby's, *The Howard and Jean Lipman Collection of Important American Folk Art & Painted Furniture: The Property of the Museum of American Folk Art*, New York, November 14, 1981, lot 356; Roque, *American Furniture at Chipstone*, pp. 164–65, no. 73; Christopher P. Monkhouse and Thomas S. Michie, *American Furniture in Pendleton House* (Providence: Museum of Art, Rhode Island School of Design, 1986), p. 152, no. 92; James D. Julia Auctions, *Annual Samoset 2003 Antiques & Fine Art Auction*, Fairfield, Maine, August 20, 2003, lot 608; David Hewett, "Action Galore on the Floor at NHADA's Annual Show," *Maine Antique Digest* (November 2006): C2; Pook and Pook, Inc., *Furniture, Art, & Accessories*, Dowingtown, Pa., May 11–12, 2007, lot 85; James D. Julia Auctions, *Annual Winter Antique & Fine Art Auction*, Fairfield, Maine, January 31, 2008, lot 874; Northeast Auctions, *The M. Austin & Jill R. Fine Collection*, Portsmouth, N.H., August 7, 2010, lot 603; and Northeast Auctions, *Annual Summer Americana Auction*, Portsmouth, N.H., August 6–8, 2010, lot 793.

18. Sir William Pepperell dominated much of the economy of Portsmouth. The chair in fig. 35 sold in Sotheby's, *Important Americana from the Collection of Mr. and Mrs. Adolph Henry Meyer*, New York, January 20, 1996, lot 43.

19. Safford, *Early Colonial Period*, pp. 83–85, no. 30. For Joseph Davis, see n. 11 above.

20. Research by Susan S. Nelson ("Capt. Abraham Knowlton, Joiner, and the Seminal

Woodworkers of Ipswich, Massachusetts," in *Rural New England Furniture: People, Place, and Production*, edited by Peter Benes [Boston: University Press and Dublin Seminar for New England Folklife, 2000], pp. 42–59) and Kemble Widmer II and Judy Anderson ("Furniture from Marblehead, Massachusetts," *Antiques* 163, no. 5 [May 2003]: 96–105) suggests that the economic leverage exerted by artisans in Essex County towns was considerable during the eighteenth century. See also Daniel Vickers, *Farmers and Fishermen: Two Centuries of Work in Essex County, Massachusetts, 1630–1830* (Chapel Hill: University of North Carolina Press, 1994).

21. The Ipswich overmantel is discussed in T. Frank Waters, *Jeffrey's Neck and the Way Leading Thereto with Notes on Little Neck* (Salem, Mass.: Salem Press, 1912), pp. 7, 58, 59.

22. An account of the discovery of the Gaines account book and the chair that descended with it in the Appleton family of Ipswich is in Albert Sack, "Tales of Portsmouth Furniture," in *Piscataqua Decorative Arts Society 2002–2003 Lecture Series*, vol. 1 (Portsmouth, N.H.: Piscataqua Decorative Arts Society, 2004), pp. 31–32. The side chair is illustrated in Beulah E. Larson, "Living with Antiques: A Salt-Box in Tulsa, Oklahoma," *Antiques* 94, no. 2 (August 1968): 210; and Sotheby's, *Important Americana*, New York, January 19–21, 1996, lot 1385. Earlier articles about Gaines chairs include Stephen Decatur, "George and John Gaines of Portsmouth, New Hampshire," *American Collector* 7, no. 10 (November 1938): 6–7; Helen Comstock, "An Ipswich Account Book, 1707–1762," *Antiques* 66, no. 3 (September 1954): 188–92; and Helen Comstock, "Spanish-Foot Furniture," *Antiques* 71, no. 1 (January 1957): 58–61. Robert E. P. Hendrick, "John Gaines II and Thomas Gaines I, 'Turners' of Ipswich, Massachusetts" (master's thesis, University of Delaware, 1964). Hendrick illustrated the banister-back chair that descended with the account book along with a very similar pair of banister backs in the collection of the Ipswich Historical Society (fig. 40 in this article). He attributed all three chairs to the Ipswich Gaines shop and suggested that the pair may have descended in the Appleton family. No accession documents or other records at the Ipswich Historical Society support that theory (see correspondence between Hendricks and Elisabeth Newton dating from the early 1960s). Sack, "Tales of Portsmouth Furniture," p. 32: "This armchair [fig. 30] is quite similar to a side chair that came with the Gaines account book from the Appleton family—a banister back chair with a carved crest and Spanish feet." Contrary to what Sack wrote, the banister back does not have Spanish feet, and the carving has no relationship to that of chairs attributed to John Gaines III of Portsmouth.

23. The chair illustrated in fig. 42 has been in the collection of the Ipswich Historical Society for many years but was never identified in accession records.

24. Tobias Lear III was married in 1733 and built his house in Portsmouth circa 1740. Adamson, "Politics of the Caned Chair," pp. 186, 195, figs. 11, 27. The front feet of the chair illustrated in Wallace Nutting, *Furniture of the Pilgrim Century, 1620–1720* (Boston: Marshall Jones Co., 1921), p. 246, are restored, and it is unclear if the set had Spanish feet originally. Wallace Nutting may have acquired his chair when he owned the Wentworth-Gardner House in Portsmouth, which is immediately adjacent to the Tobias Lear House. Nutting does not appear to have been aware of the history of the Lear cane chairs. Hendrick, "John Gaines II and Thomas Gaines I," p. 107, cites the "India back" reference. For another related side chair, see Gordon Russell, *The Things We See: Furniture*, 2nd ed. (Harmondsworth, Middlesex: Penguin Books, 1953), p. 14, no. 26.

25. Forman, *American Seating Furniture*, pp. 281–356; and Gonzales and Brown, "Boston and New York Leather Chairs," passim. For an image of the chair illustrated in fig. 44 before restoration, see Luke Vincent Lockwood, *Colonial Furniture in America* (New York: Charles Scribner's Sons, 1913), pp. 40–41, fig. 463. This chair sold as lot 1036 in Northeast Auctions, *Annual Americana Auction*, Portsmouth, N.H., August 3–5, 2006. For a Boston armchair with nearly identical turnings, carving, and proportions, see Forman, *American Seating Furniture*, p. 341, fig. 180.

26. Brock Jobe and Myrna Kaye, *New England Furniture: The Colonial Era* (Boston: Houghton Mifflin Co., 1984), pp. 325–28, no. 85. Benno M. Forman "Salem Tradesmen and Craftsmen Circa 1762," *Essex Institute Historical Collections* 107, no. 1 (January 1971): 62–81.

27. Typically chairs with Spanish feet and turned stretchers have a blocked rush seat that sits on top of the legs.

28. Jobe and Kaye, *New England Furniture*, pp. 325–28, no. 85; Forman "Salem Tradesmen," pp. 62–81.

29. For more on the production of this type of seating, see Benno M. Forman, "Delaware Valley 'Crookt Foot' and Slat-Back Chairs: The Fussell-Savery Connection," *Winterthur Port-*

folio 15, no. 1 (Spring 1980): 41–64; and Robert F. Trent, *Hearts and Crowns: Folk Chairs of the Connecticut Coast, 1720–1840* (New Haven, Conn.: New Haven Colony Historical Society, 1977), pp. 25–29, 63–66.

30. Forman, "Salem Tradesmen," pp. 35–36. Three other Salem banister-back armchairs survive with a crest executed by the carver of the example illustrated in fig. 83 (David B. Warren, Michael K. Brown, Elizabeth Ann Coleman, and Emily Ballew Neff, *American Decorative Arts and Paintings in the Bayou Bend Collection* [Houston: Museum of Fine Arts, Houston, 1998], p. 8, no. F14; *The Decorative Arts of New Hampshire: 1725–1825*, edited by Charles E. Buckley [Manchester, N.H.: Currier Gallery of Art, 1964], no. 3; Northeast Auctions, *New Hampshire Auction*, Portsmouth, N.H., August 2–3, 2002, lot 284).

31. For decades this chair was attributed to New York (V. Isabelle Miller, *Furniture by New York Cabinetmakers: 1650–1860* [New York: Museum of the City of New York, 1956], pp. 19–20, no. 19; and Robert Bishop, *Centuries and Styles of the American Chair: 1640–1970* [New York: E. P. Dutton & Co., 1972], p. 55, no. 53). Elmer C. Howe advertised the armchair illustrated in fig. 58 in *Antiques* 11, no. 6 (June 1927): 448. He had shops in both Boston and Marblehead, Massachusetts.

32. While counterintuitive, it is possible that the change from molded to turned banisters was part of this simplification.

33. Jobe and Kaye, *New England Furniture*, pp. 328–30, no. 86, note the similarities between the two shop traditions and cite several of the same objects. Nutting, *Furniture Treasury*, 2: 2089.

34. For another chair nearly identical to the example shown in fig. 64, see Robert F. Trent's catalogue entry on pp. 70–72, no. 21, in *American Furniture with Related Decorative Arts: 1660–1830*, edited by Gerald W. R. Ward (New York: Hudson Hills Press, 1991).

35. Forman, *American Seating Furniture*, pp. 229–45, 258–67. For an additional example, see Adamson, "The Politics of the Cane Chair," p. 174, fig. 1. The chair illustrated in fig. 67 sold as lot 229 in Skinner, *American Furniture & Decorative Arts*, Boston, Massachusetts, February 18, 2007. Bowett, *Early Georgian Furniture*, pp. 157–58, fig. 4:24.

Appendix
of Crest Details

The numbers refer to the figures of the overall images in this article.

Figure 72 Detail of the crest of the chair illustrated in fig. 1.

Figure 73 Detail of the crest of the chair illustrated in fig. 4.

Figure 74 Detail of the crest of the armchair illustrated in fig. 22.

Figure 75 Detail of the crest of the chair illustrated in fig. 23.

Figure 76 Detail of the crest of the armchair illustrated in fig. 30.

Figure 77 Detail of the crest of the armchair illustrated in fig. 31.

Figure 78 Detail of the crest of the armchair illustrated in fig. 34.

Figure 79 Detail of the crest of the chair illustrated in fig. 36.

Figure 80   Detail of the crest of the chair (left) illustrated in fig. 41.

Figure 81   Detail of the crest of the chair illustrated in fig. 42.

Figure 82   Detail of the crest of the armchair illustrated in fig. 44.

Figure 83   Detail of the crest of the armchair illustrated in fig. 48.

Figure 84   Detail of the crest of the armchair illustrated in fig. 51.

Figure 85   Detail of the crest of the chair illustrated in fig. 55.

Figure 86   Detail of the crest of the armchair illustrated in fig. 62.

Figure 87   Detail of the back of the crest of the armchair illustrated in fig. 62.

Figure 88   Detail of the crest of the chair illustrated in fig. 67.

Figure 89   Detail of the crest of the chair illustrated in fig. 68.

Figure 90   Detail of the crest of the chair illustrated in fig. 70.

Figure 91   Detail of the crest of the chair illustrated in fig. 71.

Figure 1   Chest of drawers with doors, Boston, Massachusetts, 1640–1670. White oak, red oak, chestnut, maple, black walnut, red cedar, cherry, cedrela, snakewood, rosewood, and lignum vitae with red oak, white oak, and white pine. H. 48⅞", W. 45¾", D. 23¾". (Courtesy, Yale University Art Gallery, Mabel Brady Garvan Collection; photo, Gavin Ashworth.)

*Peter Follansbee and
Robert F. Trent*

Reassessing the London-Style Joinery and Turning of Seventeenth-Century Boston

▼ THE JOINERY AND turning traditions of seventeenth-century Boston are now perceived as central factors in the interpretation of seventeenth-century New England furniture, but before 1969, few scholars sought to identify specific schools of New England joinery. The few traditions that were identified, like that associated with Thomas Dennis of Ipswich, Massachusetts, were considered without reference to other schools of joinery. Through a revolutionary series of research initiatives and informed guesswork, furniture scholar Benno M. Forman developed a rationale for identifying the diagnostic traits of a Boston school of joinery and turning and suggested several probable makers. While subsequent scholars have questioned the dates assigned to certain objects and attributions to specific craftsmen, none has rejected Forman's methodology.[1]

Assuming that the founders of the Boston tradition arrived on the Shawmut Peninsula in the late 1630s and began making furniture almost immediately, surviving objects suggest that these artisans and their apprentices made furniture in the London style for more than seventy years (figs. 1, 2). It is only logical to posit that there was significant development

Figure 2   Detail of the chest of drawers with doors illustrated in fig. 1. (Photo, Gavin Ashworth.)

within this school and that immigrant craftsmen who arrived in that city after 1630 may have had an influence.

During the course of his research, Forman identified what appears to be the dominant school of London joinery from 1630 to 1670. To date, no English furniture scholar has significantly expanded on or refuted his work. While British furniture histories routinely illustrate joined chests of drawers with doors and profuse mother-of-pearl, bone, and exotic wood inlays, most English scholars have studiously avoided attributions. Among the most notable exceptions are Victor Chinnery and Adam Bowett. Chinnery's "Laudian" school, along with a few surviving architectural fixtures and photographs of lost monuments like the interiors of Holland House published in *Country Life*, remains one the few irreducible groups of London joinery. Bowett has commented on the South American, Caribbean, and Asian hardwoods used on the façades of English chests of drawers with doors, but he too has refrained from attributing any of those objects to London. This reticence is puzzling, since London is, by far, the most likely center for the production of such early and stylistically elevated objects. Perhaps some English scholars still consider these chests of drawers with doors crude precursors of later Carolean veneered furniture rather than its immediate and necessary antecedent.[2]

This essay will review Forman's attributions and key issues pertaining to the Boston school, some of which are in dispute. Among these are the identity and London origins of the makers, comparison between English chests of drawers with doors and a seminal American example, the use of exotic woods, and later manifestations of the Boston tradition. In some instances, we will be qualifying Forman's assertions. In others, we will be amplifying his work, informed by objects that have appeared since his death in 1982.

The London-Trained Joiners of Boston

Publications on Boston furniture of the seventeenth century have focused on Henry Messinger and Ralph Mason as the principal joiners in that town. Both men had several sons who followed them in the trade, and Messinger's daughter Sarah married Ralph Mason's son Richard (1630–1674), who was also a joiner. Although these two families constituted a small joinery "dynasty," several other woodworkers were active during the same period. The numerous chests, chests of drawers, and cupboards that survive in the "Boston" style are clearly from several shop traditions. Further evidence of a wide range of furniture forms exists in the probate records of Suffolk County. Linking these documents to surviving artifacts is difficult, and a further challenge is linking them to the artisans noted in period records.[3]

Many woodworkers identified in period documents left little if any evidence of their work. John Davis is the earliest joiner currently known to have worked in Boston. The principal record of him is a 1640 house contract between Davis and Samuel Dix mentioned in Thomas Lechford's notebook. Davis was also mentioned in the Boston church records on February 1640/41.

Mrs. Anne Hibbon was excommunicated for her "irregular dealings with our brother John Davisse" in not admonishing him for overcharging, as she conceived it, and for her "causeless uncharitable jealousies and suspicions against him and sundry of the brethren that are joiners and other neighbors of the same calling as if they were of a combination.

Accusations regarding price fixing were common in Massachusetts after immigration ceased with the outbreak of the civil war in England.[4]

Apprenticeship contracts identify John Crabtree as another joiner working in Boston in the mid-1630s. Perhaps the most interesting records pertaining to him are suits for £20 in 1646 and £40 in 1648, both filed against Barbadian joiner Thomas Gray. These records indicate that Crabtree had business dealings in Barbados, which could be significant given the fact that imported woods are relatively common on early Boston chests and chests of drawers. Crabtree died in 1656.[5]

Boston joiner Thomas Scottow (1615–1661) was baptized in Great Yarmouth, Norfolk, England, on April 30, 1615. Presumably, he immigrated with his mother, Thomasine, and brother Joshua, who arrived in New England by 1634. Thomas would have been nineteen at that date, which was too young to have completed his apprenticeship according to English law. He could have begun serving his term in England and finished in Boston, or he could have served a shortened apprenticeship in New England. The earliest reference to Thomas working independently as a joiner is a 1638 deed.[6]

Attempts to curtail short apprenticeships in Boston began as early as June 20, 1660:

[It] is found by sad experience that many youths in this Towne, being put forth Apprentices to severall manufactures and sciences, but for 3 or 4 yeares time, contrary to the Customes of all well governed places, whence they are uncapable of being Artists in their trades, besides their unmeetness att the expiration of their Apprentice-ship to take charge of others for government and manuall instruction in their occupations which, if nott timely amended, threatens the welfare of this Towne.

[It] is therefore ordered that no person shall henceforth open a shop in this Towne, nor occupy any manufacture or science, till hee hath completed 21 years of age, nor except hee hath served seven yeares Apprentice-ship, by testimony under the hands of sufficient witnesses. And that Indentures made betweene any master and servant shall be brought in and enrolled in the Towne's Records within one month after the contract made, on penalty of ten shillings to bee paid by the master att the time of the Apprentice being made free.[7]

Thomas Scottow remained in Boston until his death in 1661. His probate inventory listed a "chest of drawers" valued at £2, a "settle with drawers" at £1, a "chest" at £1.10, and several objects of presumably greater age, including a "Court Cubboard old cloth & cushion" valued at £1.10 and "5 old basse Chaires" at 8s. Among the tools inventoried in his shop were twenty-five planes, one "long saw," three "hand saws," one pair of compasses, three augers, two hold fasts, three benches, thirty-one chisels, two axes, one froe, and "files, & other tooles." Scottow also had a "lathe and six

turning tooles" in the cellar of his house, "parcels" of wood, "bolts & pan-nells" in the yard, and "lumber" and "boards" in his shop.[8]

John Scottow (1644–1678) followed his father in the joiner's trade, but he was only seventeen when Thomas died. Presumably, he began training with his father and completed his apprenticeship with another master. Although John's career may have spanned less than thirteen years, the fashionable furniture listed in his inventory—most notably the chests of drawers and leather chairs—and the high values assigned to the chest of drawers, tools, and materials in his shop suggest that he was among the upper echelon of Boston joiners:

> 2 boxes 6s and 1 Chest of Drawers 30 / £1:16:00
> In the Garrett / 6 new frames 24s one Bedsteed 10 / one stand 5 /
> In the west low roome 2 small tables 8 / 1 Chest 25 / £1:13:00
> Linnen in sd Chest 9 napkins new 9s ½ doz (ditto) 4s Napkins 3s
> 1 tablecloth 6 towels 5s four pr of pillowbeers 16 / £1:17:07
> 5 Chaires 14s one Cradle 9s £1:03:00
> In the East Low Room one Bed wth furniture & bedsteed cupboard, cupboard cloth and Cushion, £2:10:00
> Chest of Drawers 30 / Square table 30 £3:00:00
> 9 Leather chaires £4/5 two Lookeing glasses 7s £4:12:00
> At his Shop: 4 boxes 7 / three Chests 18s two bedsteeds 32s £2:17:00
> 1 Chest of Drawers £3:00:00
> Boards, planks, timber & Joyners tooles £20:06:05[9]

"Ralph Mason, 35 yeres, Joyner" arrived in New England in July 1635, along with his wife, Anne, and their three small children. Immigrants had to swear an oath of allegiance to the crown and present proof of such conformity at the time of emigration. Ralph Mason's certificate was from the "Ministr & Justice of peace of St Olives Southwarke," a parish on the south bank of the Thames in London.[10]

Two records from the Worshipful Company of Joiners and Ceilers of London appear to refer to Mason. The first dates between June 12 and September 1, 1628—"Item [received] of Raph Mason late the apntice of James Holt a silver spoone and for his admission . . . [3s. 4d.]" (fig. 3)—and the second pertains to Mason taking an apprentice on the "Last Sept. 1628—

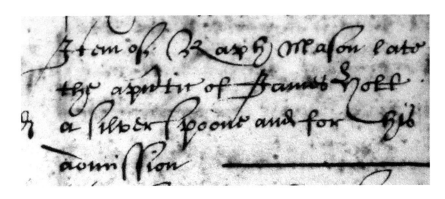

Figure 3   Admission record for Ralph Mason, Master's and Warden's Account Books, Worshipful Company of Joiners and Ceilers, London, 1621–1828. (Courtesy, Worshipful Company of Joiners and Ceilers, Surrey, England; photo, Peter Follansbee.)

Item of Raphe Mason for presenting Richard *Praynte*." These are the only references to Mason that predate his immigration. Records for London apprentice bindings begin in 1621, but Mason's indenture to James Holt (or any other joiner) is not among them. Judging by his age at the time he emigrated, Mason was a little older than usual when admitted to the Worshipful Company of Joiners and Ceilers. *An Act touching divers orders for artificers, laborers, servants of husbandry and apprentices* (1563) established guidelines for indentures, including the minimum age at which an apprentice could complete his term: "after the custom and order of the city of London for seven years at the least so the term and years of such apprentice do not expire afore such apprentice shall be of the age of 24 year." It is noteworthy that Mason was allowed to take an apprentice shortly after being admitted to the Worshipful Company of Joiners and Ceilers. Most tradesmen were not allowed to take an apprentice until they had been freemen for three years.[11]

The earliest reference to Mason in New England is a February 19, 1637/38, grant for land in Muddy River, which is present-day Brookline, Massachusetts. The Shawmut Peninsula settled as Boston had already been divided into house lots by that date. In June 1658 Mason agreed to make furniture for the Muddy River town house as partial payment for additional land:

> The Cedar swamp att Muddy river is lett to Ralph Mason his heyres and assignes for fifty yeares next ensuing, after the first of March next, in consideration whereof, hee shall pay yearly every first of March fourty shillings in wheate and pease proportionately; and hee is to pay fourty shillings this summer, and a fayre livery Cupboard for the towne house.[12]

Ralph Mason's probate inventory, dated January 27, 1678, included a "parcel of old Joyners tooles" valued at 5s.; a "worke bench, 6 old plain stocks, 5 old plain Irons, one great piercer bit, 1 new narrow chizell, a bolting plain, a hatchet, 2 bookes, a jointer and iron and turning chizell in the custody of Samuel Mason" appraised at £1.17.3; a "cupboard" valued at £1.10; "some cross plains in the custody of Jacob Mason" appraised at 5s.; a "small table" valued at 2s.; "three old chairs and an old stoole" appraised at 2s.; and an "old chest, some tubbs & other lumber" valued at 12s. The low value assigned to these tools and the references to some being in the custody of Mason's sons imply that he had either ceased or limited his joinery work.[13]

Ralph Mason's four sons—Richard, Samuel, Jacob, and John—all became joiners. In 1660 the eldest, Richard (1630–1674), married Sarah Messinger. Richard probably trained with his father, Ralph, but the possibility also exists that he served his apprenticeship with Sarah's father, Henry. Although New England apprenticeship contracts from this period are scarce, English records provide insights into prevailing customs. References to joiners apprenticing their sons to other woodworkers are common. Some families lacked the means to raise, educate, and train their children. In some English settings, civic or guild restrictions limited the number of apprentices a tradesman could have at one time, so if a joiner had two or more sons near each other in age, one might be bound to another craftsman. Last, sending a son to train with another craftsman might indicate a desire to align shops and dominate the joinery customs of their town.[14]

Richard Mason worked in Boston, presumably until he died in his mid-forties. His probate inventory, dated May 22, 1674, included the following:

One bedstead and curtains & chest drawers	02 :10 :00
One cabinet and couberd	01 :10 :00
One chest three Joynt stools & a tabell	01 :07:00
One Box five chears & a cradle	00:15 :00
Four playns	00 :12 :00
One chest and one coubard	03 :10 :00
Twenty two plates	00:08:00
A kneding trough & a lamp	00:06:00
A parcell of tools	01 :15 :00
Tow benshes	00:02:00[15]

Samuel Mason (1632–1691) was referred to as a "joiner" in a deed from 1671. Considering that he probably worked in Boston for almost forty years, he left little record of his trade. No probate records for him or his brother John (1640–1696) survive.[16]

Jacob Mason (1644–1694/95) married a woman named Rebecca in 1674. Forman noted that Jacob was called an "instrument maker" in Samuel Sewall's diary, but that description could have meant many things. His February 16, 1694/95 probate inventory, compiled by Boston joiner John Nichols, listed furniture and some unspecified tools: "1 large cedar chest" valued at £1.10, "1 Case of Drawrs" at £1.10, "1 small Table & joint stool" at 5s., "5 old flagg Chairs" at 6s., and "Barrells, tubbs &," "Timber," and "Tooles" at £3.10.[17]

The earliest record for Henry Messinger (d. 1681) in Boston is a 1639/40 grant for land at Muddy River. His first child, John, was born in Boston on January 24, 1641. He and his wife, Sarah, remained there for the rest of their lives, eventually rearing eight children. Although several deeds refer to Messinger as a "joiner," few documents pertaining to his trade are known. His tax rate was adjusted in 1645 in exchange for Messinger's mending the schoolmaster's fence. In 1661 he was called on to "secure ye foundation of ye Towne house from damage as also any other pt of ye house."[18]

The first publication to draw attention to Henry Messinger was Esther Singleton's *Furniture of Our Forefathers* (1913). She named several joiners found in period records and included information from Messinger's will and that of his son Henry (1645–1686). Forman later asserted that Henry Sr., Ralph Mason, and John Davis were London joiners, but at present only Mason can be shown to have trained there. Since then other scholars, most notably Robert Trent, whose work built on what Forman had begun, have considered Messinger and Mason the two most important joiners in Boston.[19]

Henry Messinger Sr. and Ralph Mason are the first two joiners listed on the "Petition of the Handycraftsmen," which was signed by 129 tradesmen and presented to the General Court in 1677. The petition requested protection from "the frequent intruding of strangers from all parts, especially of such as are not desirably qualified." The petitioners—shoemakers, coopers, tailors, and joiners—felt that their livelihoods were being jeopardized by men who "never served any time, or not considerably for the learning of a

Trade." The placement of names on documents of this type was often hierarchical, suggesting that the other joiners who signed the petition deferred to Ralph Mason and Henry Messinger Sr. as leading artisans.[20]

The Messinger name is most common in the area around Wigton, Cumberland, England, yet no baptismal record for a child named Henry has been found. There are a small number of baptisms for Henry Messingers in other counties, but none can be linked to the Boston joiner. Similarly, the surname Messinger does not appear in the records of the Worshipful Company of Joiners and Ceilers of London between 1621 and Henry's arrival in New England.[21]

Henry Messinger's probate inventory, dated April 30, 1681, sheds some light on his success as a joiner (app. 1). He owned a variety of fashionable forms including leather chairs, upholstered (serge) chairs, elbow chairs, chests, and "a press cubberd wth drawers." The listing for a "[family] cote of Armes & Joynrs Armes" valued together at 40s. is intriguing, since the "Joynrs Armes" could be those of the Worshipful Company of Joiners and Ceilers of London. In Messinger's shop were "all sorts of Joyners Tools" valued at £5; a "table and Chest of Drawers not finished" appraised at £1; and "Timber within and without Doors wrought and unwrought" valued at £10. A "parcel of glue and *Nurces* skins" valued at £2.10 was in a chamber over the hall. This reference to sharkskin, which was used as an abrasive, is unique among New England inventories. André Félibien's *Des principles architecture* (1st ed. 1676) notes the use of "*sharkskin* for polishing wood in irregular figures." Some of the tropical woods found on seventeenth-century Boston case furniture have interlocked or "irregular" grain, whereas most of the native oak, cedar, maple, and walnut used during the period did not require the use of abrasives.[22]

When Henry Messinger died in 1681, his sons John, Henry, Simeon, and Thomas were all practicing joiners. Since John was born in 1641, he could have been working on his own from the early 1660s. Thomas's career could not have overlapped that of his father since he was born in 1662 and probably completed his apprenticeship circa 1683. The most detailed document concerning John Messinger's work is a court case involving ship captain William Hudson. In 1676 John's apprentice Ebenezer Ingoldsby provided testimony regarding woodworking projects ranging from joined forms to oven lids and beetles. Born in Boston in 1656, Ingoldsby was nearly twenty when he appeared before the court and nearing the end of his term. Deeds from the mid-1680s describe him as a joiner, but his name does not appear in any other Boston records.[23]

Henry Messinger Jr. died on November 17, 1686, at the age of thirty-two (fig. 4). His will, which refers to Benjamin Threeneedle as his "eldest apprentice," indicates that he had two apprentices at that date. The inventory of his shop listed "Timber, Boards, planks [and] workeing tooles . . . [appraised] by Mr Cunnibell and Tho: Warren, Joyners At Eleven pounds 16/8 . . . [and] A parcel of glew -12-10." Henry's wife reported "Money [received] since the death of my husband for worke done for Some Frenchmen 2-05-00."[24]

Figure 4 Gravestone of Henry Messinger Jr., Granary Burying Ground, Boston, Massachusetts, 1686. (Photo, Peter Follansbee.)

Simeon Messinger (1645–ca. 1695) and Thomas Messinger (1661–d. after 1697) left little written record of their careers. A 1676 deed referred to "the shop that Simeon Messneger ye joyner works in at the further end of ye Garden . . . facing and fronting to ye Streete going from-ward ye Town house toward ye Prison in Boston . . . not the part toward Jeremiah Bumsteads." The only record pertaining to Thomas Messinger's work is a November 24, 1691, receipt totaling £1.7.8 for making the window shutters on the first Anglican meetinghouse in Boston.[25]

David Saywell (d. 1672), who may have been from Salisbury, Wiltshire, England, first appeared in Boston records in 1660, when he married Abigail Buttolph. He was subsequently mentioned in several deeds, one of which involved local turner Thomas Edsall. As was the case with John Davis and Thomas Scottow, Saywell worked in Boston only a short time. Nevertheless, he appears to have flourished in the joiners' trade. His inventory listed a cupboard valued at £5 along with "New bedsteeds," "24 paire of iron screws & nuts" (possibly for the bedsteads), "joint stooles chaire frames," two chests, three tables, two desks, two boxes, two cabinets, and "some new worke in the shop not finisht." His timber, lathe, benches, tools, and material were appraised at nearly £20.[26]

Jeremiah Bumstead (Bumpstead) (1636–1709) was born at Bury St. Edmunds, Suffolk, England, in 1636, immigrated to New England with his parents by 1640, and relocated to Boston shortly thereafter. He probably trained in Boston, but his master has not been identified. Bumstead married Hannah Odlin before 1664, when their first child was born. He was described as a "joiner" in Suffolk County deeds between 1669 and 1704. Several of these records reveal that Bumstead owned property next to that of Henry Messinger Sr. The two men apparently had a tumultuous relationship, since "Thomas Varrin, aged about 16 years . . . [testified] That he has heard Jerimyah Bumstead caull henery Messinger senior a wicked base mallitious fellow and . . . a prateing Logarhed." In 1685 Bumstead was allowed to "sell beere & Cyder by retayle, in consideration of the wounds & lamnesse he received in ye time of the Indian warr." Forman assumed that Bumstead's career as a joiner was over at that point, but subsequent references to the latter as a "joiner" suggest that was not the case. Bumstead's sister Mercy married Boston joiner John Roleston.[27]

John Cunnable (1649/50–1724) was described as a "Citizen and Joyner of London" in a debt record for £48 owed to ironmonger John Russell and recorded there in November 1673. That debt was still outstanding when Russell filed suit in Boston thirty-six years later. Cunnable arrived in New England shortly after 1673 and lived in Boston for most of his life. Judge Samuel Sewall mentioned work done by Cunnable including making a window and stairs for the former's house in the 1690s. Cunnable died in April 1724. His inventory listed "1 Oval table" valued at 25s., "1 Square ditto" at 15s., "1 Case of Draws" at 50s., several "Strait Slate chairs," "five back'd Ditto," and "1 Arm'd Ditto." Tools were not included, having been bequeathed to his son Samuel (1689/90 1746). The younger Cunnable and his son Samuel (1717–1797) were both called "housewright" and "joyner" in contemporary records.[28]

Benjamin Thwing (1619–1672) arrived in Boston in 1635 as a sixteen-year-old servant to his sister's husband, Ralph Hudson, a woolen draper from Yorkshire. In 1638 Hudson left Thwing £10 in his will, stating that it should be paid "when [the latter's] time should be out." Thwing must have served the remainder of his apprenticeship with a joiner, but his master's identity remains a mystery. A 1670 deed between Thwing and his son Benjamin (1647–1680) refers to the elder man as a "joiner" and the younger as a "carpenter." Another son, John (b. 1644), married Maria Messinger, daughter of Henry Messinger Sr., but there is no evidence that the former worked in the joinery trade. Benjamin Sr.'s inventory included "One Cheste 6s; one meal trough 1s; one Livery cup board not finished 5s; two chairs 3s; one small table one box 6s."[29]

The lack of detailed records for Bumstead, Cunnable, and Thwing suggests that in the Boston joinery trade they were less influential than David Saywell, Thomas and John Scottow, Henry Messinger Sr. and Jr., and Ralph Mason and his sons. There were many other furniture makers working in Boston during the seventeenth century of whom even less is known. Forman recorded more than one hundred joiners as well as turners and cabinetmakers, the latter beginning with John Clarke in 1681. As the seventeenth century drew to a close, furniture forms began to change in Boston, and other areas of New England followed. John Cunnable's architectural work may reflect that shift, particularly if he was unable to adapt to new styles and methods of furniture construction.[30]

The London-Trained Turners of Boston

Turning was an important facet of the furniture-making trades in seventeenth-century Boston. Much of the applied ornament on early Boston chests and cupboards—pillars, half-columns, feet—is turned, and some of it represents the work of specialists who sold piecework to joiners, chair makers, master builders, shipwrights, and others. The most common work probably consisted of woodenware and nautical components like blocks and pulleys.

London court records from the early 1630s outline demarcations between the trades of joiners and turners in that city:

> [The] Compy of Turners be grieved that the Compy of Joyners assume unto themselves the art of turning to the wrong of the Turners. It appeareth to us that the arts of turning & joyning are two several & distinct trades and we conceive it very inconvenient that either of these trades should encroach upon the other and we find that the Turners have constantly for the most part turned bed posts & feet of joyned stools for the Joyners and of late some Joyners who never used to turn their own bedposts and stool feet have set on work in their houses some poor decayed Turners & of them have learned the feate & art of turning which they could not do before. And it appeareth unto us by custom that the turning of Bedposts Feet of tables joyned stools do properly belong to the trade of a Turner and not to the art of a Joyner and whatsoever is done with the foot as have treddle or wheele for turning of any wood we are of the opinion and do find that it properly belongs to the Turner's and we find that the Turners ought not to use the gage or gages, grouffe plaine or plough plaine and mortising chisells or any of them for that the same do belong to the Joyners trade.

Outside London, the same craftsman often performed turning and joinery. Thomas Quilter of Great Dunmow "[combined] the twin crafts of joiner and turner" and divided "his 'working tools' equally between his two sons, giving each "a turning lathe and a grindstone unhanged." Quilter directed that his "elder son is to have the larger grindstone if he will teach his brother joining and turning in the best manner he can."[31]

In Boston some joiners, like Scottow and Saywell, owned lathes and did their own turning, whereas others commissioned piecework from specialists or had a professional turner working in their shop. Presumably, joiners working in the London style would have patronized turners working in the London style. Assuming that a joiner trained in a city where the two trades were separate, he might not have known how to turn.

Thomas Edsall has been described as one of the earliest turners in Boston and credited for providing piecework for the Mason-Messinger shops. Forman did not cite but must have used Charles Pope's *Pioneers of New England* as a source in creating Edsall's biography. According to Forman, Edsall was forty-seven when he sailed from London onboard the *Elizabeth and Anne* in April 1635; however, the name on the passenger list is "Thomas Hedsall," and there is no further reference to an "Edsall" or "Hedsall" until Thomas Edsall married Elizabeth Ferman in Boston in 1651 or 1652. Genealogist Robert Charles Anderson subsequently concluded that "Hedsall" and "Edsall" could not have been the same man, based on the unlikely circumstance that a man who left London in 1635 could have lived in Boston for nearly sixteen years without having been mentioned in records. As further evidence, Anderson noted that this immigrant would have been sixty-three when he married, and that the "Thomas Edsall" who married Ferman was mentioned frequently in the town records after 1652.[32]

Forman speculated that Thomas Edsall was either the brother or the son of London turner Henry Edsall, who took his first apprentice in 1627 and served as warden and master of the Worshipful Company of Turners in the 1650s and 1660s, but there is no concrete evidence to substantiate that claim. Moreover, several men with similar last names are mentioned in seventeenth-century English records, as is the case with Henry (b. 1619) and Thomas (b. 1612) Edsall of Sunninghill, Berkshire. Until further evidence comes to light, Forman's assertion that Thomas Edsall was "unquestionably the most important turner" of his era in Boston and subsequent efforts to link him with the Messinger and Mason shops must be discounted.[33]

The most detailed record pertaining to Edsall's work in Boston is a court ruling against Henry Harris, who may have been an apprentice who ran away or a journeyman who owed Edsall work. As Forman noted, this document provides insight into the amount of work a tradesman was expected to produce per week:

> According to a covenant . . . dated the 19th day of March, 1666/7 . . . I judge and order the said Harris either to dwell with & serve the said Edsell eight whole weeks beginning on the 17th Day of this June [1672] & to make every of the said weekes fifteen chair frames [illegible] good and merchantable or else shall make one whole hundred and twenty such frames in the whole eight week [illegible] the said Edsell finding & allowing unto him the said Harris sufficient place, tooles & stuff to make them.

Later in 1672 Harris won a suit against Edsall, receiving £12.4.7.[34]

Another turner identified by Forman was Nathaniel Adams Sr., who died in Boston in 1675. Adams's inventory shows that lathe work for furniture (fifteen new chairs and forty-eight unbottomed chairs) accounted for only a small percentage of his shop's production and sales. As yet, there is no documentation that Nathaniel Adams Sr. was associated with any of the joiners mentioned in this study.[35]

The London Chest of Drawers

How Forman arrived at the conclusion that London joinery and London-trained joiners were the source for the archetypal Boston seventeenth-century chest of drawers is not entirely clear. He was impressed with the dovetailed drawers of Boston case pieces and their strong resemblance to those of English chests and cognizant of a 1632 London lawsuit between that city's joiners and carpenters restricting dovetailing to the former trade. Forman's research on sixteenth- and seventeenth-century immigrant woodworkers in London showed that many of those craftsmen resided in Southwark, across the Thames from the city's center. He also demonstrated that foreign artisans who specialized in making inlaid gunstocks and sword hilts produced similar ornament for London chests and cabinets. Forman eventually concluded that all case pieces with this class of ornament were from London and that the city's joiners literally *invented* the chest of drawers.[36]

The latter theory may not be entirely correct. A group of northern Italian chests of drawers referred to as *canterali* in Genoa during the period are usually dated 1580–1620, although Italian furniture scholars have not

provided substantial documentation for that range. "Virtuosos," or connoisseurs, at the Stuart courts who traveled to Italy may have introduced the *idea* of a chest of drawers as a specifically Italianate furniture form. No English versions of these heavily carved *canterali* are known, but a few English patrons commissioned copies of Italianate *sgabello* chairs for grottoes from London craftsmen.[37]

The earliest English object resembling a chest of drawers with doors belongs to a small group of courtly cabinets made for the uppermost echelons of the Carolean court. Referred to as the "Laudian" school by Victor Chinnery, these cabinets have dovetailed cases filled with small boxes or drawers and doors with large appliqués that form niches with pediments, a conceit popular throughout Germany during the period. Among the better-known members of this school are a cabinet made for William Laud during his tenure as bishop of London between 1628 and 1633 and a press owned by Charles I (fig. 5). Paneling in the Jerusalem Chamber at Westminster Palace, commissioned by Laud from London joiner Adam Brown in 1629, is also in the same style. The most pertinent object of the Laudian school is a case piece composed of a cabinet over a chest of drawers with

Figure 6 Cabinet and chest of drawers, London, England, ca. 1628–1630. Woods not recorded. H. 59½", W. 41½", D. 16". (Courtesy, Edwin Willson and David Gill, Mary Bellis Antiques, Hungerford, Berkshire.)

Figure 7 Interior view of the cabinet and chest of drawers illustrated in fig. 6. The upper section has a dovetailed board case, whereas the lower section has joined construction.

doors (figs. 6, 7). The cabinet and chest sections are shallow, and the wide drawers in the lower case were obviously intended to hold rolled-up deeds and other large legal documents rather than textiles. Some scholars have posited that the chest dates later than the cabinet. While differences between the two sections are apparent, their ornamental details are similar. This suggests that the chest section was commissioned within a few years of the cabinet, if not contemporaneously, and that furniture forms close to a chest of drawers were being made in London by the early 1630s.[38]

Some scholars have questioned the earliest dates assigned to seminal Boston chests like the example illustrated in figure 1. Their criticism was based largely on London chests of drawers with bone and mother-of-pearl inlay, many of which bear dates ranging from 1647 to 1663 on the ornament (fig. 8). Although those dates are useful in determining when such inlays were fashionable, they provide no benchmark for determining when London joiners began making chests of drawers. Court documents published by Forman support the use of chests of drawers in that city by 1638. Before sailing from London to take his post as the president of Harvard College, Rev. Joseph Glover commissioned a lavish set of household goods. He died on the voyage, and his widow, Elisabeth, married the new president of Harvard College, Henry Dunster, soon afterward. Years later, Glover's heirs sued Dunster for bequests and residues from their parents' estates. Part of the case centered on furnishings that were in Mrs. Glover's house in

Figure 8 Chest of drawers with doors, London, England, 1650–1670. Oak, ebony, cocobolo (a pale tropical hardwood), mother-of-pearl, bone, and possibly ivory with unidentified secondary woods. H. 51¼", W. 46½", D. 25½". (Sotheby's, *A Celebration of the English Country House*, New York, April 15, 2010, lot 43.) Several of the inlaid and ebonized oak plaques are missing, and the applied half-columns and feet are replacements.

Cambridge before her second marriage. Testimony offered by a maid who worked in the Glover household in 1638 referred unequivocally to textiles that were stored in a chest of drawers, which presumably accompanied the Glovers on their voyage to New England. The earliest reference to a chest of drawers in London is the 1640 inventory of alderman Anthony Abdy, who had one example in a chamber over the hall and another in the chamber over the parlor. Chests of drawers first appear in Boston inventories in 1643. In that year, appraisers valued an example owned by the late John Atwood at £3.1, a considerable sum. Other early references to chests of drawers are found in the inventories of London merchants who settled in New Haven in Connecticut, where London-trained joiners also worked.

The 1647 inventories of Thomas Gray and Francis Brewster each listed a chest of drawers. Similarly, Stephen Goodyear, one of the London merchants who founded New Haven, died in 1658 owning two chests of drawers, one of which was described as "old."[39]

The Boston Chest of Drawers

Wood extraction and preparation are significant factors in evaluating London-style joinery and its Boston derivatives. Forman believed that the Shawmut Peninsula was largely deforested in the early seventeenth century, owing to the Native American practice of burning undergrowth to facilitate hunting. That led him to conclude that Boston joiners, like their London counterparts, made furniture primarily from imported wood, which they sawed into working dimensions. In reality, the acquisition and preparation of wood in both cities will not be fully understood until more London examples have been examined in detail. In London, where wood was at a premium, timber entered the city through various sources. Among these were the so-called wainscot fleets, which arrived from Scandinavia and northern Europe, once or twice a year, with cargoes of oak balks, joists, and planks. Some of this imported timber was sawn into boards in the Netherlands before being shipped to London, and some was imported in riven form as well. Once wainscot entered the London woodworking trade, it was either sawn or riven into usable sizes. In English urban centers, pit sawing appears to have been the most common means of processing wood. In the Netherlands, water- or wind-powered sawmills often took the place of pairs of sawyers. By contrast, riving involved cleaving ring-porous hardwoods radially, using wedges and beetles to section trunks and lighter froes and wooden clubs called mauls to split out smaller pieces. Riven stock is automatically aligned on the medullary ray plane, whereas sawn stock can be radial or transverse in orientation.[40]

Forman's contention that London artisans worked exclusively with sawn stock is refuted by the chest of drawers illustrated in figures 8 and 9 and by records of riven timber for carpentry in that city's marketplace (see app. 2). The question of how commonly riven wood was used in London joinery remains unclear. It is unlikely that the city's joiners could have obtained unseasoned oak to rive, unless such wood was brought down the Thames from inland sources or via the sea from the West Country.

Although clearly based on London work, the Boston chest of drawers with doors illustrated in figure 1 provides little information regarding the extraction of its stock. The interior surfaces have been planed smooth, removing all evidence of pit sawing or riving. Although one might assume components oriented on the medullary ray plane were extracted by riving, that is not necessarily the case. The most significant attribute of radial stock is that it will not warp across its width. This is an important consideration in drawer fronts that are intended to receive applied ornament, because warping could promote loss. Stock aligned with the medullary ray plane is also preferable for drawer sides, which need to remain stable to avoid binding. While it is true that almost all riven oak is aligned with the

Figure 9 Detail of the chest of drawers with doors illustrated in fig. 8, showing evidence of riving on the interior of the upper case. Most of the framing members and some of the panels are made of riven lumber, while the drawer bottoms, rear panels, and the top of the upper case are made of sawn lumber.

Figure 10   Rear view of the chest of drawers with doors illustrated in fig. 1. (Photo, Gavin Ashworth.)

Figure 11   Detail showing the drawer construction of the chest of drawers with doors illustrated in fig. 1. (Photo, Gavin Ashworth.) The drawers are dovetailed at the front and nailed at the back.

radial or medullary ray plane, the same orientation can be obtained by quarter sawing.

London and Boston case pieces typically have wide, thin framing members and relatively small panels (fig. 10). The panels of London case pieces are sometimes made of multiple boards, a feature also seen in London-derived furniture from the New Haven Colony and *kasten* from New York. London-trained joiners may have used broad framing members to regulate the dimensions of panels. Wide, thin sections of clear panel stock were the most difficult components to produce, especially if extracted by pit or frame sawing. This problem would have been particularly acute in cities like London, where timber for furniture making was largely imported. As the stiles and rails of the chest of drawers with doors illustrated in figure 1 suggest, London-trained joiners in Boston continued using Old World techniques and modes of construction after they arrived in New England, despite having ready access to oak and other ring-porous hardwoods.[41]

In both the London and Boston joinery traditions, makers used half-blind dovetails to connect the drawer sides to the fronts and nails to secure the rear corners (fig. 11). The number of dovetails varies according to drawer height. Thus, shallow drawers often have only one dovetail, slightly larger drawers usually have two, and very deep drawers—presumably intended for table linens or seasonal storage of bedding—sometimes have three. Dovetailed drawers also appear in joined case pieces attributed to Braintree, Cambridge, and northern Essex County, but it is unclear if their dovetailing was influenced by Boston practice.[42]

Another feature shared by London case pieces and their Boston counterparts is an exceptionally thin top, which is set in a shallow rabbet (usually 1/4"–3/8" deep) in the cornice moldings of both one- and two-piece forms. In London such tops are often made from three boards. To reinforce the tops, makers often attached a strut to the front and rear rails below. Why London joiners used thin tops is a puzzle, since the savings in material was offset by the labor needed to saw or rive thin stock. Surprisingly, the chest of drawers with doors illustrated in figure 1 and a related chest of drawers (fig. 17) do not have fore-and-aft struts, whereas most other Boston joined case pieces do.

The lipped tenon found on some Boston case pieces is another feature seen in London work. In most cases, mortise-and-tenon joints are positioned in the stock so the rails and stiles are flush with each other. The archetypal London lipped tenon is positioned farther to the rear, thus setting the face of the rail ahead of the face of the adjoining stile. This feature seems to

Figure 12   Detail of the chest of drawers with doors illustrated in fig. 8, showing the lipped tenon on one end of the lower front rail of the lower case. (Photo, Gavin Ashworth.)

Figure 13   Detail of lipped tenons on a chest with two drawers, Plymouth Colony, Massachusetts, 1650–1690. (Courtesy, Plimoth Plantation, Plymouth, Massachusetts.)

Figure 14   Detail of the chest of drawers with doors illustrated in fig. 1, showing the lipped tenon of the upper front rail of the lower case. (Photo, Gavin Ashworth.)

have evolved in order to place the front base molding ahead of doors (fig. 12). Another version of this lipped tenon has long been associated with the lower cases of chests with drawers and cupboards made in Plymouth Colony, Massachusetts (fig. 13), but on those objects the lipped tenon serves no apparent function. The Boston chest of drawers with doors has lipped tenons, but they are not in the same location as those on the London examples. Their use on the upper front rail of the lower case may have reflected the maker's desire to position the large waist molding of the case forward of the doors (fig. 14). Further evidence that the lipped tenon is a London joinery detail can be found on an armchair that belonged to Edward

Figure 15 Armchair attributed to Kenelm Winslow, Plymouth, Massachusetts, 1640–1660. Red oak. H. 42", W. 24", D. 15". (Courtesy, Pilgrim Society, Pilgrim Hall Museum, gift of Abby Frothingham Winslow, 1882.)

Figure 16 Detail of the back of the crest of the armchair illustrated in fig. 15. (Photo, Peter Follansbee.)

Winslow (1595–1655) and is attributed to his brother, London-trained joiner Kenelm Winslow (1599–1672) (figs. 15, 16). On the chair, the tenons are cut in the top of the rear stiles and fit into mortises cut in the crest rail. Because the tenon extends up behind the crest rail and prevents wracking, it provides a measure of structural support.[43]

The large chest of drawers illustrated in figure 17 is the only other London-derived two-part chest of drawers from seventeenth-century Boston with three drawers in the lower case. Although similar in proportion, this object and the chest of drawers with doors (fig. 1) have structural differences critical to dating them. The interior surfaces of the chest are rougher, with marks left from riving, and the sides of its drawers are laminated (fig. 17). This could indicate that the maker had a shortage of wide riven stock, or that he was following the prevailing London practice of glu-

Figure 17 Chest of drawers, Boston, Massachusetts, 1650–1680. Oak, chestnut, cedrela, black walnut, and ebony with oak and white pine. H. 51¼", W. 47³⁄₁₆", D. 23¹⁄₁₆". (Courtesy, Museum of Fine Arts, Boston, bequest of Charles Hitchcock Tyler.)

ing up smaller-dimensioned materials to conserve wood. The chest also shares with other Boston case pieces the "paneling" of the front stiles (the chest of drawers with doors is an exception because the doors cover the stiles of the lower case). To render this detail, joiners planed channels with fine edge moldings along the entire length of the front faces of the stiles, then used mitered stops to create the illusion of panels. Several other eastern Massachusetts shop traditions used this technique, but only on drawer fronts. Much of the carcass of the two-part chest is made of riven cedrela (Spanish cedar), an imported wood often used for moldings, glyphs, and other appliqués; the rear framing members and the rails between the drawers are the only structural oak in the case. Except for the sides of the rear stiles, none of the oak shows in the finished object.

Other Furniture Forms Attributed to Boston

The cupboard illustrated in figure 18 is the only indisputable Boston example known, and contemporary London examples are rare. By 1670 cupboards were being displaced by chests of drawers, and the growing popularity of the latter furniture form explains why joiners began to install drawers in the lower cases of some cupboards. The Boston cupboard shares several traits with other London-derived case pieces, including a strut under the top boards of the upper case, dovetails at the front corners of the drawers, and large, academically correct cove and Roman ovolo moldings. The

Figure 18   Cupboard with drawers, Boston, Massachusetts, 1670–1690. Oak, maple, walnut, cedar, and chestnut with oak and white pine. H. 55⅝", W. 49⅜", D. 21¾". (Chipstone Foundation; photo, Gavin Ashworth.) The frieze ornaments and the top of the upper case are restored on the basis of those elements on the chest of drawers illustrated in fig. 17.

Figure 19   Rear view of the cupboard with drawers illustrated in fig. 18. (Photo, Gavin Ashworth.)

Figure 20   Detail of the cupboard with drawers illustrated in fig. 18, showing the underside of the trapezoidal compartment in the upper case. (Photo, Gavin Ashworth.)

cupboard deviates from conventional London and Boston practice in having elaborate applied ornament on the sides of the lower case and is unique in its use of ebonized curly maple to simulate a tropical hardwood.[44]

The maker of the Boston cupboard used different methods to enclose the rear of the two case sections (fig. 19). The rear of the upper case has a large pine panel with feathered edges that engage grooves plowed on the inner edges of the four framing members. The rear of the lower case has three vertical boards that meet in lap joints and feathered edges that are set in grooves in the vertical framing members and nailed into rabbets in the horizontal framing members. Another distinctive feature involves the framing of the trapezoidal compartment (fig. 20). Rather than attaching the rails of the compartment to the rear posts with mortise-and-tenon joints, the maker merely nailed them in place from behind. This is substandard practice, considering the more normative use of pentagonal posts on Boston leaf tables with trapezoidal frames (figs. 26, 27).[45]

Although furniture scholars were not aware of the Boston cupboard during Forman's lifetime, two chests with applied ornament on the front panels informed his theories. On the example illustrated in figure 21, two of the panels have crossets at the corners, and the third features a round motif

Figure 21 Chest, Boston, Massachusetts, 1650–1690. Red oak, black walnut, red cedar, and maple with oak and white pine. H. 26⅛", W. 47⅝", D. 21½". (Courtesy, Historic New England; photo, Richard Cheek.) The lower drawer, framework, and feet are missing.

Figure 22 Chest, Boston, Massachusetts, 1650–1690. Oak, cedrela, and walnut with oak and white pine. H. 30½", W. 45", D. 20½". (Chipstone Foundation; photo, Gavin Ashworth.)

Figure 23 Detail of the scratch-stock molding on the interior of the chest illustrated in fig. 22. (Photo, Luke Beckerdite.)

with four circular, molded segments separated by voussoirs—a design common in London chests of drawers but unique in Boston work. The other chest (not illustrated) has three crosseted panels.[46]

Other chests that have appeared since Forman's death shed additional light on Boston versions of that form. The example illustrated in figure 22 has an applied Roman ovolo above a false drawer and an ogee molding on the front edges of the lid and till. The bottom of the till protrudes past the interior side and is also molded (fig. 23). As is the case with the chest of drawers with doors (fig. 1), the interior surfaces of the chest are smooth and neat. The maker used planes and scrapers to remove all evidence of riving and/or sawing and scratch-stock cutters to produce the moldings on the framing members. A fragmentary Boston chest has a different ornamental scheme, featuring a crosseted panel in the center and side panels that are further accented with lozenge-shaped appliqués (fig. 24). Boston chests of this type are rare, which is surprising when one considers that the form is one of the most common in other New England joinery traditions.

Figure 24 Chest, Boston, Massachusetts, 1660–1690. Oak, walnut, and maple with oak. H. 19¾", W. 46¼", D. 20". (Private collection; photo, courtesy of the owner.) The chest is missing one or two drawers below the storage compartment. The lid is replaced.

Figure 25   Chest, Boston, Massachusetts, 1670–1690. Red oak and black walnut with white pine and hemlock. H. 36¼", W. 36½", D. 21¼". (Courtesy, Metropolitan Museum of Art, gift of Mrs. Russell Sage, 1909; photo, Gavin Ashworth/Art Resource, NY.)

Another curious furniture form from Boston is a narrow chest with drawers (fig. 25). Six examples with one or two drawers are known. Their proportions and design suggest that they were used as chamber tables or dressing tables. Their dovetailed drawer construction and applied ornament is squarely in the Boston tradition, and the example shown in figure 25 has applied half-columns similar to those on the lower case of the Boston cupboard (fig. 18). These case pieces may be antecedents for the numerous chamber tables with an open shelf beneath a case section that were made in several shops on the South Shore of Massachusetts.[47]

Two Boston leaf tables are extraordinary rarities within the surviving corpus of New England furniture (figs. 26, 27). Tables of this type appear to have been used initially for drinking wine or dining, rather than gaming. Celia Fiennes may have seen a comparable example when she visited Hampton Court in 1698. Her diary mentions a "Clap table," which was the Dutch term for any folding, or leaf, table. The word "clap" obviously referred to

Figure 26   Round leaf table, Boston, Massachusetts, 1660–1690. Oak, black walnut, cedrela, and maple with oak and white pine. H. 28¾", W. 29", D. 29" (open). (Chipstone Foundation; photo, Gavin Ashworth.) The table is missing the molding around the lower shelf and its turned feet.

Figure 27   Round leaf table, Boston, Massachusetts, 1660–1690. Red cedar, cedrela and maple with oak and white pine. H. 33¼", W. 40¼", D. 20". (Private collection; photo, Gavin Ashworth.) The top, feet, fly rail, and pendants are restored.

the sound a leaf made when closed against the legs or frame. Fiennes also noted that the "back room" at Hampton Court contained "a little Wanscoate [oak] table for tea, cards or writeing." This suggests that small tables, like the Boston examples, performed several functions, regardless of their shape or top design.[48]

The Boston table illustrated in figure 26 has an oak frame, a black walnut top, and walnut, cedrela, and maple applied ornaments. The sources for this furniture form in England are ambiguous, but Dutch leaf tables, which often have a draw leg or a hinged fly leg, may have been an influence. The fly legs on Dutch tables of this genre were generally turned from two pieces of laminated stock with a paper interface, then separated like the applied half-columns on case pieces; one half remained stationary, and the other half rotated out to support the leaf and back to abut its mirror image and create the illusion of a single turning. In contrast, almost all English examples are framed with an auxiliary post, or leg, and both Boston tables are constructed in that fashion. This required an extraordinarily thick rear rail in order to house the fly leg post when the tables are shut. Another interesting feature of the Boston tables is the pentagonal shape of the posts where the rails join to form trapezoids. This allowed makers to secure the rails to the posts at approximately ninety-degree angles.

Both of the Boston leaf tables are sophisticated in design and construction, which suggests a connection to the upper echelon of London's joinery trade. They have dovetails at the front corners of their drawers and are composed of native and exotic woods. The table illustrated in figure 26 is the only Boston object with carved brackets, and its legs have multiple rings reminiscent of the "Ordre Français" designed by sixteenth-century French architect Philibert de l'Orme. The other table is even more architectural, having arches and classically correct Doric columns with pronounced entasis (fig. 27). It is made primarily of red cedar and cedrela with maple bosses and cedrela glyphs. The red cedar probably came from Bermuda or the Carolinas, whereas the cedrela came from the Caribbean. Extensive riving evidence on this table indicates that the cedar was treated like a ring-porous hardwood.[49]

A square table base formerly owned by pioneer collector Dwight Prouty (fig. 28) may also be a seventeenth-century Boston product. It is distinguished among early New England examples in having turned stretchers and is the earliest table from that region with bilaterally symmetrical balusters. Pinning evidence in the frieze rails indicates that the base probably had a multiboard, clamped oak top, much like those surviving on three other New England square tables. The posts and stretchers are approximately 2⅝" square, and the rails are made of riven stock that tapers substantially across the grain. The maker used the thicker dimension at the top, since that was the pinning surface for the top boards. The brackets are integral with the rails and have ogees generated with scratch-stock cutters.

Two square tables currently attributed to Boston are later in date and have maple posts, dry-brushed grain painting, and single baluster turnings on the posts. Nevertheless, there seems to be a relationship between the turnings of all three objects. Heavy balusters with pronounced, filleted collarinos

Figure 28   Square table, Boston, Massachusettts, 1650–1680. Oak. H. 27⅞", W. 34", D. 34⅛". (Courtesy, Shelburne Museum, gift of George G. Frelinghuysen; photo, Gavin Ashworth.) The top and the bottom portions of the feet are missing.

are relatively rare in New England turning, although they are common in the Middle Atlantic region and the South. This suggests that two different shop traditions used the same turner. The later tables have medial struts to support the top boards, much like those seen on seventeenth-century Boston chests of drawers.[50]

The cabinet was another form favored by Boston joiners working in the London style. The large example illustrated in figure 29 is the only Anglo-

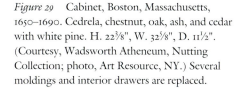

Figure 29   Cabinet, Boston, Massachusetts, 1650–1690. Cedrela, chestnut, oak, ash, and cedar with white pine. H. 22⅜", W. 32⅝", D. 11½". (Courtesy, Wadsworth Atheneum, Nutting Collection; photo, Art Resource, NY.) Several moldings and interior drawers are replaced.

Figure 30   Cabinet, Boston, Massachusetts, 1660–1690. Mahogany and cedrela with oak and white pine. H. 18⅝", W. 17½", D. 9". (Chipstone Foundation; photo, Gavin Ashworth.) One foot, several moldings, the edges of the bottom board, and the hinges are restored.

Figure 31   Cabinet, Boston, Massachusetts, 1660–1690. Oak, walnut, cedar, and lignum vitae with oak and white pine. H. 16½", W. 16½", D. 8½". (Private collection; photo, Gavin Ashworth.)

American example with two doors, and the only one to approach the size and architectural grandeur of its European prototypes (fig. 6). The strong horizontal emphases of the surbase and frieze and the lack of turned feet suggest that the cabinet may have been intended for use on a table or, perhaps, that it originally had a tall base resembling a table frame. Certainly the carrying handles on the ends suggest that it was moved on a regular basis, perhaps back and forth from a countinghouse to a sailing vessel.[51]

Two smaller Boston cabinets, possibly used for storing writing materials and implements, also survive. The example illustrated in figure 30 is extraordinary in being made of mahogany and cedrela. This object may be earlier than a Salem, Massachusetts, chest with a mahogany plaque bearing the date 1700, making the cabinet the earliest piece of American furniture with that wood. British and American one-door cabinets of this general type often have turned feet, but that was not the case with the Boston example illustrated in figure 31. It has an unusually elaborate door, with an oak panel and framing members and walnut and cedar appliqués. With its raised pyramidal mount, L-shaped plaques, and crosseted corners, this door would have been described during the period as having a "cushion" panel. Flanking the panel are applied walnut half-columns.

Use of Exotic Woods and Applied Ornaments

Forman was the first scholar to recognize the use of exotic woods in seventeenth-century Boston furniture. His research focused on cedrela, but many other exotic species have been identified since his death. Indeed, several scholars have noted that black walnut, often referred to during the period as "Virginia walnut," was regarded as an exotic in both England and New England because that wood was imported from the southern colonies. The same was true of cedar and cypress. In 1682 Thomas Ashe wrote that

Figure 32 Detail of the large and small applied half-columns on the chest of drawers with doors illustrated in fig. 1. (Photo, Gavin Ashworth.)

the Carolinas were "cloathed with odoriferous and fragrant . . . Cedar and Cyprus Trees, of . . . which are composed goodly Boxes, Chests, Tables, Scrittores, and Cabinets. . . . Carolina [cedar] is esteemed equal . . . for Grain, Smell and Colour . . . [to] Bermudian Cedar, which of all the West Indian is . . . the most excellent."[52]

Exotic woods were commonly reserved for ornamental appliqués, like the exceptional Tuscan-Doric half-columns (fig. 32) on the Boston chest of drawers with doors (fig. 1). As is the case with many Boston half-columns, these have a pendant vase at the bottom and a turned urn at the top. A second type, exemplified by the half-columns on the lower case of the Boston cupboard with drawers (fig. 18), has an unconventional urn element. Whereas some Boston case pieces have appliqués made of exotic woods, others have half-columns, bosses, and other components made of maple and finished to resemble ebony. Mimicking exotics in that fashion was the norm in other eastern Massachusetts shops. In Boston case furniture, cushion panels and inset panels on drawers and stiles are often made of exotics (fig. 33). While some inset panels are plaques, others are thin enough to be considered veneer.

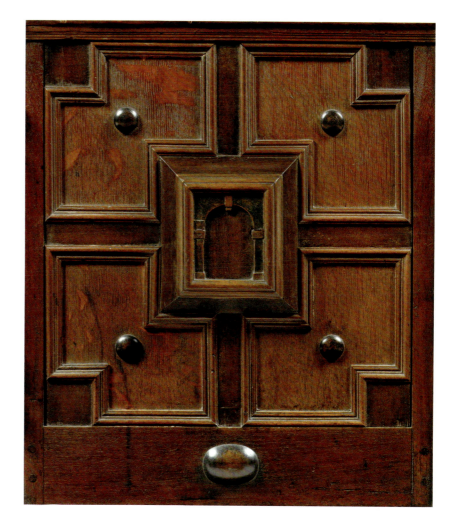

Figure 33 Detail of a panel on the chest of drawers with doors illustrated in fig. 1. (Photo, Gavin Ashworth.)

223   LONDON-STYLE JOINERY AND TURNING

Figure 34   Chest of drawers, Boston, Massachusetts, 1690–1710. Cedrela with oak and white pine. H. 34", W. 33⅛", D. 21⅜". (Private collection; photo, Gavin Ashworth.)

Figure 35   Chest of drawers, Boston, Massachusetts, 1670–1700. Walnut with oak and white pine. H. 35¾", W. 37⅝", D. 21⅞". (Private collection; photo, Gavin Ashworth.)

Figure 36 Detail of the chest of drawers illustrated in fig. 35, showing the hewing marks on the interior surface of a side panel of the upper case. (Photo, Luke Beckerdite.)

Figure 37 Chest of drawers, Boston, Massachusetts, 1670–1700. Walnut with oak and white pine. H. 35¾", W. 37¾", D. 23⅛". (Private collection, photo, Mark Heffron.) This chest has all of its original hardware.

Figure 38 Detail of the chest of drawers illustrated in fig. 37, showing the spectral mortise on reused lumber. Reused lumber occurs on London case pieces but has not previously been recorded in Boston work.

Exotics used in Boston furniture include black walnut, red cedar, cedrela, snakewood, rosewood, and lignum vitae. What is not clear is how those species arrived there. Boston merchants and timber dealers could have imported exotics circulating in the Dutch timber trade via London or acquired them directly from the Caribbean, through legitimate trade or through acts of piracy. Certainly New England merchants obtained large amounts of Spanish-American silver specie, through means both fair and foul. Further, New England shippers competed with Dutch carriers throughout the Atlantic and may have learned about cargoes of exotic woods in that manner.[53]

Several Boston chests are made of cedrela (fig. 34), and some hewing marks on the interior surfaces left by the enslaved, mixed-race logging crews who cut down the trees in the jungles of the Caribbean and Central America and squared them up into balks for export can still be seen (fig. 36). The Boston chest illustrated in figure 37 has such marks, but it is made of walnut and recycled oak, as witnessed by a spectral mortise pocket on the interior (fig. 38). Although a cousin of mahogany, some species of cedrela are ring-porous and suitable for riving. Cedrela's popularity in the seventeenth century probably reflected its relative low cost, availability in wide widths, fine pore structure, and pale color. It also contrasted dramatically with darker woods, like walnut or rosewood, and ebonized surfaces.[54]

A black walnut chest of drawers that descended in the Pierce family of Dorchester has moldings of maple, red cedar, and possibly cedrela (fig. 39). It is identifiable in inventories extending back to the original owners and is one of the few Boston case pieces known to have descended in a family from

Figure 39 Chest of drawers, Boston, Massachusetts, 1660–1700. Oak, black walnut, red cedar, maple, and possibly cedrela, with oak, chestnut, and white pine. H. 37⅞", W. 39½", D. 23½". (Courtesy, Historic New England.)

near that city. The wood generally referred to as "red cedar" in descriptions of seventeenth-century Boston furniture is actually a juniper. The popular name refers to either Virginia red cedar (*Juniperus virginiana*) or Bermuda cedar (*Juniperus bermudiana*). The location where boards are taken from a juniper trunk determines whether those boards are clear or exhibit tiny knots. Most commercially available red cedar today is relatively free of such knots and seems to come from the lower portions of large trees that grow in mountainous areas. By contrast, the red cedar used in most early American furniture is rife with small knots. Much of that wood may have come from the lowlands of the Carolinas or Florida. Less plausibly, some of the timber used in Boston may have come from Bermuda, although wood shortages in seventeenth-century Bermuda make that scenario less likely.[55]

English observers were well aware of exotic woods, often noting their use in architecture. In 1698 Celia Fiennes wrote:

> I went to admiral Russells [house] who is now Lord oxfford . . . The hall . . . its wanscoated wth wall Nutt tree, the pannells and Rims round wth mulberry tree yt is a Lemon Coullour, and ye moldings beyond it round are of a sweete outlandish wood not much differing from Cedar but of a finer Graine, the Chaires are all the same [wood].

Much of the cedar described in period documents appears to have been red cedar from the American South or Bermuda, rather than Atlantic white cedar.

Figure 40 Chest of drawers, Boston, Massachusetts, 1670–1700. Red cedar and possibly rosewood with oak and pine. H. 35", W. 38⅝",
D. 23¼". (Private collection; photo, Gavin Ashworth.) The fronts of both case sections, the top
of the upper case, and the larger and smaller
moldings are made of red cedar. The chamfered
edges of the cushion panel appliqués on the deep
drawer are thick red cedar veneers. Because the
maker intended to cover the drawer fronts completely with ornaments, he made the cores out
of white pine.

The fourth edition of John Evelyn's *Sylva: A Discourse of Forest Trees & the
Propagation of Timber* (1706) provides one of the best period accounts of
woods used for furniture and architecture. In reference to cypress, he stated:

> Since these precious materials may now be had at such tolerable rates (as
> certainly they might from Cape-Florida, the Vermuda, or other parts of
> the West-Indies) . . . I cannot but suggest that our more wealthy citizens
> of London, every day building and embellishing their dwellings, might be
> encourag'd to make use of it in their shops, at least for shelves, counters,
> chests, tables, and wainscot, &c the fancerings (as they term it) [veneer-
> ing?] and mouldings, since beside the everlastingness of the wood, enemy
> to worms, and those other corruption we have named, it would likewise
> greatly cure and reform the malignancy and corrosiveness of the air.

Regarding red cedar, he wrote:

> After all these exotics brought from our plantations, answering to the
> name of cedar, I should esteem that of the Vermuda, little inferior, if not
> superior, to the noblest Libanon, and next, that of Carolina for its many
> uses, and lasting . . . the natural, wholesome, and ancient use of timber,
> for the more lasting occasions, and furniture of our dwellings; And though
> I do not speak all this for the sake of joyn'd-stools, benches, cup-boards,
> massy tables, and gigantic bed-steads, (the hospitable utensils of our fore-
> fathers) yet I would be glad to encourage the carpenter, and the joyner.[56]

The Boston leaf table and two-part chest of drawers illustrated in figures
27 and 40 are exceptional in having red cedar primary woods. The chest is
further distinguished by having contrasting plaques made of rosewood or
some other dense, dark tropical hardwood. The plaques are set in recesses
cut in the front stiles and drawer fronts.[57]

Figure 41   Chest of drawers, Boston, Massachusetts, 1690–1720. Red oak, white oak, white pine, and yellow pine with red oak, white oak, and white pine. H. 40", W. 40½", D. 22". (Courtesy, Metropolitan Museum of Art, gift of Mrs. J. Insley Blair, 1948; photo, Gavin Ashworth/Art Resource, NY.)

Later Boston Furniture in the London Style

The latest manifestations of Boston joinery in the London style appear to have been coeval with the dovetailed-board, veneered case pieces of the baroque, or "William and Mary" style, and include chests of drawers, chests with drawers, and chamber tables (fig. 41). Many of these case pieces lack dovetails, are made principally of softwoods, and have extensive painted decoration. Some scholars have been reluctant to attribute these objects to Boston because of the lack of dovetailed drawers, but the high correlation of other shared traits suggests that they are Boston products, and that many date from the eighteenth century. Although genealogical research has called into question attributions made by Forman and some of his students to specific makers and shop traditions, their observations pertaining to the overall school of Boston joinery remain largely valid. Undoubtedly, more objects by this school of joinery and turning will emerge, and further documentary work in England may clarify the origins of Henry Messinger and other important artisans.[58]

ACKNOWLEDGMENTS For assistance with this article, the authors thank Gavin Ashworth, Luke Beckerdite, Paul Beedham, Kathryn Bolles, Dennis Carr, Katherine Chabla, Victor Chinnery, David Gill, Constance Godfrey, the late Dudley Godfrey, Joseph P. Gromacki, Erik Gronning, Peter Kenny, Robert Leath, Susan Newton, Martin O'Brien, Jonathan Prown, Helena Richardson, Harry Mack Truax II, John and Marie Vander Sande, Nancy Sazama, Gerald Ward, and Edwin Willson. We are particularly grateful to Alan Miller and Adam Bowett for reading the manuscript and providing helpful suggestions and references.

Appendix 1

An inventory of the estate of Henry Messenger deceased taken by us whose names underwritten the 30 of April 1681

In the Parlor

A featherbed a boulster & too pillows a payer of blankets a coverlid & curtins & valling & bedstead	£08:00:00
A framed bedsted a woolbed & boulster 2 coverlits	01:05:00
A press cubberd wth drawers	
A table & seven joint stooles	01:10:00
A small round table five elbo chayrs	00:18:00
Two framde Elbo chayrs	00:08:00
Close stoole with a pewter pan in it & stone mortar	01:10:00
2 small boxes 1 case of quart bottles 10 / three stone juggs 1 Earthen 8 /	00:18:00
9 cushions & a warming pann 18 / A cote of Armes & Joynrs Armes 40 /	02:18:00
a parcel of glas & Earthen ware 12 / A silver spoon & dram cup 10 /	01:02:00
A looking glass 2/6 Eight pr of sheets & five pr of pillobeers 7:10:00	07:12:06
Three dozn napkins of several sorts five small pillobeers & cupboard cloth	02:01:00
A Large diaper table cloth & three Linnen ditto	01:00:00
A pr darnick curtains & vallents	00:10:00
Two Darnick carpets and cupboard cuishion	00:12:00
A pr andirons fire shovel and tongs 8 / a Rapier & Childs blankett 10 /	00:18:00

In the Parlor chamber

A feather bed, Boulster a pillow a pr sheets a pr blanketts Rugg and Bedsteed	04:00:00
Two Searge chaires a stand & pr of andirons	01:00:00
A small box of drawers a chest and looking glass	01:00:00

In the hall

A pr of andirons a fire shovel, tongs, a trammell pr of bellows	01:05:00
One cupboard, one chest and a screen	01:10:00
One table 3 joint stooles 4 chaires & a forme	01:00:00
Three framed chaires & 2 other chaire & one leather	00:15:00
A looking glass and a parcel of Earthen ware	00:05:00
Three Bibles and other bookes	00:10:00
A pr andirons tongs & fire shovel and tramell	01:05:00
A gridiron, fire Iron, toasting Iron and four Spits	00:15:00
Three Iron candlesticks and two frying pans	00:08:00
Five Brass kettles three skillets and a brass morter	02:10:00

Six pewter dishes, six pewter pots, two salts, three porringers a plate, seven small dishes and one chamber pot	02:05:00
Three dripping pans one sawce pan one funnell	00:07:00
A punch Bowle lign vitae	00:10:00
A parcel of wooden and Earthen ware & one piggin	00:10:00
Two pr scales and twelve pounds lead weights & meale barrel	00:10:00

In Kitchen chamber

Two spinning wheels a cradle, a table wth other lumber	01:10:00

In the Cellar

A powdering tubb with other tubbs and barrells	01:00:00

In the hall chamber

A flock bed and two feather pillows a pr blanketts a pr sheets	
two small pillows an old Rugg Bedsteed and a pillowbeer	02:10:00

In the middle room over the Hall

Another flock Bed, one Bolster a pr blanketts a pr sheets a Rugg and Bedsteed	02:10:00
A feather bed a Bolster a pillow a pr blanketts a pr sheets a Rugg a Bedstead	05:00:00
One table three chests a small box a close stool wth Earthen pan	01:10:00
A parcel of glue and Nurces skins	02:10:00

In the shop chambr

A wicker glass case, a chest of drawers a large bedsteed and trundlebedsteed	02:10:00

In the shop

All sorts of Joyners Tools	05:00:00
A table and Chest of Drawers not finished	01:00:00
Timber within and without Doors wrought and unwrought	10:00:00
Two cows and hay	06:00:00
Land and housing in all	400:00:00
About 20 gallons of trayn oyl	01:00:00

John Fayerweather Edw Wyllys
Sarah Messinger Exec made Oath in Court 5 May 1681 that this is a just and true Inventory of the Estate of her late husband
Henry Messinger decd to the best of her knowledge and that if more appears she will discover it.
Attests Js Addington
Source: Suffolk County Registry of Probate, docket no. 1172

Inventory of the Estate of Henry Messenger late of Boston, Joyner
decd taken & apprized by us whose names are underwritten, 30th Nov 1686

Impr. His wearing Apparell, hatts, shoes, stockins, shirts etc and his	
Armes, given away by will amongst his Brethren	25:4:00
It: his small wearing Linnen	3:10:00

In the Halle:

1 doz. Russia Leather chaires at 11/8	6:12:00
2 Tables at 24s a ps	1:08:00
1 pa of brasses for the chimney	1:10:00
Glasses & Earthen ware	:07:00

In the Chamber over the halle:

8 Turkey worke chaires at 14s	5:12:00
1 Chest of drawers	2:10:00
1 feather bed, boulster, pillows, ffurniture of coverings, curtains, vallents and bedstead	17:00:00
1 table 25s 1 looking glass & brasses 18	2:03:00
1 pr brasses for the chimney 20s 2 stands 8	1:08:00
5 pr of sheets 6/5 1 doz of Napkins 18	7:03:00
1 doz of diaper towells: eight coarse ones	−:18:00
5 pillowbeers	−:17:00

In the Chamber over the Kitchin

One feather bed, furniture and bedstead	6-00-00
1 [illegible]att table, one chest & deske and Trunke	1-10-00
1 case of knives	-7-00

In the Garret

1 flock bed furniture and bedstead	2-06-00
1 feather bed furniture and bedstead	5-05-00
A meale trough 6s four bushlls of wheat 16s	1-02-00

In the Kitchin

1 Table (price) eight sedge bottom chaires (price)	1-12-00
1 Hamaker and Morings (price) one Chest	2-00-00
1 looking glass and brush	-07-00
Iron ware belonging to the chimney	1-02-00
Smoothing box and heater	-05-00
Bookes 40 Pewter and Tin ware 50	4-10-00
Brass kettles and skillets	4-15-00
Iron pots and Kettle 25 lign[illegible]d vitae morter pestle [illegible]	1-15-00
Lumber in the Cellar 20s severall small things 12 s	1-12-00
Firewood in the yard	3-03-00
A dwelling house & garden and land the apprces	200-00-00
Timber, Boards, planks workeing tooles (etc) at the	
Shop, apprized by Mr Cunnibell and Tho: Warren, Joyners	
At Eleven pounds 16/8	11-16-8
A parcel of glew	-12-10
one Cow	2-00-00
Money since the death of my husband for worke done for Some frenchmen	2-05-00

Debts due to or from the estate not known

Source: Suffolk County Registry of Probate, docket no. 1554

Appendix 2

The 1607 bylaws of the Company of Carpenters provide information on various timber components used in the city. Although these specifications pertain to the building trades, they show some of the types of timber that were available in London during the seventeenth century. The quarter-boards (not the "quarters" or the "double-quarters") and the "seelinge-boards" were tapered in thickness. This most likely resulted from their having been radially riven from ring-porous woods such as oak.

> The Master and Wardens, or three of them . . . to make search in all places within the limits, for & upon timber, boards, planks, rafters, joists, quarters, laths, & other things belonging to carpentry, to be sold; to try & see that the same should contain the just length, measure & assize following, that is,
>
> Every load of timber hewed or sawn to contain in measure of solid timber fifty foot of assise, and every tunne of such timber, 40 ft. of assisse, under a penalty of 2s6d for every load or tunne put to sale contrary thereto.
>
> Every load of rafters to contain in number 30 rafters, each rafter 12 ft. of assisse in length at least; and at the greater end in breadth, 4 inches & ½ an inch, and in thickness, 4 inches; and at the lesser end in breadth, 4 inches, and in thickness, 3 inches at least, under a penalty of 2 pence for every rafter.
>
> Every load of joists to contain in number 30 joists, every joist to be in length 8 ft. 6 inches of assise, in breadth 6 inches, and in thickness 4 inches from end to end at the least, under a penalty of 2 pence for every joist.
>
> Every load of puntions, being of oak to contain 40 puntions, every puntion to be in length 6 ft. 6 inches, in breadth 6 inches, and in thickness 4 inches. Every load of puntions being of beech, to contain 50 puntions, every puntion to be in length 6 ft. 6 inches, and 5 inches square, under a penalty of 2 pence for every puntion.
>
> Every load of bedsides to contain 50 bedsides, every bedside to be in length 6 ft. 6 inches, in breadth 10 inches, and in thickness 2 inches, under a penalty of 1 penny for every bedside.
>
> Every load of double quarters to contain in number 50 double quarters, to be in length 8 ft. 6 inches, in breadth 4½ inches, and in thickness 3 inches from end to end at least.
>
> Every load of single quarters to contain 100 single quarters, each quarter to be in length as the double quarters, in breadth 3½ inches, and in thickness 2 inches from end to end at the least, under the penalty of 1 penny for every double quarter, and 1 halfpenny for every single quarter.

Every load of stable planks to be 40 planks, each plank to contain in length 6 feet 6 inches, in breadth 12 inches, and in thickness 2 inches, under a penalty of 1 penny for every plank.

All quarter-boards to be at the thinner edge the 3rd part of an inch in thickness, and at the thicker edge 1 inch, under a penalty of sixteen pence for every hundred quarter boards.

All seelinge boards to be thicker at the edge half an inch, and at the thinner edge the 3rd part of an inch, under a penalty of sixteen pence for every hundred seeling boards.

All planch boards to be in thickness an inch, under a penalty of sixteen pence for every hundred planch boards. All planks and boards to be measured & accounted after the rate of 5 score ft. of plank or board to the hundred, flat measure, being duly measured without fraud, according to the plain superficies, what length, breadth, or thickness soever may be.

All laths to contain in thickness at either end the 3rd part of an inch, and in breadth from end to end an inch & a half, or very little less, and all laths to be in length 5 ft. or 4 ft. of assise, and them of 5 ft. long to be accounted 5 score laths to every bundle, and them of 4 ft. long to be accounted 6 score and 5 laths to every bundle; 30 such bundles to be a load, being 20 bundles of them at least hart lath, and the shorter not to be packed or bound up with the longer, under the penalty of 4 pence for every bundle.

. . . if any of the Master or Wardens should find any such stuff belonging to the occupation of Carpentry to be bought between forraine and forraine contrary to the liberties of the city, the Master & Wardens to have power to seize the same. . .

. . . all manner of wayny pieces of timber that should arise out of the premises & be serviceable, there should be allowed two for one, or three for two or otherwise, as should be indifferent between buyer & seller.

Source: E. B. Jupp, *An Historical Account of the Worshipful Company of Carpenters* (London: Pickering & Chatto, 1887), pp. 145–52.

1. Benno M. Forman, "Urban Aspects of Massachusetts Furniture in the Late Seventeenth Century," in *Country Cabinetwork and Simple City Furniture*, edited by John D. Morse (Charlottesville: University Press of Virginia, 1970), pp. 1–34. Benno M. Forman, "Boston Furniture Craftsmen, 1630–1730," MS, Winterthur, Delaware, 1969, in the possession of Robert F. Trent. Benno M. Forman, "Continental Furniture Craftsmen in London: 1511–1625," *Furniture History* 7 (1971): 94–120, pls. 25–28. Benno M. Forman, "The Origins of the Joined Chest of Drawers," *Nederlands Kunsthistorisch Jaarboek* 31 (1981): 169–83. This article was republished with additions by Robert F. Trent, as Benno M. Forman, "The Chest of Drawers in America, 1635–1730: The Origins of the Joined Chest of Drawers," *Winterthur Portfolio* 20, no. 1 (Spring 1985): 1–30. A summary of critiques of Forman's last article can be found in Robert F. Trent, "Furniture in the New World: The Seventeenth Century," in *American Furniture with Related Decorative Arts, 1660–1830*, edited by Gerald W. R. Ward (New York: Hudson Hills Press, 1991), pp. 25–28 n. 8.

2. Adam Bowett, "The Age of Snakewood," *Furniture History* 34 (1998): 212–25; Adam Bowett, "Myths of English Furniture History: Anglo-Dutch," *Antique Collecting* 34, no. 5 (October 1999): 29–33; and Adam Bowett, "Furniture Woods in London and Provincial Furniture, 1700–1800," *Regional Furniture* 22 (2008): 87–114. Victor Chinnery, *Oak Furniture: The British Tradition* (Woodbridge, Eng.: Antique Collectors' Club, 1979), pp. 432–37. For related architectural work, see Howard Colvin, *The Canterbury Quadrangle of St. John's College, Oxford* (Oxford: Oxford University Press, 1988), pp. 44–46, pls. 41, 42. In a later essay, Chinnery cited some 1598 furniture designs of Johann Jakob Ebelmann of Strasburg, Germany, as a potential source for the aediculae of door panels in the Laudian group. However, it is evident that such panels were prevalent throughout Germany, so the Ebelmann source need not be considered an immediate prototype. See *Sotheby's Concise Encyclopedia of Furniture*, edited by Christopher Payne (New York: Harper Collins, 1989), pp. 50–52.

3. For previous attributions pertaining to the Messinger and Mason shops, see n. 1 above; *New England Begins: The Seventeenth-Century*, edited by Jonathan L. Fairbanks and Robert F. Trent, 3 vols. (Boston: Museum of Fine Arts, 1982), 3: 522–27, 536–38; and Gerald W. R. Ward, *American Case Furniture in the Mabel Brady Garvan and Other Collections at Yale University* (New Haven, Conn.: Yale University Art Gallery, 1988), pp. 125–28. Many upholstered chairs can be interpreted as seventeenth-century Boston work, but none has been linked to a specific joiner's shop. In his unpublished manuscript "Boston Furniture Craftsmen, "Forman attempted to identify all the turners and joiners working during that period. Another invaluable reference is Annie Haven Thwing, *Inhabitants and Estates of the Town of Boston, 1630–1800* and *The Crooked and Narrow Streets of Boston, 1630–1822* (Boston: New England Historic Genealogical Society and Massachusetts Historical Society, 2001), CD-ROM. This essay will take a narrower focus, concentrating on new research on the Mason-Messinger tradition and other Boston shops that produced case furniture in the London style.

4. For Davis's contract, see *Note-Book Kept by Thomas Lechford, Esq., Lawyer, in Boston, Massachusetts Bay, from June 27, 1638 to July 29, 1641*, edited by Edward Everett Hale Jr. (1885; reprint, Camden, Maine: Picton Press, 1988), pp. 303–4. Robert Charles Anderson, *The Great Migration: Immigrants to New England, 1634–1635*, currently 6 vols. (Boston: New England Historic Genealogical Society, 2001), 3: 301–3. Forman, "Boston Furniture Craftsmen," ch. 2, p. 2, states that Davis was "from London" but does not provide a source. Anderson suggested there might be a connection between Davis and Dix, who was from Norfolk.

5. *A Volume Relating to the Early History of Boston Containing the Aspinwall Notarial Records from 1644 to 1651* (Boston: Municipal Printing Office, 1903), p. 40.

6. Anderson, *The Great Migration*, 6: 38. Scottow's deed is in *Boston Records, 1634–1660, and the Book of Possessions* (Boston: Rockwell and Churchill, 1881), p. 38. The first apprenticeship contract for a joiner in New England specified a term of considerably less than the customary seven years. On January 6, 1633/34, Samuel Jenney was bound to "Kenelm Winslow, of Plymouth, joyner, for . . . four yeares." This document also reveals that Winslow had trained in London, having been admitted to the Worshipful Company of Joiners and Ceilers in 1625. Thus, Winslow has the distinction of being the first London-trained joiner identified in New England records. *Records of the Colony of New Plymouth in New England*, edited by Nathaniel B. Shurtleff and David Pulsifer, 12 vols. (Boston: William White, 1855–1861), 1: 24. Peter Follansbee, "Connecting a London-Trained Joiner to 1630s Plymouth Colony," *Antiques & Fine Art* (Summer/Autumn 2007): 200–205.

7. *Boston Records, 1634–1660*, pp. 156, 157.

8. Suffolk County Registry of Probate (hereafter SCRP), no. 284, Massachusetts State Archives, Boston.

9. SCRP, no. 1047.

10. John Camden Hotten, *The Original Lists of Persons of Quality . . . Who Went from Great Britain to the American Plantations, 1600–1700* (London, 1874), p. 99. Anderson, *The Great Migration*, 5: 81–84.

11. The Worshipful Company of Joiners and Ceilers of London, Master's and Warden's Account Books, 1621–1828, Family History Library (hereafter FHL), microfilm no. 1068631, Guildhall Library, City of London. Margaret Gay Davies, *The Enforcement of English Apprenticeship: A Study of Applied Mercantilism, 1563–1642* (Cambridge, Mass.: Harvard University Press, 1956), pp. 271–74. An appendix to the history of the Worshipful Company of Carpenters of London cites the ordinances of 1608, which state that a company member is "Not to have an apprentice before he has been free three yeares . . . (and served at least one year with a

freeman of the Company)" (E. B. Jupp, *An Historical Account of the Worshipful Company of Carpenters* [London: Pickering & Chatto, 1887], p. 421). Similar guidelines applied to all the trade companies of London at the time.

12. *Boston Records, 1634–1660*, p. 32: "Also to Raph Mason a great Lott at Muddy Ryvare for six heads." For the allotments in Boston, see "Focus on Boston," in Robert Charles Anderson, *The Complete Great Migration Newsletter: Volumes 1–15* (Boston: New England Historic Genealogical Society, 2007), pp. 67–68. *Boston Records, 1634–1660*, p. 147. Two years later, Mason was still working the cedar swamp: "Upon consideration of the great expences Ralph Mason and his associates have beene att already, and are like further to bee att in subduing the Cedar Swamp att Muddy river, Itt is agreed that ten yeares shall bee added to their lease upin the same rent mentioned therein" (*Boston Records, 1634–1660*, p. 158).

13. SCRP, no. 1033. The "cross" planes were probably "crease" planes—a period term for molding planes. The same is true of Mason's "bolting" plane. W. L. Goodman, "Tools and Equipment of the Early Settlers in the New World," *Chronicle* 29, no. 3 (September 1976): 40–51.

14. Evidence of joiners apprenticing their sons to other joiners can be found in Clifford L. Stott, "English Background of George and Margery (Hayward) Wathen of Salem, and Their Nephew, William Sargent of Gloucester, Massachusetts," *New England Historic Genealogical Register* (January 1994): 67–78.

15. SCRP, no. 690. On the microfilm, "plates" is in a hand different from the rest of the line, implying that the transcriber could not read the original and someone helped finish this line. While it is tempting to read "planes" instead of "plates," the value assigned is only 8 shillings, whereas four planes above it are valued at 12 shillings.

16. Forman, "Boston Furniture Craftsmen," ch. 3, p. 2.

17. *The Diary of Samuel Sewall, 1674–1729*, edited by M. Halsey Thomas, 2 vols. (New York: Farrar, Straus and Giroux, 1973), 1:327. SCRP, no. 2293.

18. *Boston Records, 1634–1660*, p. 46: "The 27th day of the 11 moneth, 1639 [January 1639/40]) . . . Also to Henry Messenger a great Lott at Muddy River for 2 heads." For John's birth, see "Records of Boston," *New England Historic Genealogical Register* 2 (January–April 1848): 274. See also Harley Brice Messinger, Glenn Messinger, and Richard Messinger, *The Descendants of Henry Messinger of Boston, 1637* (Yarmouthport, Mass.: privately published, 1994); and Helen S. Ullman, "The Three Messengers: Henry, Andrew, and Edward, Clearing the Decks," *New England Historic Genealogical Register* 152 (July 1998): 353–72. *Boston Records, 1634–1660*, p. 86: "This 27th of 8th mo., 1645. It's Ordered that the Constables shall sett off six shillings of Henry Messenger's Rates, for mending the Schoole Masters his part of the partition fence betweene their gardens." See also *Boston Records from 1660–1701* (Boston: Rockwell and Churchill, City Printers, 1881), p. 4.

19. Esther Singleton, *Furniture of Our Forefathers*, 3rd ed. (New York: Doubleday, Page, 1913), p. 177, has excerpts from Henry Messinger's probate inventory. See also n. 1 above.

20. "Fac-Simile of a Petition of the Handycraftsmen of Boston in 1677, Against the Intrusion of Strangers," *Bulletin of the Boston Public Library* 4, no. 4 (January 1894): 305–6. Ultimately, the court appointed a committee to look into this matter. No record exists of any action taken by the committee. See *Records of the Governor and Company of the Massachusetts Bay in New England*, edited by Nathaniell B. Shurtleff, 5 vols. (Boston: William White, 1853), 5: 143. The joiners listed in the petition are, from top to bottom: Ralph Mason, Henry Messinger Sr., William Parsons, Samuel Mason, John White, John Scottow, Sollomon Raynsford, Manassas Beck, John Temple, Obediah Wakfeld, Henry Messinger Jr., Digory Sargent, John Baker Jr., Simeon Messinger, and John Messinger.

21. There was a woodworking craftsman in London named Anthony Messenger (1558– d. after 1632). He became prominent in the Worshipful Company of Carpenters, serving his apprenticeship there from 1577 to 1584:

> John Jackson ys admitted to have as his apprentice Anthonie Messenger of the age of Nyntene years the sone of John Messenger of Walton in the countie of Comberland husbandman for the terme of seaven years begyninge at the feaste of the Purification of St Marie the Virgin laste paste before the date hereof (fridaye . . . last daie of Januarie 1577).

Anthony Messenger became a freeman in 1584, took his first apprentice in 1592, and eventually became a warden, then master of the Worshipful Company of Carpenters (*Records of the Worshipful Company of Carpenters*, edited by Bower Marsh, 7 vols. [London: Phillimore & Co., 1913–1968], 6: 86, 201, 303). He had a wife named Anne but no children. Messenger died in 1634 and was buried at St. Alphage, London Wall. His last apprentice, also named Anthony

Messenger and possibly a relative, was turned over to Thomas Rushall (Lists of Freemen, MS 21,742/1 [transcript], Guildhall Library, London).

22. For Messinger's will and inventory, see SCRP, no. 1172. André Félibien, *The Principles of Architecture, Sculpture, and Painting, and Other Related Art. With a Dictionary of Terms Proper to Each of These Arts*, 3rd ed. (Paris, 1699), chap. 18. For another period reference to abrasives, see Joseph Moxon, *Mechanick Exercises; or the Doctrine of Handy-works Applied to the Arts of Smithing, Joinery, Carpentry, Turning, Bricklaying*, 3rd ed. (1703; reprint, Dedham, Mass.: Toolemera Press, 2009), p. 213:

> Lastly, [turners] . . . hold either a piece of Seal-skin or *Dutch* Reeds (whose outer skin or Filme somewhat finely cuts) pretty hard against the Work, and so make it smooth enough to polish.
>
> Hard Wood they polish with *Bees-wax, viz.* by holding *Bees-wax* against it, till it have sufficiently toucht it all over, and press it hard into it by holding hard the edge of a Flat piece of hard Wood made sizeable and suitable to the Work they work upon, as the Work is going about. Then they set a Gloss on it with a very dry woole Rag, lightly smear'd with Sallad Oyl.

It is unclear how sealskin would have provided abrasive action. Moxon may have meant sharkskin rather than sealskin. He also referred to the use of glue, which figures prominently in Boston joinery. Applied moldings and turnings are almost invariably glued in place. Some makers even glued up stock, as seen in the drawer sides of the chest of drawers illustrated in fig. 17.

23. Forman, "Boston Furniture Craftsmen," app. E, cites a document dated October 3, 1676, in the collection of the Massachusetts Historical Society:

> Ebenezer Ingoldsby aged 20 yeares or thereabout testifieth and sayeth that he knoweth that his master John Messinger did sell and deliver the two forms first mentioned in his booke unto Captayne Hudson and I know that my master helped Sam: Joy and that my master mended the 23[illegible] well, and he made two oven lids and mended the parlor floare and windows & made a beetle and mended the [illegible] floare and made the 2 roughs for the Green house and mended the castle windowes and put up boards against the chimney & mended the benches that the Capt had the table & made the windows & casements and three boards of the floor in the castle chamber where my Mr his [*sic*] & he made the floare & benches in the Bar[?] & found boards & made the windows & hanged doores & made & doare for the bar & a[illegible] in the wine celler all these things I know were done by my master for Capt Hudson and his order and my Master was very often called to bring his bookes to the Capt to worke.

On that date, John Messinger sued William Hudson, for debt, in the amount of £5.8.

24. SCRP, no. 1554: "I [Henry Messinger Jr.] give to my Eldest apprentice Benjamin Threeneedle the remainder of his time he hath yet to serve with me; and if his friends thinke he have not sufficient cloathing I would have my wife give him one suit of Apparell." Messinger's inventory listed household furnishings by room (see app. 1).

25. For Simeon Messinger, see *Suffolk Deeds*, 14 vols. (Boston: Rockwell and Churchill, City Printers, 1880–1906), 4: 2. Messinger, Messinger, and Messinger, *The Descendants of Henry Messinger of Boston*, pp. 15, 16.

26. In his will "David Saywell of Boston in New England joiner" bequeathed to "my honoured & aged ffather Reinhold Saywell in Salisbury in old England the just summe of three pound." This reference to Salisbury, Wiltshire, provides a starting point for further research concerning Saywell's training. SCRP, no. 614. *Suffolk Deeds*, 7: 252.

27. Bumstead's birth is cited in the International Genealogical Index. Several deeds are cited in Thwing, *Inhabitants and Estates of the Town of Boston*, n.p. The remarks concerning Henry Messinger are in Forman, "Boston Furniture Craftsmen," chap. 3, pp. 1, 2, citing Suffolk Superior Court Files 10: 149. For his liberty, see *Boston Records, 1660–1701*, p. 179. Jeremiah Bumstead son and namesake (1678–1747) maintained a diary from 1722 to 1727, but it does not mention joinery. The younger Jeremiah bought and sharpened saws, mended pikes, did paving work, and various other tasks. His diary notes his receipt of a 12-foot section of "spechelwood" and a 6-foot piece of "Redwood" ("Diary of Jeremiah Bumstead of Boston, 1722–1727," *New England Historic Genealogical Register* 15 [July 1861]: 193–315).

28. Edward J. Connable and John Newcomb, *Genealogical Memoir of the Cunnabell, Conable or Connable Family: John Cunnabell of London, England and Boston, Massachusetts, and His Descendants, 1650–1886* (Jackson, Mich.: Daily Citizen Book Printing House, 1886), pp. 10–45.

29. *New England Historical Genealogical Register* 64 (July 1910): 284. *New England Historical*

Genealogical Register 3 (January 1850): 53. Walter Eliot Thwing, *The Thwing Family: A Genealogical, Biographical and Historical Account of the Family* (Boston: David Clapp & Son, Printers, 1883), pp. 13–18.

30. Forman, "Boston Furniture Craftsmen," chap. 8.

31. Henry Laverock Phillips, *Annals of the Worshipful Company of Joiners of the City of London* (London: privately printed, 1915) pp. 27, 28. See also A. C. Stanley-Stone, *The Worshipful Company of Turners of London: Its Origin and History* (London: Lindley-Jones & Brother, 1925), pp. 89–90: "William Gryme was charged for putting his apprentice to work at the trade of Turning within a joiners to make Turner's work for the joiner, and was ordered to take him home" (November 12, 1622); "Christopher Bere was charged with working in a joiner's house and teaching them the trade of Turning" (July 6, 1630). F. G. Emmison, *Elizabethan Life: Home, Work and Land* (Chelmsford, Eng.: Essex County Council, 1976), p. 82.

32. Charles Henry Pope, *The Pioneers of Massachusetts* (1900; reprint, Bowie, Md.: Heritage Books, 1991). Anderson, *The Great Migration*, 3: 306.

33. For Henry Edsall, see www.originsnetwork.com/help/aboutbo-lonapps-details.aspx#tur. Roland Champness, *The Worshipful Company of Turners of London* (London: Lindley-Jones & Brother, 1966), app. D, pp. 251–60. For Henry and Thomas Edsall birth records in England, search www.familysearch.org/eng/search/frameset_search.asp. A Boston birth record for Thomas's son Henry is cited in *A Report of the Record Commissioners of the City of Boston Containing Boston Births, Baptisms, Marriages, and Deaths, 1630–1699* (Boston: Rockwell and Churchill, City Printers, 1883), p. 46. Forman, "Boston Furniture Craftsmen," pp. 2–4.

34. Edsall rented a house from David Saywell, but the latter owned a lathe and presumably did his own turning (*Suffolk Deeds*, 7: 252). Forman, "Boston Furniture Craftsmen," pp. 2–4, citing Suffolk County Superior Court Files, 12: leaf 48. *New England Historic Genealogical Register* 106 (January 1952): 30.

35. Forman, *American Seating Furniture*, p. 51. Suffolk County Probate Record Books, 5: 273–75:

7 doz. of Large wooden Platters 8s. pr. doz.	£2-16-00
6 doz. of hollow turnd ware 6s. pr. doz.	1-16-00
8 grosse of taps [for kegs] at 5s. pr. grosse	2-00-00
5 grosse & 5 doz. of trenchers at 8s. pr. grosse	2-03-04
4 grosse of woodden Spoones 4s. pr. grosse	0-16-00
1 doz. of woodden Sives	0-09-00
15 new Chaires at 2s. pr. ps.	1-10-00
48 chaires unbottomed at 18d. pr. ps.	3-12-00
4 grosse of Sive Rimmes at 3s. doz	7-04-00
timber at the wharfe	5-00-00
a pcell of Sive rimmes	0-10-00
a pcell of wheele rimmes	1-00-00
a pcell of flagges for Chaire Bottoms	0-10-00
a pcell of turner's tooles	3-00-00
a great woollen wheele	0-05-00
5 doz. & 3 wicker fanns at 5s. pr. pc.	15-00-00
3 wicker basketts	0-04-00
2 wicker Cradles	0-10-00
a pcell of Shovells & three half bushells	0-05-00
8 pare of Bellowes at 3s. pr. ps.	0-16-00
7 Haire Sives & two Lawne Sives at 15d. pr. ps.	0-11-03
. . . a pcell of refuse Sive bottoms	0-10-00
Severall peeces of old Lumber, Stuffe and Blockes only hewed for torneing	1-10-00
20 hundred of Lanthorne's hoarnes at 7s. pr. hundred	7-10-00

For examples of goods sold in a London turner's shop, see Paul S. Seaver, *Wallington's World: A Puritan Artisan in Seventeenth-Century London* (Stanford, Calif.: Stanford University Press, 1985).

36. Forman, "Urban Aspects," pp. 15–17.

37. For examples of late-sixteenth-century northern Italian chests of drawers, see Augusto Pedrini, *Il mobilo: Gli ambienti e le decorazioni del rinascimento in Italia, secoli XV e XVI* (Florence: Azienda Libraria Editoriale Fiorentina, 1948), p. 138, fig. 353; Angela Comolli Sordelli,

Il mobile antico dal XIV al XVII secolo (Milan: Görlich Editore, 1967), p. 75, pl. 3; p. 76, pl. 1; p. 99, pls. 2 , 3; p. 100, pls. 1, 2; Maurizio Cera, *Il mobile italiano dal XVI al XIX secolo: Gli stili, le forme, il mercate* (Milan: Longanesi & C., 1983), pls. 59, 60; and *At Home in Renaissance Italy*, edited by Marta Ajmar-Wollheim and Flora Dennis (London: Victoria and Albert Museum, 2006), p. 27, figs. 1, 15. English *sgabello* chairs are discussed in Peter Thornton, *Seventeenth-Century Interior Decoration in England, France and Holland* (New Haven, Conn.: Yale University Press, 1978), p. 185.

38. See n. 2 above.

39. The Dunster inventory was cited by Forman in "The Chest of Drawers in America," p. 8. The authors thank Adam Bowett for the 1640 London inventory reference. The originals of the London probate records are in the Guildhall Museum, London, MS 03760. An excellent survey of London inventories is Eleanor John, "At Home with the London Middling Sort: The Inventory Evidence for Furnishings and Room Use, 1570–1720," *Regional Furniture* 22 (2008): 27–52. The New Haven inventories are from the New Haven Probate Records (old series), 1: 1, 19, 78, New Haven County Courthouse, New Haven, Conn.

40. Forman, "Boston Furniture Craftsmen," pp. 1–4. Adam Bowett, "Furniture Woods in London and Provincial Furniture, 1700–1800," *Regional Furniture* 22 (2008): 83–113.

41. For pieced-out panels in New Haven joinery, see Patricia E. Kane, *Furniture of the New Haven Colony: The Seventeenth-Century Style* (New Haven, Conn.: New Haven Colony Historical Society, 1973), pp. 32–33. For pieced-out panels in New York Dutch *kasten*, see Peter M. Kenny, Frances Gruber Safford, and Gilbert T. Vincent, *American Kasten: The Dutch-Style Cupboards of New York and New Jersey, 1650–1800* (New York: Metropolitan Museum of Art, 1991), pp. 38–43.

42. For dovetailing of Boston drawers, see Forman, "Urban Aspects," pp. 15–17; and Forman, "The Chest of Drawers in America," pp. 13–14. For dovetailed drawers in other eastern Massachusetts joinery schools, see Robert F. Trent, "The Joiners and Joinery of Middlesex County, Massachusetts, 1630–1730," in *Arts of the Anglo-American Community in the Seventeenth Century*, edited by Ian M. G. Quimby (Charlottesville: University Press of Virginia, 1975), pp. 130–33; Peter Follansbee and John D. Alexander, "Seventeenth-Century Joinery from Braintree, Massachusetts: The Savell Shop Tradition," in *American Furniture*, edited by Luke Beckerdite (Hanover, N.H.: University Press of New England for the Chipstone Foundation, 1996), pp. 94–96; and Robert F. Trent, Peter Follansbee, and Alan Miller, "First Flowers of the Wilderness: Mannerist Furniture from a Northern Essex County, Massachusetts, Shop," in *American Furniture*, edited by Luke Beckerdite (Hanover, N.H.: University Press of New England for the Chipstone Foundation, 2001), pp. 35–38.

43. The use of lipped tenons in Plymouth Colony joinery may relate to the presence of London-trained joiners working there (Follansbee, "Connecting a London-Trained Joiner," pp. 200–205).

44. Six or seven New Haven, Connecticut, cupboards (some of which incorporate drawers in the lower case) are the only other London-derived cupboards made in the English colonies of North America (Kane, *Furniture of the New Haven Colony*, pp. 24–31, 50–55, nos. 8–11, 21–23).

45. The Boston cupboard was first discussed in Peter Arkell and Robert F. Trent, "The Lawton Cupboard: A Unique Masterpiece of Early Boston Joinery and Turning," *Maine Antique Digest* 16, no. 3 (March 1988): 1C–4C. Trent's observation that the base molding and drawer dividers of the cupboard were installed with lipped tenons is incorrect. Subsequent examination revealed that what Trent had thought was a scribed line for the joint was a glue line between the rails and the moldings. The relationship between the Boston cupboard and some Cambridge, Massachusetts, cupboards is discussed in Robert F. Trent and Michael Podmanicsky, "An Early Cupboard Fragment from the Harvard College Joinery Tradition," in *American Furniture*, edited by Luke Beckerdite (Hanover, N.H.: University Press of New England for the Chipstone Foundation, 2002), pp. 229–42. The iconographic background of the trapezoidal section and other similarly shaped architectural and furniture forms is discussed in Glenn Adamson, "Mannerism in Early American Furniture: Connoisseurship, Intention, and Theatricality," in *American Furniture*, edited by Luke Beckerdite (Hanover, N.H.: University Press of New England for the Chipstone Foundation, 2005), pp. 22–62.

46. The first Historic New England chest was illustrated and discussed in Brock Jobe and Myrna Kaye, *New England Furniture: The Colonial Era* (Boston: Houghton Mifflin Co., 1984), pp. 115–20, no. 6. The other Historic New England chest is illustrated in Forman, "Urban

Aspects," p. 13, fig. 6. The second chest is now housed in the Historic New England property Cogswell's Grant in Essex, Massachusetts.

47. This group of case pieces is discussed in Ward, *American Case Furniture of Yale University*, pp. 67–69, no. 9; and Frances Gruber Safford, *American Furniture in the Metropolitan Museum of Art*, vol. 1, *Early Colonial Period: The Seventeenth-Century and William and Mary Styles* (New York: Metropolitan Museum of Art, 2007), pp. 234–39, nos. 98, 99. A Plymouth Colony chamber table is illustrated in Robert Blair St. George, *The Wrought Covenant* (Brockton, Mass.: Brockton Art Center–Fuller Memorial, 1979), p. 64, fig. 75.

48. For a seventeenth-century oak example of a *klaptisch*, see K. Sluyterman, *Huisraad en Binnenhaus in Nederland in Vroegere Eeuwen* (s'Gravenhage, Netherlands: Martinus Nijhoff, 1918), pp. 86–87, figs. 146–48. Clap tables have a tip-top on cleats, like that of an eighteenth-century round tea table. The base consists of a battered, two-legged trestle, combined with a fly leg. For a split-leg, half-round octagonal table with a T-shaped stretcher and diagonal frieze rails, see ibid., p. 87, fig. 150. It seems that these smaller round leaf tables were the ultimate source for the concept of the large oval leaf table with two leaves and two fly legs that became popular in London circa 1660. *Through England on a Side Saddle in the Time of William and Mary, Being the Diary of Celia Fiennes* (London: Field & Tuer, 1888), pp. 306–7.

49. The table illustrated in fig. 26 and its French design source are discussed in Adamson, "Mannerism in Early American Furniture," pp. 38–42, figs. 17–23.

50. Safford, *American Furniture in the Metropolitan Museum of Art*, pp. 122–24, no. 46; and Ward, ed., *American Furniture with Related Decorative Arts, 1660–1830*, pp. 40–42, no. 7.

51. For a one-door cabinet attributed to Boston, see Fairbanks and Trent, eds., *New England Begins*, 2:293–94, no. 293.

52. See Philip Zea, "Furniture," in *The Great River: Art and Society of the Connecticut Valley, 1635–1820*, edited by Gerald W. R. Ward and William N. Hosley Jr. (Hartford, Conn.: Wadsworth Atheneum, 1985), p. 187. Thomas Ashe, *Carolina, Or a Description of the Present State of that Country* (London, 1682) in *Narratives of Early Carolina, 1650–1708*, edited by Alexander S. Salley Jr. (New York: Charles Scribner's Sons, 1911), p. 142.

53. Research and restoration conducted by Robert F. Trent and Brian Considine in 1980 identified exotics on the chest illustrated in fig. 17: cedrela (primary wood), ebony (applied columns), and black walnut (knobs). In the mid-1980s Gerald W. R. Ward and R. Bruce Hoadley identified the following exotics on the chest of drawers with doors illustrated in fig. 1: red cedar, cedrela, snakewood, rosewood, and lignum vitae. Since then, other scholars have been more cognizant of the use of exotics on seventeenth-century Boston case furniture. According to Adam Bowett, who has identified numerous exotics used in London chests of drawers and is writing a monograph on British cabinet woods, cedrela is rarely encountered in seventeenth-century English case pieces. This suggests that Boston merchants were obtaining that wood directly from the Caribbean. Exotics are common on Parisian and Netherlandish furniture of this period. For Parisian examples, see Jacqueline Boccador, *Le mobilier français du moyen âge à la renaissance* (Saint-Juste-en-Chaussée: Éditions d'Art Monelle Hayot, 1988), pp. 240–64; Jacques Thirion, *Le mobilier du moyen âge et de la renaissance en France* (Dijon: Éditions Faton, 1998), pp. 94–119; *Un temps d'exuberance: Les arts décoratifs sous Louis XIII et Anne d'Autriche* (Paris: Galeries Nationales du Grand Palais, 2002), pp. 212–47; *Parrures d'or et de pourpre: Le mobilier à la cour des Valois* (Paris: Somogy Éditions d'Art et Château de Blois, 2002), pp. 41–51; Agnès Bos, *Meubles et panneaux en ébène: Le décor des cabinets en France au XVIIe siècle* (Paris: Éditions de la Réunion des Musées Nationaux, 2007), passim; Mechtilde Baumeister and Stéphanie Rabourdin-Auffret, "A Seventeenth-Century Parisian Ebony Cabinet Restored by Herter Brothers," *Postprints of the Wooden Artifacts Group* (Minneapolis, Minn.: American Institute for Conservation, 2005), pp. 3–22; Th. H. Lunsingh Scheurleer, *Pierre Gole: Ébéniste de Louis XIV* (Dijon: Éditions Faton, 2005), passim. For Parisian ebony cabinets owned by Englishmen, see Anthony Radcliffe and Peter Thornton, "John Evelyn's Cabinet," *Connoisseur* 197, no. 794 (April 1978): 254–62; *The Geffrye Museum: A Brief Guide* (London: Geffrye Museum Trust, 2998), pp. 12–14; and "Object Lesson: Gordon Turnbull on Boswell's Ebony Cabinet," *Yale Alumni Magazine* (May–June 2005): 58–59. Dutch furniture made of exotic woods is discussed in Sluyterman, *Huisraad*, pp. 114, 115, 130, 131, 193, figs. 192, 193, 213, 214; Reinier Baarsen, *Nederlandse Meubbelen, 1600–1800* (Zwolle: Waanders Uitgevers, 1993), pp. 24–49, nos. 9, 14, 16, 19, 21; Reinier Baarsen, *Furniture in Holland's Golden Age* (Amsterdam: Rijksmuseum, 2007), pp. 81–109, 147–67; and C. H. de Jonge, *Holländische Möbel und Raumkunst* (Stuttgart: Verlag Julius Hofmann, 1922), pp. 75–100. The standard

monograph on Boston merchants is Bernard Bailyn, *The New England Merchants in the Seventeenth Century* (Cambridge, Mass.: Harvard University Press, 1955).

54. For descriptions of the various species of cedrela, see Franklin R. Longwood, *Commercial Timbers of the Caribbean* (Washington, D.C.: United States Department of Agriculture, 1962), p. 45; and Martin Chudhoff, *Tropical Timbers of the World* (Madison, Wis.: Forest Products Laboratory, 1984), p. 47.

55. Arkell and Trent, "The Lawton Cupboard," p. 2-C, fig. 3. Nancy Carlisle, *Cherished Possessions: A New England Legacy* (Boston: Society for the Preservation of New England Antiquities, 2003), pp. 98–100. For red cedar, see John Bivins Jr., *The Furniture of Coastal North Carolina, 1700–1820* (Winston-Salem, N.C.: Museum of Early Southern Decorative Arts, 1988), pp. 76, 77, 86.

56. *Through England on a Side Saddle*, pp. 27–28 and 125. Fiennes commented on many other cedar interiors. John Evelyn, *Sylva: A Discourse of Forest Trees & the Propagation of Timber, Volume One* (London, 1706; reprint, London: Arthur Doubleday & Co., 2009), pp. 233, 237–239, 247.

57. The chest of drawers has a restorer's label, "John Allen, Antique Furniture, 2132 Washington Street, Boston Highlands," and pencil inscriptions, "This 250 years old Repaired April 1877 Reign of Queen Elizabeth sold by John Allen & Sons Antique Furniture dealers Boston Highland Mass." and "Brot to Scituate Mass by the early English settlers." Another Boston chest of drawers made completely of juniper is illustrated in Sotheby's, *Sinking Springs: The Appell Family Collection*, New York, January 18, 2003, lot 1002.

58. For previous discussions of this group of objects, see Jobe and Kaye, *New England Furniture: The Colonial Era*, pp. 120–23. John B. Vander Sande and Marie-Teresa Vander Sande, "First Period Low Chests with Raised-Field End Panels," *Newburyport Maritime Society/Custom House Museum Antiques Show* (1989), pp. 19–23. Safford, *American Furniture in the Metropolitan Museum of Art*, pp. 269–75.

Book Reviews

Briann G. Greenfield. *Out of the Attic: Inventing Antiques in Twentieth-Century New England*. Amherst and Boston: University of Massachusetts Press, 2009. xii + 265 pp.; 31 bw illus., index. $26.95 pb.

Once upon a time, there was a graduate program in a small eastern state that prepared students for museum careers. Taking advantage of privileged access to one of the country's most notable collections of Americana, each year instructors in the program initiated the new crop of students into the art and mystery of the study of historic objects, including familiarization with period styles, the nature of materials, construction techniques, and all the rest. Or nearly all the rest. Most instructors seemed content to confine their teaching to close examination of the objects. Only one or two thought it was also important to orient students to the marketplace, current prices, and major dealers. There was, however, notable precedent for this more encompassing approach. An earlier and much esteemed director of the program, Charles F. Montgomery, once a collector and dealer, later a curator, and finally a professor, had taken students on field trips to antiques shows, where they encountered firsthand the reigning hierarchies of value and the prevailing prices assigned thereto. Some few educators, then, have recognized that the study of American antiques cannot be separated from the marketplace. The entire enterprise is embedded in and shaped by an economic framework.

How money has mattered is a central theme of Briann Greenfield's engaging and informative examination of the changing nature and fortunes of American antiques over the course of the twentieth century. *Out of the Attic* traces the shift in the appreciation of old objects from a system of valuation based on family ancestry and historical association to one governed by aesthetics and the preferences of elite collectors. Greenfield, trained at Brown and now associate professor of history at Central Connecticut State University, is primarily interested in cultural process. Although objects are central to her story at every stage, Greenfield treats them as somewhat interchangeable, at least for the purposes of her account. Therefore, readers looking for explicit commentary on particular furniture styles, forms, regions, or makers will not be rewarded. Instead, Greenfield offers a systemic analysis of the dynamic triangle trade connecting dealers, collectors, and museum folk. The topic is immense and, over the years, has involved literally thousands of players in one or another of these capacities and at every level of engagement, whether part-time or full-time, high-end or low. Anyone who has been a player, however small or peripheral, realizes that the American antiques phenomenon is enormous, highly complex, and in a constant state of flux. It has spread so widely across the American cultural landscape over the years and involved so many participants that a comprehensive account is simply not feasible. Greenfield, therefore, wisely decided to offer five case studies, each of which illuminates one part of the larger whole.

One background chapter and four case studies, to be more accurate. The first chapter is less a case study than a matter of setting the stage for what follows. Here Greenfield examines the uneven and never totally complete shift from associational values to aesthetic. Put simply, early on, colonial-era objects were valued as relics, as pieces of one or another true cross. Over time, the importance of historical connection declined and objects became increasingly understood as art. As a broad explanation of what took place, Greenfield's description is accurate, but she recognizes that the matter has always been more complex and that aesthetics, narrowly defined, has never been the sole criterion shaping value.

Because the cultural and economic importance of antiques is socially constructed, value is what a quorum of significant players says it is—and is willing to pay. The shift from association to today's reigning system of aesthetics has been a complicated, uneven, and sometimes contradictory process. So much so, in fact, that at one point Greenfield invokes the spirit of Kenneth Roberts, whose 1928 *Antiquamania* playfully exposed some of the muddled thinking about antiques prevalent when he wrote. The dogma of the day was that associations were no longer of prime importance—but there was one critical and necessary exception: objects had to be of American origin. Roberts's instructive invented dialogue between Father and young Rudolph illustrates the confusion the former generated while on the one hand claiming that "sentiment and association have no market value" (p. 36) and on the other trying to explain why aesthetically inferior American Chippendale chairs were worth more than English examples. Young Rudolph did not have to be much of a philosopher to recognize the flaw in the argument. Indeed, the high valuation attached to objects of American origin only demonstrated that sentiment and association were still important but had shifted from the purely local or parochial, where they were once lodged, to the national, where they helped expand the American antiques phenomenon and allowed American antiques to become instruments in international cultural and political competition.

Although some schools of philosophy might argue to the contrary, aesthetics are largely culturally determined—and that means economically determined as well. For an informative exercise, peruse the early years of *Antiques* magazine and note well the sorts of objects that appear in both articles and advertisements. Then dip back into a few issues of the magazine every succeeding decade or so and observe the process of sorting, sifting, classifying—and ranking. One might expect that with the passage of time, the range of goods included would expand, but just the opposite took place, especially in the advertisements. The changing fortunes of various classes of antiques make for fascinating stories, but the most important tale of all may be the ways that big money has shaped and limited the canon of Americana. *Out of the Attic* provides a glimpse into some of that process.

Greenfield's case studies center on New England or New Englanders. Like authors before her, she acknowledges that yet more attention to New England may be annoying to some. New England is not the center of America or the origin of all things great and good. But, also like others before her, Greenfield is attracted to the rich accumulation of materials, textual and artifactual, that enable a fuller account to be made of New England than of any other place. The fact is that several generations of New Englanders and New England sympathizers have loaded the documentary dice so that New England wins most of the time. With reservations noted, this book becomes yet another addition to the very long list of New England–centered antiques publications, and a fine one at that.

Greenfield's case studies examine representative examples of the major classes of players taking part in the American antiques drama: dealers, collectors at both the middle level and the high end, and museum curators. In the first instance, Greenfield documents the important contributions of Jewish dealers to the trade, and in doing so makes an important contribution of her own. Dealers have been underrepresented in the literature on antiques, which has tended to valorize rich collectors but has taken the trade for granted. Not surprisingly, if the trade has been little spoken of, Jewish prominence within it has also gone largely unmentioned (if occasionally disparaged). Yet Jews have not only been numerous in the antiques business but have also occupied leading positions. In fact, the history of the American antiques phenomenon could not be truthfully written without recognizing Jewish dealers' critical roles.

Part of the explanation for Jewish prominence in the antiques business revolves around the peculiar nature of the immigrant Jewish population at the turn of the twentieth century. Unlike many non-Jewish immigrants from rural areas of Europe, Jewish males often arrived in this country with competence in commerce or in a saleable trade. Determined to settle, succeed, and prosper, many Jews possessed a powerful work ethic, an eagerness to learn, and a willingness to seize opportunity. Although Greenfield makes no mention of it, classic outsider theory would argue that Jews' relative distance from the larger American society and culture allowed them to become astute analysts of the tastes and customs of the dominant groups in their new country, knowledge they put to considerable market use.

The featured players in Greenfield's account are familiar, Sack, Ginsburg, Levy, Liverant, and a few others. All came from relatively modest backgrounds and gradually rose within the trade, shaping it as they grew. Greenfield's narrative, sprinkled with instructive anecdotes, describes the origins and early days of various firms and their evolving and expanding presence in the marketplace. Although she casts her net broadly and paints an inclusive picture of the trade during the first half of the twentieth century, Sack and Liverant receive the most attention. Or, more accurately, the Sacks and the Liverants, since both are extended family operations. Today the Sack firm is at a low ebb, but Liverant still goes on, now in its third generation, selling antiques from its distinctive headquarters "in a former Baptist meeting house" (p. 61) on South Main Street in Colchester, Connecticut.

The Sacks and Liverants have attracted considerable press notice over the years. They have also generated a fair amount of copy and visibility on their own. In his later years, Zeke Liverant cultivated something of a country character persona, sitting at the front of his shop, chatting amiably with visitors, offering old-timey witticisms about string too short to save and the like, and generally presenting himself as a living link with the early days of the antiques business. If visitors were local, odds are that he knew their house, had been inside it at some point in the past, and could describe it. And he may have even bought and sold some of its earlier contents somewhere along the line.

The Sacks were more assertive about self-promotion through publication, with their readily recognizable and prominent advertisements in *Antiques*, multiple printings of *Fine Points of Furniture* (the infamous "good, better, best" book), and luxury volumes illustrating objects sold by the firm. Because Greenfield's focus is on careers rather than objects, she has nothing to say about *Fine Points*, which is unfortunate, since it is a vivid example of how a prominent dealer took a leading role in constructing the hierarchy of aesthetic-economic value that remains largely in place today. Initially published in 1950, *Fine Points* has gone through twenty-four printings, according to Albert Sack's current website, and may compete with Wallace Nutting's *Furniture Treasury* for the honor being the most influential book in the field.[1]

As a codicil to her discussion of Jewish dealers, Greenfield offers a few pages on the business of repairs and reproductions. For many, Jews and others, the route into the antiques business had been through furniture repair. From repairing one might move into dealing or into the specialist terrain of restoration or, taking another tack altogether, into the domain of reproductions. The region around Hartford, Connecticut, often considered the cradle of the study of American furniture, was also home to an early manifestation of the furniture reproduction business. The firm of Nathan and then Harold Margolis dominated the Hartford market in the first half of the twentieth century. One of the great surprises for first-time attendees to Hartford-area auctions comes in witnessing the high prices Margolis pieces bring, often far in excess of what bidders are willing to offer for middling period originals. Part of the reason for its high valuation is that Margolis furniture is not only exceptionally well made but also of relatively recent manufacture and therefore sturdy and usable. But another piece of the explanation, documented in Eileen Pollack's 2004 Cooper-Hewitt master's thesis, is that goods by Margolis (and by the competing Fineberg firm) have powerful resonance with Hartford-area Jews, connecting them on the one hand to the broad current of American historical design and on the other to a significant local episode in the history of Jewish immigration, acculturation, and commercial success. In other words, while these objects are undeniably aesthetically pleasing, much of their appeal is, yet again, a matter of "sentiment and association."

The next two chapters deal with two sets of museum builders, one very successful, the other less so. In the latter category we meet George and Jessie Gardner of Providence, Rhode Island. Their names may not be widely known today but that is not because they did not once seek fame and visibility. Greenfield describes the couple as avid collectors by the 1920s, passionately devoted to antiques and sharing a deep belief in their cultural significance. They found considerable personal satisfaction in assembling their collection of antiques and over time determined that they would do whatever was necessary to keep it intact after their deaths. Their solution was to build a museum to house it.

Greenfield suggests that the Gardners may have had the example of Pendleton House in mind as a possible model for their own venture. Charles L. Pendleton had given his collection of American antiques to the Rhode Island School of Design in 1904, and the school had built an impressive neo-Georgian building to house it. The Gardners looked not to RISD but to neighboring Brown University as their collaborator. The problem was that they were relatively small-time. Indeed, that is at least part of the reason for their inclusion in *Out of the Attic*. The big players typically get most of the press, but in concentrating only on them, we are likely to get a distorted view of the entire picture. Like the art world more generally, the antiques world can be fairly described as a "very dense cultural enterprise."[2] It includes winners as well as losers, those who were able to realize their visions and those who had to settle for less. The Gardners viewed themselves as philanthropists and promoters of genteel culture, but they had only an upper-middle-class pocketbook. Achieving their goal became even more difficult when George had a stroke and could no longer participate in the project (he died in 1936) and then when the bottom fell out of the stock market in 1929 and the Gardners' funds shriveled. What had seemed possible a few years before became a struggle at every step, with Jessie now assuming full responsibility for managing restoration of the apparently derelict 1806 building destined to house their collection. In the end, Jessie finally created Gardner House, but the effort required constant oversight and proved both exhausting and disappointing. As for the Gardners, in Greenfield's account they come across as neither completely endearing nor villainous, but people of middling means reproducing the cultural values and prejudices of their age and class. Although Greenfield tells an engaging story, those wondering about specifically what the Gardners collected will have to look elsewhere. Greenfield tells us that the collection was not top tier, but it would be instructive today to know what, exactly, it contained. At present, Gardner House provides lodging for guests of Brown University, not quite what its originators had in mind when they first started dreaming of it in the 1920s.

The other museum makers had greater success, and there is no doubt about what their collection contained, for it is still in place to be seen. These are the Flynts, Henry and Helen, who reconstructed the now quaint and charming village of Deerfield in the so-called Pioneer Valley of Massachusetts. Deerfield is a real place with a real history. It long has been one of the most self-consciously historical villages of New England, with a deep tradition of antiquarian activity. George Sheldon and the Pocumtuck Valley Memorial Association appear prominently in accounts of the early interest in the colonial American past. The full story of the Flynts is perhaps less well known. Greenfield performs a valuable service in presenting the major features of their story.

Unlike the Gardners, the Flynts were very rich. Their activities at Deerfield dramatically illustrate the shift from the local, antiquarian values of Sheldon and his kind to what Greenfield describes as "an aesthetically driven history based on the standards of a nationally based antique community" (p. 142). If local antiquarianism stressed the importance of place and of connections to a personal past, the Flynts' vision all but erased the local specificities of the historical Deerfield as part of a larger agenda that enlisted American antiques in the service of combating the communist critique of American capitalism. Greenfield argues that the Flynts' Deerfield is an artifact of the cold war. Hers is not an isolated or deviant opinion. The institution's official narrative necessarily acknowledges as much, for Henry Flynt's own writings are rich in rightist ideological pronouncements.[3] Although the logic is no clearer than Father's when he tried to straighten out young Rudolph on the value of American Chippendale chairs, Henry Flynt believed that the exhibition of pre–Revolutionary War rich peoples' furnishings would somehow reveal the superiority of the American way of life.

And that puts the buildings and the collections into a larger cultural and political context. Like the Gardners, the Flynts reenacted the values and prejudices of their class. Unlike the Gardners, however, they had the money to give their political agenda physical form. The Deerfield that Henry Flynt manufactured promoted nationalism (and exclusivism), celebrated the origins of America's professional classes, to which he belonged, and argued, through both display of artifacts and supporting publications, that elegant homes and fine antiques were proof of American cultural superiority. George Sheldon liked ordinary objects with stories. Henry and Helen Flynt liked elegant, expensive goods that conformed, whenever possible, to Sack's "better" and "best" categories.[4] Sheldon honored objects with local associations and cared little for aesthetics or condition. The Flints bought what they thought was beautiful, even if there was little evidence such objects had been owned in Deerfield. Their intention was less to learn from the eighteenth century than to present it as an age of cultural refinement and taste. Indeed it was, but only for some. In the end, the story of the Flynts' Deerfield is a tale of gentrification with a political agenda. Today's Deerfield is, in fact, historically accurate, but it is an artifact of a much more recent period than many visitors assume.

Greenfield's last vignette examines the Smithsonian Institution in its various organizational phases and the role of New Englander C. Malcolm Watkins in assembling a material record of America's past at the national museum. Here again, class and money play critical roles. Although the Smithsonian has high name recognition, for many decades its actual achievements in the realm of representing history were fairly meager. The history wing of the Smithsonian, the National Museum of American History, entered an extended period of energy, imagination, and accomplishment by the 1970s. Before then, however, the historical division of the institution was decidedly underpowered, with small staff, limited funds, and a hodgepodge of collections that rendered making any coherent national historical statement difficult in the extreme.

While the story of the Flynts at Deerfield illustrates the mischief that can happen when people have money, the story at the Smithsonian is just the opposite. Without money, Watkins and other curators in similar positions became necessarily dependent on donors, an arrangement with its own set of problems and mandatory negotiations and compromises. Greenfield explores at some length Watkins's relationship with collector-donor Edna Greenwood of Massachusetts and the ways the two worked in a generally happy collaboration to extend the Smithsonian's holdings of early American artifacts. Greenwood was not as wealthy as the Flynts and in any case had interests that reached far beyond the merely elegant. She collected household and preindustrial artifacts in nearly all available categories, providing Watkins with collections that made it possible to evoke a fuller and more egalitarian picture of Americans' past. Watkins would have little sympathy with the Flynts' transformation of Deerfield. His preference was for an inclusive history rather than an elitist one; commonplace objects admirably served his purposes. Nonetheless, because of his own New England background, his familiarity with the material culture of the region, and his network of collectors there, Greenwood among them, Watkins ultimately helped to perpetuate the dominance of New England in the narrative of colonial American material life.

In a short epilogue, Greenfield wonders about the future of antiquing. She is not alone. Prophecy is a dubious business, but recent history suggests that all is not well in the antiques world, certainly not as well as it was a short decade ago. Somewhere circa 2001, the antiques business took a few body punches; the business has been reeling ever since. Not all dealers feel the pain, but a number are struggling, many so-called hobby dealers have dropped out, long-established shows fold or open with fewer exhibitors, and attendance at them is generally down. All cultural behaviors are artifacts, of course, and few artifacts have eternal appeal or continue to function forever at the same level of intensity.

Furthermore, the young people who are supposed to replace the current collectors as they die off are nowhere to be seen. If David Brooks is correct in the picture he paints of how the affluent young spend their money, such folk are not much interested in antiques.[5] Objects that speak to rugged and vigorous outdoor activity, such as trail bikes and sporting gear, attract their attention, as do expensively updated kitchens and bathrooms. And there are always artisan guitars to buy. The crystal ball remains cloudy on the future of antiques.

In the meantime, the business hangs on, established dealers are still selling, and wonderful things continue to appear on the market. Museums are not dead and people still visit historic houses. So it is not over yet. If this is no longer the golden age of antiques, it is nonetheless a phase of a complex cultural enterprise that is well over a century old and has a fascinating history. Briann Greenfield, a talented storyteller, has drawn a few instructive strands from the larger fabric and written about them in graceful and accessible prose. Her recognition of the importance of the marketplace and the power of money help demythologize a phenomenon sometimes viewed too innocently. As is so often the case, truth is more interesting than fiction, perhaps especially when fiction actually is the truth.

Kenneth L. Ames
Bard Graduate Center

1. An expanded successor volume, *The New Fine Points*, appeared in 1993.

2. Michael D. Hall, *Emerson Burkhart: An Ohio Painter's Song of Himself* (London: Scala Publishers, 2009), p. 17.

3. See, for instance, Amanda E. Lange, *Delftware at Historic Deerfield, 1600–1800* (Deerfield, Mass.: Historic Deerfield, 2001), p. 7.

4. The furniture collection is well documented in Dean A. Fales Jr., *The Furniture of Historic Deerfield* (New York: E. P. Dutton, 1976).

5. David Brooks, *Bobos in Paradise: The New Upper Class and How They Got There* (New York: Simon & Schuster, 2000).

Joseph Cunningham. *The Artistic Furniture of Charles Rohlfs*. New York: American Decorative Art 1900 Foundation; New Haven, Conn.: Yale University Press, 2008. xxi + 283 pp.; 321 color illus., 16 bw illus., appendix, bibliography, index. $65.00.

In the literature of the American arts and crafts movement, the work of Charles Rohlfs has generally appeared as an afterthought. Robert Judson Clark mentioned Rohlfs only briefly in his seminal exhibition catalogue, *The Arts and Crafts Movement in America, 1876–1918* (Princeton, 1972), and subsequent scholars of the movement—Leslie Greene Bowman, Wendy Kaplan, Janet Kardon, to name just a few—devoted minimal pages to Rohlfs in their important publications of the 1980s, 1990s, and early 2000s. Yet Rohlfs's quirky furniture and metalwork now resides, as Bruce Barnes indicates in his foreword to this handsome new exhibition catalogue, *The Artistic Furniture of Charles Rohlfs*, in "almost every major American museum that collects American decorative art from the period around 1900" (p. xvi). Thus, this in-depth study by independent scholar Joseph Cunningham is long overdue and will fill a gap in the libraries of scholars, curators, and collectors who share a fascination with Rohlfs's idiosyncratic vision.

That vision—which Rohlfs himself never fully articulated—has made his work hard to categorize and may explain why scholars for the past three decades have tended to gloss over his contribution to American craft. Though arising out of the aesthetic movement, Rohlfs was not mentioned in the exhaustive publication that spurred interest in that subject, *In Pursuit of Beauty: Americans and the Aesthetic Movement* (Metropolitan Museum of Art, 1986). And, though parallels between Rohlfs's work and art nouveau abound, Rohlfs does not figure in Paul Greenhalgh's recent and otherwise definitive *Art Nouveau, 1890–1914* (Abrams, 2000). Even David Cathers, writing in the first edition of his important primer (1981) on arts and crafts furniture makers in New York State, did not mention Rohlfs, who resided in Buffalo. A designer and craftsperson, Rohlfs drew on eclectic contemporary and historic sources, but he eschewed outright associations with the arts and crafts movement generally and the mission style more specifically. In short, Rohlfs defied pigeonholing.

Providing a comprehensive overview of this enigmatic man's life and work is thus the goal of *The Artistic Furniture of Charles Rohlfs*. An exhibition catalogue accompanying shows held at the Milwaukee Art Museum and four other institutions between June 2009 and January 2011, the book includes gorgeous nine-by-twelve-inch color details along with smaller black-and-white, sepia, and color images. In his foreword Barnes justifies inclusion of such luxurious images: "this book covers the life of Rohlfs in roughly chronological order, but the focus is on the objects he designed, rather than his life and times" (p. xvi). Barnes, who edited the book, provides an executive summary of its contents, highlights some of Rohlfs's biographical background, acknowledges supporters of and contributors to the traveling exhibition, and provides background on the American Decorative Art 1900 Foundation, of which Barnes is founder and president. As a foremost Rohlfs connoisseur, Barnes discusses his motivations for both collecting and promoting this "complex and exciting" (p. xvii) work.

In the acknowledgments section that follows, Cunningham expands on Barnes's comments while explaining his scholarly approach, that is, making himself "aware of the known examples of [Rohlfs's] works," which required "advertising in relevant publications and reaching out to more than a hundred dealers, collectors, curators, and scholars who are active or knowledgeable in this field" (p. xxi). Serious collectors will appreciate the thoroughness with which Cunningham applies this firsthand exposure to Rohlfs's works.

Sarah Fayen, assistant curator of the Chipstone Foundation and adjunct assistant curator at the Milwaukee Art Museum, provides a balanced introduction that addresses Rohlfs's background (son of a piano cabinetmaker), education and training (night courses at the Cooper Union), and early work as a professional pattern maker (for iron foundries and stove manufacturers). She considers his marriage to his older and more successful novelist wife, Anna Katherine Green, as well as his amateur acting career. She ponders his evolution from what was, essentially, an early industrial designer into a maker of "artistic furniture," exploring his emerging design philosophy, his sense of self, and his collaborative relationship with his talented wife and partner. Fayen attributes Oscar Wilde's 1882 appearance in New York to Rohlfs's recognition of an affinity between, as she aptly puts it, "drama on the stage and drama in design" (p. 6). Because of evident gaps in the Rohlfs archives, Fayen often speculates, but she draws conclusions that seem logical and well grounded.

Fayen's introduction provides a satisfying overview of topics into which Cunningham delves at greater depth, but it also raises numerous questions.

What was the background of the aesthetic movement in Buffalo? How did aestheticism come to that city and how did the Rohlfses become involved with the "artistic" set? What role did vernacular forms—the turned chair, the trestle table, the settle bench—play in Rohlfs's oeuvre? Given Rohlfs's fascination with cast metal in his early foundry work, why does none of it appear in his later furniture or metalwork? And, where did he learn to forge metal by hand? How does Rohlfs's acceptance of what Fayen terms "faux-honest construction" (p. 17) justify his dedication to design reform, which prided itself on such concepts as integrity, sincerity, and directness? Finally, how did Rohlfs's amateur acting career connect to, say, the Little Theater movement that was an important part of reformist organizations including the Detroit Society of Arts & Crafts?

Cunningham's eleven chapters that follow embrace the macrocosm of Rohlfs's life and the microcosm of Rohlfs's work. Chapter 1 explores Charles's and Anna Katherine's early biographies up through the first years of their marriage. Chapter 3 covers their European grand tour in 1890 and, after their return to the United States, the dramatization of Anna Katherine's first novel, *The Leavenworth Case* (1878), into a stage play in which Charles appeared as the villain. The first part of chapter 4 speculates on Rohlfs's "transition, around 1897, from actor to cabinetmaker and wood-carver" (p. 65), describes his various work spaces, and his short-lived connection with Chicago retailer Marshall Field and Co. (1899–1901). Chapter 6 discusses Rohlfs's emerging design philosophy as presented in articles, interviews, and lectures: "Rohlfs defined great design," Cunningham informs us, "as useful, well planned, beautifully executed objects of decorative art imbued with spiritual power" (p. 107). The first part of chapter 8 considers critical assessment of Rohlfs's work in the international design press and his participation in Buffalo's "Pan-American Exposition" of 1901. Chapter 9 focuses on Rohlfs's contributions to the "Exposition of Modern Decorative Art" held the following year in Turin, Italy, his growing international reputation, and his household milieu. Chapter 10 advances to the year 1904 (when Rohlfs significantly did not participate in the St. Louis world's fair), chronicling his manufacturing of small household items—chafing dishes, candle stands, hanging shelves, and so forth—his foray into commissioned interiors for Adirondack camps and those in his own Norwood Avenue home. Chapter 11 explores the last decades of Rohlfs's life in a Voyseyan home (newly built on Park Street), its interiors filled with his own works that he either desired to keep or was unable to sell, and his civic pursuits after he "ended his career as a furniture-maker" (p. 229) circa 1911.

The sociocultural background provided by these chapters helps put into context Rohlfs's eccentric works. But, to reiterate Barnes's statement in the foreword, the book's focus is clearly "on the objects he designed, rather than his life and times." As a result, these chapters raise more questions than they answer. Their descriptive nature often stops short of the critical analysis necessary to link the sociocultural background to Rohlfs's design philosophy or aesthetic approach. Sometimes, Cunningham offers more information than we really need: is it essential, for example, to know the exact time that the Rohlfs family arrived at their hotel in Liverpool? At other times, he leaves us longing for a more substantive interpretation of the facts presented. A concluding paragraph, for example, summarizing the overarching implications of the grand tour on Rohlfs's subsequent work would be a welcome addition. In light of Rohlfs's Germanic heritage, the family's extensive trip to Germany must have been especially meaningful.

This delving into Rohlfs's sociocultural background again raises a variety of unanswered questions, some of which are conceptual. What, for example, did Rohlfs actually study at the Cooper Union? (It would be helpful to know more than just course titles.) What did he read, both at school and later in life? What tomes and periodicals filled Rohlfs's personal library? (Interior photographs of his various homes clearly show overflowing bookcases.) Did he, for example, peruse Louis Sullivan's *The Tall Office Building Artistically Considered* (1896) or his later books? (This seems likely, considering Rohlfs's proximity to Adler and Sullivan's Guaranty Building [Buffalo, 1894–95] and his purported interest in Sullivan's ornament.) How did the spiritual element that Cunningham perceives in Rohlfs's work relate to the concept of "expression," which design theorists and critics discussed and debated during this era?

Questions of a more technical or aesthetic nature include the following: for an individual labeled the "best draughtsman" (p. 183) in his classes at the Cooper Union, why did he take such a casual approach to sketches and working drawings during his career? Why did Rohlfs's lighting fixtures rely on old technology, that is, candlepower, when other reformist designers on both sides of the Atlantic were exploiting the newer, cleaner electricity? Regarding Rohlfs's approach to ornament: could the impressive *Bed with Canopy* (ca. 1900) owe its iconography to the so-called language of flowers, which was an obsession with decorative artists in the nineteenth century? Might images—see the *Outline for Raised Panel*—have any connection to the inkblots made famous by Swiss psychoanalyst Hermann Rorschach (1884–1922)? And, might Rohlfs's fascinating work process presage what contemporary author Mihaly Csikszentmihalyi has termed "flow," or the psychology of optimal experience?

Cunningham devotes the remaining chapters (or parts thereof) to a loving analysis of the objects—furniture, clocks, vessels, luminaries—that emanated from Rohlfs's studio and filled his home and those of his clients. These analyses are like extended catalogue entries turned into impassioned prose. Because Cunningham intersperses these descriptions with the broader, sociocultural sections, he forces the reader to shift from sweeping overview to focused detail and back again. This introduces variety as the reader moves from absorbing dry facts of Rohlfs's life to appreciating sensual descriptions of form and ornament, wood grain and surface finish, joints and fittings. The book might have been improved, though, both conceptually and stylistically, by combining "like" material with "like" and incorporating smoother transitions.

Doubtless, this is a beautiful tome, which may be one reason that the Decorative Arts Society (DAS) awarded it the Charles F. Montgomery

Prize for 2008. Its large format, exquisite photographs, careful layout, and ample white space are visually striking. Scholars may lament, however, the delicate sans serif font, which is difficult to read, the minuscule superscript numbers indicating notes, the placement of the notes at the volume's end, and the notes' odd, abbreviated format, requiring simultaneous perusal of the one-page bibliography. In view of the ample white space that borders most pages, endnotes could have appeared as marginalia, along with captions. This would have drawn attention to some of the truly obscure sources that Cunningham took the trouble to locate and consult. The passages devoted to object analysis raise a further set of questions: what is the link between Rohlfs's ornament and conventionalized motifs from the past that seem to abound in his work, such as the rinceau, the paired reverse-curve, the lamb's-tongue molding, auricular elements, the ogival, and the crocket, to name just a few? Similarly, what is the connection between his high-backed chair forms and, say, the caquetoire of the French Renaissance? Did Rohlfs consciously evoke the thong-strung seats of the ancient Greek klismos or the monopodia supports seen in late-renaissance/mannerist pattern books? What was Rohlfs's awareness of patent furniture—such as the revolving bookcase form—which surely must have influenced some of his not-always-successful experiments in furniture engineering and invention?

It is a credit to its authors that *The Artistic Furniture of Charles Rohlfs* inspires such query and debate. Long after the accompanying exhibition has been dismantled, this catalogue will continue to attract a wide range of readers. A proof of its merit will be if it inspires a new generation of Rohlfs scholars and collectors to delve further into the conceptual, aesthetic, and technical underpinnings of his curious work.

Beverly K. Brandt
Herberger Institute for Design & the Arts
Arizona State University

Edward R. Bosley and Anne E. Mallek, eds. *A New and Native Beauty: The Art and Craft of Greene & Greene*. London and New York: Merrell, in association with the Gamble House/USC, 2008. 272 pp.; numerous color and bw illus., bibliography, index. $75.00.

The catalogue *A New and Native Beauty: The Art and Craft of Greene & Greene*, edited by Edward R. Bosley and Anne E. Mallek, accompanied an exhibition of Charles and Henry Greene's designs marking the centennial of their David and Mary Gamble house in Pasadena, California. In the book, eleven scholarly essays take a variety of approaches toward the Greenes' work, investigating, for example, its inspirations, its individual components, and its historiography. Despite a somewhat peculiar structure and an occasional tendency toward description rather than critical analysis, the catalogue is a significant addition to the literature on these designers.

In the first essay, "The Beauty of a House: Charles Greene, the Morris Movement, and James Culbertson," Mallek uses the Culbertson house in

Pasadena, which the Greenes worked on intermittently from 1902 to 1915, as a case study to examine their relation to William Morris and the English arts and crafts movement. She stresses Charles Greene and Culbertson's shared Anglophilia and admiration for the romantic aspects of English arts and crafts, simultaneously demonstrating the client's important role in the creation of Greene and Greene's houses. The second essay, by Virginia Greene Hales and Bruce Smith, summarizes the brothers' biographies, drawing on the special knowledge Hales has as a grandchild of Henry Greene. Hales and Smith argue that Charles was the more artistically oriented, while Henry was the more practical; nevertheless, Henry had a central role in the firm's creations, necessitated in part by the sheer number of commissions the brothers had when their architectural practice was at its height.

Bruce Smith's "Sunlight and Elsewhere: Finding California in the Work of Greene and Greene" focuses on the Greenes' efforts to develop a new Californian style of architecture between 1895 and 1904. In this period, Pasadena was still quite rustic, and Americans viewed all of California in romantic terms, as an alternative place. As a result, as the Greenes sought to design buildings appropriate for the state, they chose models that were considered exotic, such as those from the Japanese and Spanish mission traditions, using them to create architecture for Southern California's sunny climate. The Greenes' buildings became, in turn, one of the ways the region defined itself.

In "The Forest, the Copper Mine, and the Sea: The Alchemical and Social Materiality of Greene and Greene," Margaretta M. Lovell notes the Greenes' careful specifications for a remarkable variety of materials in their work, in order to appeal to the senses of touch, hearing, and smell as well as sight. She argues persuasively that this use of materials reveals the Greenes' simultaneous modernity and antimodernity. On the one hand, they incorporated materials from many different international sources into their designs, combining, for example, African ebony with local Californian abalone and American and African copper, materials they likely saw on display at world's fairs. Such wide-ranging elements indicate the Greenes' participation in the modern, capitalist economy. On the other hand, the Greenes used materials to distinguish the masters' and servants' areas of the house, installing, for example, oak floors in the masters' quarters and maple or fir in the servants'. These architectural differences upheld traditional power structures, revealing the Greenes' antimodernity.

The next three essays examine individual components of the Greenes' houses. Edward S. Cooke Jr.'s contribution, "An International Studio: The Furniture Collaborations of the Greenes and the Halls," traces the development of the Greenes' furniture aesthetic. Their first furniture was heavily influenced by Gustav Stickley, whereas their later pieces synthesized elements drawn from neoclassical, traditional Chinese, and contemporary German sources. This change in the Greenes' furniture occurred after 1906 and was made possible by their partnership with Peter and John Hall, who had the mastery of construction techniques necessary to execute the Greenes' ideas successfully. The Halls were especially attentive to details of joinery and wood expansion, concerns that were characteristic of contemporary

Scandinavian design and thus demonstrate the influence of the Scandinavian craftspeople working in their shop. Cooke's detailed discussion of such aspects of construction, including X-ray analysis of a Blacker house chair, is particularly helpful.

In the next essay, "'The Spell of Japan': Japonism and the Metalwork of Greene and Greene," Nina Gray surveys the Greenes' metalwork, moving from exterior elements such as strapwork and lanterns to interior furniture and fireplace accoutrements. Like Cooke, she asserts that Greene and Greene's mature designs in metal were only achievable because they found talented craftspeople who were capable of executing them successfully, in this case George Burkhard and Rudolph Lensch of the Art Metal Company. Gray describes the Japanesque aspects of the Greenes' metalwork, focusing in particular on its relation to traditional Japanese sword guards, or *tsuba*. Nevertheless, as several of the other catalogue essays demonstrate, Japanism influenced all the Greenes' creations, not just their metalwork, so Gray's essay title seems misleading.

Julie L. Sloan then treats the brothers' stained glass in her essay, "'A Glimmer of Vivid Light': The Stained Glass of Greene and Greene." Like Cooke and Gray, she argues that the Greenes' innovative glass designs after 1906 were viable only because they partnered with master craftspeople, in this case, the glaziers Harry Sturdy and Emil Lange. Sloan effectively contextualizes the Greenes' glass within contemporary practice in this medium, while also discussing the technical developments—such as the use of copper foil and iridized glass—that made the Greenes' mature productions possible.

Ann Scheid, in "Independent Women, Widows, and Heiresses: Greene and Greene's Women Clients," analyzes the social background of the Greenes' female clients, most of whom were midwestern progressives, the daughters of men who had made their fortunes in industry in western Pennsylvania and Ohio. These women were educated and independent, and their strong ideas about how their houses should look affected the Greenes' designs. Thus, like Mallek's essay, Scheid's discussion demonstrates that Greene and Greene houses were collaborative affairs, with the clients playing important roles in shaping the form that the buildings ultimately took.

Next, Alan Crawford addresses "Charles Greene and Englishness." Charles Greene had been exposed to English arts and crafts design through his travels in England and his reading of design periodicals such as *International Studio*. Nevertheless, as Crawford argues persuasively, Greene's designs were less influenced by these realities than by his romantic, nineteenth-century-based picturesque idea of England and by the stereotyped English house form that was recognizable to his American clients.

David C. Streatfield then surveys "Divergent Threads in the Garden Art of Greene and Greene." The Greenes believed that gardens should be integrally related both to the house and to the surrounding landscape. As a result, they worked to develop their own appropriately Californian picturesque garden aesthetic, inspired by such apparently contradictory traditions as Spanish mission, English Tudor, Italian formal, and Japanese. Streatfield demonstrates that the Greenes' work in this area was collaborative as well:

since they knew little about horticulture, it is likely that they described the effects they wanted to nurseryman George Chisholm, who chose the plants best suited to execute their designs.

In the final essay, "Out of the Woods: Greene and Greene and the Modern American House," Edward R. Bosley addresses the changing reception of Greene and Greene's work in the first half of the twentieth century. Although the popularity of the International Style after World War I made the Greenes' regionalist, handcrafted designs seem antimodern, by the 1930s this attitude was beginning to change. Pioneering Greene and Greene scholars such as Jean Murray Bangs ensured that the brothers' architectural plans and drawings were saved and their designs published in such leading periodicals as *House Beautiful*. As a result, by the early 1950s the Greenes' work was seen as protomodernist rather than antimodernist, and it influenced later twentieth-century design.

Each of the catalogue authors, then, offers helpful insights into the Greenes' work. Nevertheless, there are aspects of the overall publication that hinder the reader's understanding of their arguments. First, the book's structure is somewhat idiosyncratic. Hales and Smith's chapter on the Greenes' biographical background is not first but second in the book, with the result that the reader must attempt to follow the first essay—Mallek's on the Culbertson house—with no sense of the brothers' family background, relation to each other, architectural training, or overall career trajectories. Mallek's essay also overlaps significantly with Crawford's, which strangely appears much later in the catalogue. Both authors address the English influence on the Greenes' work, but in fact, as various writers argue throughout the catalogue, the English strand was only one of a number of significant influences on Greene and Greene. Japanism, the German concept of *Gesamtkunstwerk* (the environment as a total work of art), contemporary Scandinavian design practice, and the Spanish mission and Native American architectural traditions of Southern California also inspired these architects. With no essays on these other aspects, the book falsely suggests that the English influence on the Greenes was the most important. Moreover, since no author offers a comprehensive treatment of these other strands, the background information on each is repeated in different essays unnecessarily; Mallek, Smith, and Gray, for example, all summarize the history of Japanism.

The catalogue also does not include enough comparative illustrations, a lack that significantly deters the authors' efforts to describe the many different influences on the Greenes' work and their relation to their contemporaries. Although more photographs might involve added expense and some sacrificing of the book's dramatic design, these compromises would give the reader much-needed concrete visual examples against which to judge the Greenes' buildings. Without such comparative material, the authors' points seem vague and unsubstantiated. The reader also misses an object list of the exhibition for which this publication served as a catalogue. This omission is especially regrettable given the challenges of creating a show on architecture, a medium that by its very nature is not easily exhibited in a museum context. Curators of design from all eras and regions would benefit

from knowing which objects were chosen to make the Greenes' buildings accessible to a museum audience.

Despite these drawbacks, the book's emphasis on the collaborative nature of the Greenes' work advances scholarship on these architects and, indeed, on design in general. The catalogue essays work together to debunk two related myths: first, that the Greenes' remarkable designs were the achievement of the more artistic Charles alone; and second, that the brothers themselves were solely responsible for them. In reality, Charles and Henry Greene worked with each other and with their clients and craftspeople to create their houses.

The catalogue's most successful essays are those, like Lovell's and Crawford's, that acknowledge the contradictions inherent in the Greenes' work and move beyond mere description and promotion of the Greenes' role in architectural history to critical analysis. Bosley writes in his introduction that the catalogue's text is not "the last word on Greene and Greene, but rather the next in a continuing discussion leading to a fuller recognition of their legacy" (p. 13). This book certainly persuades the reader of the importance of studying Greene and Greene. It is to be hoped that future scholars will move beyond this need to legitimize their work to ever more nuanced investigations of its complex nature.

Ellen E. Roberts
The Art Institute of Chicago

Paul Fitzsimmons, Robert Tarule, and Donald P. White III. *Discovering Dennis: The Search for Thomas Dennis among the Artisans of Exeter*. Exeter, Eng.: Marhamchurch Antiques, 2009. 50 pp.; color illus. £10.00.

Thomas Dennis just won't stay dead. The most-studied joiner of early New England continues to generate interest and debate nearly seventy-five years after first being identified as the maker of a large body of carved furniture from Ipswich, Massachusetts. *Discovering Dennis: The Search for Thomas Dennis among the Artisans of Exeter* is a catalogue of an exhibition and sale of more than twenty-four examples of English furniture from Devon, held at the Guild Hall in Exeter on November 4 and 5, 2009. The assembly of this group was spearheaded by Paul Fitzsimmons, owner of Marhamchurch Antiques in Bude, Cornwall. Fitzsimmons's shop specializes in medieval to seventeenth-century furniture and woodwork, with a particular focus on the carved works from Devon.

The catalogue features short essays and entries by Robert Tarule and Donald P. White III. The authors maintain that close examination of these twenty-four examples of Devon (specifically Exeter) oak furniture has led them to link them with the furniture attributed to Thomas Dennis in Massachusetts. This is not new research; the Devon-to-Ipswich link has been known to American furniture scholars since Helen Park's 1960 article "Thomas Dennis, Ipswich Joiner: A Re-examination," in which she identified William Searle as a joiner in Ipswich and cited his birthplace of Ottery St.

Mary. The devil is in the details, they say, and it is details that *Discovering Dennis* cites, while claiming to be able to identify English objects made in the same shop in which Dennis was trained.[1]

It will be helpful first to run down the evolution of the Thomas Dennis story. Irving Whitehall Lyon pioneered some of the techniques still used today in furniture studies; his preface to *The Colonial Furniture of New England* (1891) outlined his approach to the subject:

> About the year 1880 the writer commenced a somewhat systematic study of this old furniture. This included among other things an examination of specimens; an inquiry into what others knew or had written; and an examination of old records, such as inventories of household furniture, old newspapers, account books, and diaries. The furniture of England and Holland for the corresponding period was also studied to some extent.[2]

Both Irving W. Lyon and his son Irving P. Lyon relied on probate records to study seventeenth-century furniture and its makers. Irving P. applied his father's methods to link the carved furniture of Ipswich, Massachusetts, to Thomas Dennis, a joiner who lived in Ipswich between circa 1667 and his death in 1706. Lyon outlined the descent of several pieces in the family, then made connections between these and other related works. Ultimately, he went overboard with this attribution and credited Thomas Dennis with nearly every piece of Essex County furniture, but the first two sections of his study are still mostly valid.[3]

Once Lyon had gone to an extreme with his theories concerning Dennis, other scholars picked up the material and the story unfolded from there. Homer Eaton Keyes and Park both published follow-up articles in *Antiques*, refuting parts of Lyon's work, and expanding the knowledge base concerning Essex County furniture of this period. Robert F. Trent's introduction to the compilation of these articles in an anthology entitled *Pilgrim Century Furniture* (1976) is not called "The Thomas Dennis Problem" for a lark. Trent pulled out a quotation from Keyes's article that is worth repeating: "an artist trained under the old apprentice system . . . could never quite escape from his conditioned self. Certain grooves worn in his brain by years of practice would force him, unwittingly and unvaryingly, to treat minor forms in a virtually identical manner."[4]

Park's article also cited records pertaining to William Searle, such as his death in Ipswich in 1667, and found that the Searle family genealogy recorded his birth in Ottery St. Mary, Devon. Searle's birth date is variously given as May 28, 1611, or January 23, 1634. We know that *a* William Searle married Grace Cole in Ottery St. Mary on April 12, 1659. This couple immigrated to Massachusetts in 1663, settling first in Boston, then in Ipswich. Once Park brought Searle into the mix, much ink was spent trying to sort out the sequence of events. The main points are Searle's death sometime before August 16, 1667; the date of his probate inventory; and the marriage on October 26, 1668, between Grace (Cole) Searle, widow, and Thomas Dennis, joiner, who by then had moved to Ipswich, where he spent the rest of his life. There has yet to be found any additional link between William Searle and Thomas Dennis, other than a deed of sale dated September 26, 1663.[5]

All the authors who have trod this ground have cited various documents in New England: William Searle's estate inventory, Essex County court records, then records generated by the children and grandchildren of Thomas Dennis. After Park, the next up was Benno M. Forman, who also covered much of this material. Forman's book *American Seating Furniture, 1630–1730* (1988) illustrated a carved chest from Devon, dated 1671, that clearly resembles Ipswich furniture. Attempts to sort the surviving artifacts, assigning some pieces to Searle, and others to Dennis, were made principally by Forman, Trent, and Robert Blair St. George.[6]

Then, some years later, came Robert Tarule's dissertation (1992) and, from it, the book *The Artisan of Ipswich* (2004). Tarule's approach to studying these objects from the perspective of a maker dovetails nicely with Keyes's statement about the work habits of a traditional craftsman being consistent and recognizable. This point becomes a key feature of *Discovering Dennis*.[7]

That brings us to the catalogue under consideration here. Before discussing the contents, a quick detour concerning the layout and execution of the book is in order. The catalogue, for several reasons, is difficult to read. The design is dense and crowded, and uses white type on a dark gray background. The size of the type changes randomly throughout: one entry is in a tiny font, the next in something considerably larger. Further, a photograph of a chest or carving is printed behind almost all of the text, making both difficult to see. These photos add nothing other than irritation. A plainer design would have made things better for everyone. The placement of endnote markers is also erratic, making them hard to find or at least difficult to follow. The essays by White make numerous references to objects by their catalogue numbers, such as "front panels of another chest (cat. 6)," yet no numbers appear on the pages showing the objects in the exhibition. This again makes things hard to follow, and I can imagine that many readers will tire of trying to figure out which chest is which, and then give up.

There are more layout problems. The text on pages 36–42 discusses a chest front and three complete chests, but the lengthy paragraph describing these objects is just copied and pasted—four times. Even worse, the text is formatted differently each time, and thus trying to read through it to make sure it's not new text is difficult, to say the least.[8]

In addition to the poor design, the copyediting was faulty as well. There are places where notes and citations that are clearly still in draft form nevertheless made it into print. For example, on page 25 we need to decipher the following: "This chest (incised with the initials 'MC' make this a single quote mark on the front panels). . . ." If this sort of thing happened once, that would be unfortunate, but it is not an isolated incident in this publication. So it amounts to sloppy copyediting. Very simple things also warrant correction; for instance, the Peabody Essex Museum in Salem, Massachusetts, is repeatedly referred to as the Essex Institute, its name before the 1992 merger with the Peabody Museum of Salem.

Now to content. The foreword is Tarule's essay on Dennis's career, both in the seventeenth century and in furniture histories written in the twenti-

eth century. Tarule quickly runs through the historiography of the carved furniture. He cites Forman's follow-up of Park's interest in William Searle. In 1970 Forman had corresponded with W. F. Bennett, of the Ottery St. Mary District Council, asking specifically about records pertaining to either William Searle or Thomas Dennis. The research came up empty regarding Dennis, but Bennett sent Forman several citations concerning Searle, among them a birth record from May 28, 1611, and, according to Bennett, this William Searle married Grace Cole in 1659. Park cited a family genealogy in which 1634 was given for the year of William Searle's birth. And in fact, there is an extant record of a William Searle, born January 23, 1635, in Ottery St. Mary, to John Searle and his wife Margaret. An Ipswich chest in the Chipstone collection has the date 1634 inscribed in the center panel. Most accept that this date was carved into the chest after it was made, yet some writings have noted that it corresponds to Searle's birth date. Others, Forman among them, stick to the 1611 date, making Searle forty-eight years old at the time of his first marriage. Tarule follows with the earlier date for Searle's birth. This becomes significant, because in one situation Searle is Thomas Dennis's senior by twenty-seven years or more, but if 1634 is his birth date, then he and Dennis are separated by only six years at most. The whole William Searle issue needs to take the 1634/35 birth record into consideration; further research might help clarify which William Searle emigrated in the early 1660s.[9]

Tarule notes the short career of Searle in New England (four years) and the lengthy time Dennis spent in Ipswich, making Dennis the more likely candidate for the creator of much of the surviving furniture, a logical conclusion. He then goes through many of the public records pertaining to Dennis, and here his writing is much like what is found in *The Artisan of Ipswich*: "we can almost see him going from door to door," and so forth. In this section, Tarule writes that "for all we know about Thomas in New England, he is invisible in England. At the moment Exeter seems as likely as Ottery St Mary, but there may have been other regional centers" (p. 4). Here, an editor would have been a plus. One thing that is lacking is any mention of where in England the authors have "looked" for Thomas Dennis documents; identifying what records have been searched would be a start. The two sentences quoted above are related but are not really about the same thing. One says the authors have found no record of Thomas Dennis in England; the other seems to refer to a possible center for the carved style featured on the objects in the catalogue. The best thing about this is the phrase "At the moment," which implies that the authors are willing to concede that further research might change their findings. Indeed, Fitzsimmons was quoted as saying this is "a work in progress—about discovering Thomas Dennis among the Exeter woodworking community, not Dennis discovered." Unfortunately, this sentiment did not make it into the catalogue itself.[10]

Tarule then goes through some of the woodworking steps found in *The Artisan of Ipswich*, comparing the New England material with the Devon material. This is his strength. However, during this discussion, we read a clunky transition: "Thomas seems to have returned to a technique he knew from the Old World" (p. 5). I would like to know why it's a *return*? If we put these petty details aside, we can appreciate Tarule's contribution. He runs down the use of two different-sized joints in the chests from Devon and Ipswich. To this reader, here is the greatest finding of the catalogue: the very sort of thing that Homer Eaton Keyes was writing about in 1938. There follows a list of characteristics of the Dennis chests' construction features that are quite significant when they are then found on the Devon work.

White's essay "Understanding Exeter" starts with a discussion about the variety displayed in the carving repertoire of Thomas Dennis and its possible sources, particularly the notion that English decorative arts in the early seventeenth century were influenced by a combination of immigrant artisans and imported objects. Among other elements, White mentions Dennis's use of humanoid grotesques on the wainscot chairs at the Peabody Essex Museum and the Bowdoin College Museum of Art. Further, White says that the diverse nature of Dennis's carving can be equated with high-level English design of the sixteenth and early seventeenth centuries, which sets his work apart from the "generally provincial and homogenous character of the relief carved ornament executed by other joiners active in seventeenth-century New England" (p. 6). Some further garbled writing clouds the author's intention. What are we to make of the following: "The determinative factor that shaped Dennis' approach to the design of joined furniture was not simply that he was an immigrant. More precisely, the specific place or place in which he lived, received his training, and worked in England and what he learned and experienced before departure" (p. 7). Many readers will simply tire of this lack of editing and skim the remainder of the catalogue.

What White is driving at is a lead-in to a theory that once Thomas Dennis was in Ipswich, he relied on his "memories" to produce the vivid and varied carved works assigned to his shop tradition. White goes to an extreme length to illustrate this point, stating that just four decades before Dennis arrived in New England, the English were living in bark- and reed-covered huts. Thomas Dennis hadn't even been born when the English settlers were living in huts in Ipswich. Clearly, what the author wants to convey is that in New England the artificial landscape was not as fully developed as it was back in England. Having only a few decades' worth of material culture in place in New England, versus centuries' worth in old England, the artisans working in New England relied on their training. Thomas Dennis is not alone in this regard—that is the case with every tradesman-craftsman who came to New England during this period.

Thus we get to the description of Exeter. Drawing on several reference materials, White paints a picture of Exeter in the sixteenth century leading into the seventeenth. Its position as the fifth-largest city in England in the 1650s was in part a result of its textile trade with the Continent. White discusses the presence of immigrant masons and joiners working in Exeter and explores the impact their work had on Exeter's joinery tradition. As mentioned, the endnote markers are difficult to find or follow, and it seems that those between numbers 4 and 8 are missing. It is in note 7 that White lists the work of Anthony Wells-Cole, whose 1981 article "An Oak Bed at Mantacute [*sic*]: A Study in Mannerist Decoration" pinpointed Exeter as the most likely source for work of this style and identified the Garrett and Hermon/Harmon families of joiners working there in the late sixteenth and early seventeenth centuries. Wells-Cole's article remains a must-read for anyone exploring this material. In it he traces the strapwork motif, citing its use on several monuments, pulpits, and on furniture, then explores documentary sources to identify the joiners who are possibly responsible for its development.[11]

White's essay is essentially a synopsis of Wells-Cole's article, down to the citations of extant examples of stonework and woodwork exhibiting this strapwork motif. The conclusion to this section admits that it is unknown whether Thomas Dennis trained in one of these Exeter joiners' shops or was just somehow exposed to their works. To the authors, what is certain, however, is that these works represent the immediate predecessors to the work of Thomas Dennis. Interestingly, nothing is said of William Searle, who can be placed by documentary record just a few miles from Exeter.

The last introductory essay is "Anatomy of an Exeter Chest." Exeter was heavily damaged during bombing in World War II; the few surviving sections of paneled rooms are now mainly in museums. White claims that the movable furniture that remains illustrates the fabric of an Exeter style. The carved motives and the "vibrant polycromy [*sic*] applied to the dropped-ground of relief carving in reds, oranges, blues, and greens composed from exotic and/or costly pigments including vermillion, hematite, ultramarine, and celedonite demonstrate Exeter's trading connections across regional borders and oceans" (p. 10). The long list of colors and pigments is quite dramatic and exciting. What is lacking is any clarification as to whether any of the surviving furniture or woodwork has been tested to show use of these pigments—the note cites Helen Howard's *Pigments of English Medieval Wall Painting*. If the reader is not careful, she might come away thinking that this furniture was painted with these pigments. In fact, this author is not aware of any studies done on the pigments used on *any* English furniture of this period. New England pieces have been studied to some degree, and new research in this regard is under way at both the Museum of Fine Arts, Boston, and the Winterthur Museum. If the "Exeter" work has been tested, then publishing those findings would be a great boon to studies of related works. On the next page, White says that he believes that different pigments were used in New England compared with those used in old England.[12]

A discussion of timber shortages and use follows. This is perhaps some of the most useful information in this section. Finally, a description of an "Exeter" chest is found in the second-to-last paragraph. The wrap-up discusses the fact that of the carved chests in the catalogue, none is a direct quote of an existing one attributed to Thomas Dennis. Knowing the Dennis material, one would not expect a carbon copy; variety is what this shop tradition is noted for. White lists a number of links between the chests in the catalogue and the known New England works, but here the catalogue numbering system fails us. To flip back and forth to see the pieces discussed here is too awkward.

As to the catalogue itself, it starts off with a bang, an object that is unprecedented in the real world. Titled "Joined Oak three tier cupboard of monumental proportions, constructed for an elite-level household," this entry describes an object that is hard to believe. This piece gives the impression that it is a concoction, a piece of furniture made up of a selection of parts, and the authors present a most imaginative interpretation. In a sense, they, too, think of it as a made-up piece, but made up by the best joiners Exeter produced. Phrases like "Exeter at its most elaborate" reveal the authors' high regard for this object. Noting the use of reused furniture components, they write:

> Shockingly how about uncharacteristically, virtually every framing member was originally intended for another purpose. Stiles, rails, and muntins exhibit open mortises, unexplained panel grooves, and previously bored pinholes. . . . None of the components appear to have ever seen use in a completed object as the extra pinholes, mortises, and panel grooves are undisturbed and the second generation of work was done while the oak was still green. These components were most likely harvested opportunistically from a pile of discarded work pieces that accumulated in the shop as a result of mistakes or breakage. . . . [p. 13]

One question that immediately comes to mind is this: how did a joiners' shop capable of the best-quality work make enough mistakes and create enough discards to frame an entire cupboard, and make those mistakes so quickly that they could build that cupboard from green wood? It's a stretch, to say the least. Certainly there is first-rate work exhibited in the cupboard; the carved drawer fronts are probably a match for the work done on the Corporation pews in Totnes, Devon. The lion masks also relate closely to that work.[13]

The first two chests presented (pp. 15–18) are deemed of great significance, based on their relation to surviving architectural woodwork in the Victoria and Albert Museum. Both chests are noted for the quality of timber found in them, slow-grown clear oak. In the discussion of the first of these (p. 15), we read that the maker(s) of this chest were more accustomed to framing fixed woodwork, because the "[u]se of massive bottom rails (nearly double the width of the top rails) in the chest's framing is consistent with architectural practice. . . ." That may be so, but it must be thickness the authors are talking about here, because the top rail is greater in height than the bottom rail in the photograph. One question about the second chest (pp. 17–18) that might be explored is the blank area on the front stiles, at the height of the top rail. It stands out prominently on a chest that is otherwise decorated over almost all its façade. The strapwork decoration on the top rails of both chests is pointed out as relating to similar treatments on several of Thomas Dennis's pieces: the two wainscot chairs, the Staniford chest at Winterthur, and the Dennis family box with drawer at the Bowdoin College Museum of Art.

The next chest (pp. 19–20) identifies another feature linking these English works with those from Ipswich: the fitting of floorboards of the chest into a notch in the rear stiles. The text says that the original floorboards are now lost, but the detail photo on the next page, which has no caption, seems to show a chest with its original floorboards fitting into a notch in the rear stiles, with a thicker floor installed underneath the thinner original floor. Is this the chest in question? This small detail is one of those habits of construction that is quite useful in studying the connections from one chest to another. The text states that this is the only English chest in which this feature has been noted, but it doesn't tell us how many were sampled for this detail. Further, a later entry in the catalogue states that another chest "is only the second example of an English joined chest yet discovered on which the edges of the outermost bottom boards are inserted in small grooves or 'notches' cut in the inner edges of the back stiles at the level of the lower back rail" (p. 29). One last point: they aren't grooves—those run the length of a board. Why the word "notches" is presented in quotes is not clear. The presence of these notches in the Devon chests is another of the strong points of the authors' findings, but perhaps a less severe interpretation would have actually made the point better.[14]

The following chest (pp. 21–22) includes another of the positive points of this catalogue, the use of tapered cleats, both in thickness and height, fixed to the lid with wooden pins running through the cleat and lid.

After having stated that it was never certain where Thomas Dennis trained, now the authors present us with a chest labeled as "Joined oak chest with remains of original polychromy, probably constructed in the same workshop in which Thomas Dennis apprenticed" (pp. 23–24). Here we come to a wave the authors ride for much of the rest of the catalogue—almost divine revelation in which they can "see" that this object and its six related pieces are all the work of one workshop, and Thomas Dennis trained in that workshop. This becomes rather off-putting. This writer would have preferred an analysis of the objects and the ties between them, leaving the "Thomas Dennis was here" feeling out of it.

Seven chests and a chest fragment make up the group under discussion. These are seen as the work of four artisans in one shop, over three generations. The first chest (pp. 23–24) is claimed as the earliest, and thus the master's work, based on the good-quality timber and the use of an alternating shell motif on the bottom front rail. This pattern is linked to some of the fixed woodwork from sixteenth-century Exeter. The arches carved on the front panels are cited as reflecting "the artisans' engagement with design sensibilities of the late sixteenth century which were less familiar to joiners of Thomas Dennis' generation" (p. 23). But in several passages before this point we had read that Thomas Dennis was most likely exposed to earlier works that he saw in buildings and woodwork around Exeter. ("No artisans responsible for the earliest Exeter joinery survived into Thomas Dennis' time. Dennis, however, invariably saw their work, perhaps even the V&A paneling itself, on a regular basis" [p. 15].)

The text then singles out the decorative elements used on this chest that appear with regularity on the work attributed to Thomas Dennis, including the painted background of the carvings. Noted here for the first time too is the particular molding cut into various framing parts of the chest. Its shape, described as a V-V-ogee molding, is distinctive and appears on all the Dennis chests (p. 23). The molding on this chest, the authors report, is a direct match in size and shape with that on the New England chests. Again, this sort of material is the strongest part of the publication, although some might not go as far as the authors, who see a possible "familial" connection between this chest and the Dennis examples based on the match in the moldings. There is a discussion about the "ephemeral" nature of molding planes, the argument being that use and sharpening changes their profiles over time, and therefore where this chest and the New England ones match closely they must be related. I might ask, why isn't it that they both got their plane irons from the same blacksmith or ironmonger? We know next to nothing about how joiners during this period acquired their plane irons. We do know they made their own plane bodies, but until we know more about the molding plane irons' makers, basing such a strong connection on the molding profile is perhaps too ambitious. I certainly agree that they are related, and it is a close connection, but I would then pull back to a more cautious conclusion.

The next chest (pp. 25–26), a coarser version of the preceding chest, is seen as being by a contemporary of Dennis. The top rail's guilloche-carved pattern is compared with that on the drawer front of the Dennis family box with drawer at the Bowdoin College Museum of Art. The argument put forward here is that this less-accomplished carving was made by late-seventeenth-century joiners who were further removed from the immigrant craftsmen who brought this style to Devon in the late sixteenth century. The V-V-ogee molding is cut on numerous parts of the chest. The authors keep us guessing, though. What is the meaning of the "faces of the side profiles of the stiles" or the "top profiles of all framing members"? This is again a place where an editor would have been of assistance. This chest and the previous example are said to have original paint remaining, but it can't be seen in the photos and is not discussed in the text.

The next carved and painted chest (pp. 27–28) is again attributed to "the same workshop in which Thomas Dennis apprenticed," yet it exhibits the roughest carving seen on this body of work thus far. This poor carving is "more likely" laid at the feet of "an apprentice . . . not yet able to work with the accuracy and efficiency of a mature and independent artisan" (p. 27). Lousy timber and bad carving are not enough to sink this chest, though, because its lid matches those used on the overall group, and the V-V-ogee molding is present as well. The authors note the use of elm as a framing timber on the rear section of the chest, which brings to mind the rather pedestrian joined chest at the Metropolitan Museum of Art attributed to the Thomas Dennis shop in which some framing parts are made of hard maple (*Acer saccharum*). That chest, too, has carving thought to be a beat or two behind the peak examples from the Thomas Dennis shop tradition. Attributing such work to an apprentice is speculation and is only one possible scenario—might this caliber of workmanship represent an aging joiner, with weakening eyesight, perhaps a little arthritis thrown in for good measure? These factors would affect the results achieved at the bench. Assigning second-rate examples to the apprentice is a tired form of interpretation that serves no purpose.[15]

The carved chest dated 1668, shown next (pp. 29–30), is claimed to represent the "second of three distinct later seventeenth-century joiners' workshops in Exeter. . . ." The writers maintain that this chest and one seen in Ralph Edwards's *Dictionary of English Furniture* (vol. 3, fig. 30) are part of a shop tradition "furthest removed from the practices carried by Thomas Dennis to New England." The carving on this example utilizes patterns not really seen before in this publication; some will be skeptical about the connection between it and the core group of joined works. The floorboards fit into the notches in the rear stiles; this is the principal connection between this chest and the pieces under discussion.

Further, what the text fails to really drive home is why this chest is considered "Exeter." Might the areas surrounding Exeter be able to support joiners working in a manner related to that found in Exeter itself? Consider the pioneering study by Blair St. George concerning furniture made in Plymouth Colony in New England. There, geometric decorative patterns and structural techniques are documented as being consistent across a wide-ranging area, spanning maybe forty miles along the southeastern coast of what is now Massachusetts, then Plymouth Colony. Why couldn't that phenomenon play out in Devon as well?[16]

This is perhaps one of the catalogue's biggest failings in this reviewer's eyes: no mention anywhere of the provenance of these works. All the Exeter claims are extrapolations based on Wells-Cole's study of the strapwork motif and his findings concerning the Garrett-Harmon families. Thus, anything showing characteristics descended from the "best" work must therefore also be from Exeter. This is not the route to take here; it is akin to Irving P. Lyon's assignment back in 1938 of every piece of joined furniture from Essex County to Thomas Dennis. The writers mention that this exhibition and catalogue are not to be seen as just a gathering of related, regional works of English furniture (p. 12), but that's really what's at hand here. And that is a valid and useful exercise. Fitzsimmons is to be commended for the legwork in rounding up this group of joined furniture, and careful analysis of its construction and decoration will pay dividends. Tarule and White, just by cataloging the use of two different-sized joints here make headway in the Devon-to-Ipswich connection. The seeming need to make something more of these pieces is the downfall of the catalogue. It becomes tiresome and difficult to read through it, and the photographs are not good enough on their own to reward the student of this period with the necessary visual information draw his own conclusions.

The chest dated 1672 (pp. 31–32) is another case in which the authors go to great lengths to make the point that they consider this as an important piece. Claiming that "No other known object so completely represents the use of polychromy by Exeter joiners" is rather extreme. A similar chest in an American private collection parallels this chest point by point, as does the first "Ottery St. Mary" chest known to modern researchers, the Lady

William-Powlett/Cadhay chest. These are just two examples, and there are several others. Carved boxes from the group also exhibit the painted background quite clearly. It should suffice to say that this chest retains much of its once-bright painted background. Any research identifying pigments and vehicles for these painted works would be quite welcome. The authors cite red and green pigments on both this 1672 chest and the Staniford family chest at Winterthur. As of 1986, research conducted at Winterthur on that chest explicitly concluded that the pigment that appears green contained no copper and thus is not verdigris.[17]

Again, the moldings are cut on "side profiles" and "top profiles," and, further, we have a note about "applied spandrels," which technically are neither applied nor spandrels. These are brackets, tenoned into the chest's front stiles and nailed to the lower rail. For some reason, when discussing a chest with a carved date, the last two digits are always presented in single quotes, thus 16'72'.

The joined oak chest (pp. 33–34) exhibits detailed carving of a more modeled and shaped form, combined with simple incised work on some of the framing parts. The authors note the presence of an aborted carved pattern now on the rear face of the upper rear rail "originally intended for an entirely different project. . . ." It just as well could have been for the front of this chest and, being somehow ruined, turned out to be the back. Also, it seems from the small, hard-to-read photograph that this carving extends across the juncture of the rail-to-stile joints, something that might have been addressed in the text. The use of two panels on each end of the chest, separated by a central muntin, is noted here, unusual for this group of chests in old England, but standard format for the Ipswich examples.

Three carved panels, now all that survives of a period chest, are illustrated on page 35. These are well-defined examples of the florid style associated with the overall group and are associated in the text with the example on pages 31–32.

The next seven pages cover the group of three joined chests and one chest-front fragment whose text repeats four times across the seven pages. It becomes quite difficult to try to sort out this material. These are described as "the products of a single artisan working in the first of three identified later seventeenth-century Exeter joiners' workshops." That statement in and of itself is hard to fathom, but the text gets more bogged down from there.

Perhaps the juxtaposition of the objects in the exhibition helped coordinate this subset of the group, but those of us who have only the catalogue to go by are left befuddled in several ways. We are told that this joiner was two generations behind the man responsible for cat. no. 6, and that *he* trained the maker of cat. no. 7. Then, examining these four pieces with the other four examples related to them (cat. nos. 6–8, 18) will help to "elucidate the variety and qualitative range of one joiner's practices as well as those of other artisans within a single, multigenerational workshop. The five objects also help to cement the connections between this Exeter workshop and Thomas Dennis, who evidence suggests, was among its apprentices" (p. 36).

So, did the maker of cat. no. 7 train the maker of the four objects discussed here? And, after viewing these four items with the earlier four objects, what "five objects" help connect us to Thomas Dennis? It all becomes just too dense to plumb, and the proof of these connections is never truly presented in any coherent manner. These chests are clearly related to some of the works associated with Thomas Dennis's shop, and the lozenge pattern carved on three of the four pieces is seen in the New England work as well. The authors illustrate an example from the Peabody Essex Museum on page 34; another chest at the Metropolitan Museum of Art has the same motif.[18]

Two more chests round out the English material. One chest (pp. 43–44) is said not to share enough traits to belong to the three joiners' shops just discussed. But "one chest does not constitute a fourth workshop, although there is no doubt one existed." Well, is it, or isn't it? If it doesn't belong to the others, it must belong to something. But the authors see it as indicative of many workshops linked by social and familial ties. Without any documentary evidence, it is hard to accept these bold, broad statements.

The final chest of the group does not fit any better than its predecessor in the catalogue, but for different reasons. This chest shares some features with the core group; the V-V-ogee molding (again cut on "side" and "top" profiles), the tapered cleats, the lozenge motif, and red and "green" paint. But otherwise, it bears little resemblance to the rest of the "Exeter" material. It's considerably smaller, has carving only on the front panels, uses a different floor arrangement (although not described in the text, it appears to be showing out the front of the chest) and, most important, exhibits "an almost obsessive attention to detail." This is interpreted as "a late seventeenth-century joiner on the verge of transforming into something else, perhaps a cabinetmaker" (p. 45). That statement must be challenged; to be able to read so much from one object is beyond the limits of connoisseurship. Why can't it just be a good joiner, one who fits his joints well and planes his stock carefully and cleanly?

The "Thomas Dennis fingerprint" on the New England example shown as the final entry in the catalogue (pp. 47–48) is described in detail; the V-V-ogee molding, the cleats, the floorboards-in-a-notch. In addition to these features, the chest uses the tapered cleats fastened with wooden pins, brackets, and other small details that tie it to the shop of Thomas Dennis. The applied ornament—turned half-columns/balusters, glyphs, and moldings applied to the panels—are new territory for this study. The top and bottom front rails have three repeats of carved S-scrolls. A chest decorated in a similar manner descended from Thomas Dennis Jr. and is now part of the collection at the Bowdoin College Museum of Art.

The condition notes state that the applied turned pieces are replaced; some of the molding is replaced too. It is surprising, considering the authors' knack for details, that they do not mention if the applied moldings are the same profile on this chest as on the Bowdoin example. The Bowdoin chest has no applied turnings, so there is no way to tell if these follow an old pattern or if they are made up from whole cloth.

This chest was sold twice in the past ten years, and while it is clearly part of the Thomas Dennis shop tradition, some people felt there was reason to question the carved decoration in addition to the applied work. This reviewer has never seen the chest, although now it is back in the United States as part of the collection at the Ipswich Museum (formerly the Ipswich Historical Society).

After sifting through the poor layout, lack of editing, and dense text, what are we left with? I think what remains in the end is the groundwork for further research. The small details, the use of two different-sized joints in these chests, the distinctive tapered cleats, and the notch for the floor-boards are excellent examples of little nuances of joiners' work that drive home the connections already established between the Ipswich work and the chests from Devon. These are the strongest aspects of the catalogue.

Fitzsimmons has shown a dedicated interest in rooting out and collecting this material; several examples have come to light since the exhibition, and these appear regularly on the Marhamchurch website. It would be ideal for someone to catalogue all the known examples of this florid carved furniture; there are several examples in public and private collections in both England and America that, when combined with the works shown in the catalogue, paint an even broader picture of seventeenth-century Devon oak furniture.

A further avenue to explore would be all the documentary records available for indications of joiners who might have been part of this tradition; Wells-Cole's work on the Garrett-Harmon joiners is only the tip of the iceberg. This is where new, detailed research is wanting in this endeavor. Few will accept that Exeter is the sole source in Devon for this work.

Fitzsimmons, Tarule, and White say in several places in the text that there is no record of Thomas Dennis, but they never tell us where they have looked. At Forman's request in 1970, W. F. Bennett searched Ottery St. Mary for records pertaining to Thomas Dennis, and found none. Thomas Dennis's birthdate is a little shifty. His gravestone lists him as being sixty-eight years old at the time of his death in 1706; thus, he would have been born circa 1638. He deposed in Essex County court in 1680 that he was "aged 40," so a slight adjustment results in a birth date circa 1640. Searching for birth/baptism records of this sort has become greatly simplified since Forman's time; a quick search of the Family History Library's website reveals a couple of candidates in North Devon who were born at the right time to be the Thomas Dennis of Ipswich. One is Thomas Dennis, son of Lewis Dennis, baptized on March 10, 1639, in West Down, Devon. Another possibility is the Thomas Dennis baptized on April 28, 1639, in Hartland, Devon, son of Richard. These records might be a starting point to finding Thomas Dennis in England.

In the end, we have traveled from Irving P. Lyon in 1937–38 all the way to Fitzsimmons, Tarule, and White in 2009 and yet still have far to go with this material. The principals are to be applauded for working in depth at this project, no doubt at great expense in both time and money. Fitzsimmons's enthusiasm for this oak furniture has stirred renewed interest in this subject in England, as evidenced by the Regional Furniture Society's field trips to both the exhibition and to Marhamchurch Antiques in 2009–2010. A great divide spans the research and interpretation of seventeenth-century furniture in England and America. In America, with such a small number of objects to study, we tend to delve into great detail and from there make sweeping conclusions. English work is characterized by casting a wider net, with more reserved conclusions. Perhaps this work will spur interested parties in both directions to further the work presented in *Discovering Dennis* and bring the varied approaches together.

Peter Follansbee
Plimoth Plantation

1. Helen Park, "Thomas Dennis, Ipswich Joiner: A Re-examination," originally published in *Antiques* (July 1960), collected in *Pilgrim Century Furniture: An Historical Survey*, edited by Robert F. Trent (New York: Main Street/Universe Books, 1976), pp. 84–88.

2. Irving Whitall Lyon, *The Colonial Furniture of New England* (Boston: Houghton Mifflin and Company, 1891), pp. iii–iv.

3. Irving P. Lyon's series of six articles, "The Oak Furniture of Ipswich, Massachusetts," originally appeared in *Antiques* in 1937–1938. They are all reprinted in Trent, *Pilgrim Century Furniture*, pp. 55–78.

4. Homer Eaton Keyes, "Dennis or a Lesser Light?" originally published in *Antiques* (December 1938), collected in Trent, *Pilgrim Century Furniture*, pp. 79–83.

5. Park, "Thomas Dennis, Ipswich Joiner," in Trent, *Pilgrim Century Furniture*, p. 86; the 1611 birth date comes from the records found in Ottery St. Mary. Searle's probate inventory is in George Francis Dow, ed., *The Probate Records of Essex County Massachusetts*, 3 vols. (Salem, Mass.: Essex Institute, 1916), 2: 96–97; the deed between Searle and Dennis is in the Dennis Family Papers, Massachusetts Historical Society, Boston; quoted in Robert Tarule, "The Joined Furniture of William Searle and Thomas Dennis: A Shop Based Inquiry into the Woodworking Technology of the Seventeenth-Century Joiner" (Ph.D. diss., Graduate School of the Union Institute, 1992), pp. 121–22.

6. Abbott Lowell Cummings photographed the Lady William-Powlett chest in Cadhay House near Ottery St. Mary and brought it to Forman's attention. The author thanks Robert Trent for some of the details concerning the Lady William-Powlett chest. This chest was bought at a local farm sale in the twentieth century, so its place of manufacture is not necessarily Ottery St Mary. Benno M. Forman, "The Seventeenth-Century Case Furniture of Essex County, Massachusetts, and Its Makers" (master's thesis, University of Delaware, 1968); Benno M. Forman, *American Seating Furniture, 1630–1730* (New York: W. W. Norton, 1988), pp. 135–36; *New England Begins: The Seventeenth-Century*, edited by Jonathan L. Fairbanks and Robert F. Trent, 3 vols. (Boston: Museum of Fine Arts, Boston, 1982), 3: 514–19; Robert Blair St. George, "The Staniford Family Chest," *Maine Antique Digest* (February 1983): 16B–18B.

7. Tarule, "The Joined Furniture of William Searle and Thomas Dennis"; Robert Tarule, *The Artisan of Ipswich: Craftsmanship and Community in Colonial New England* (Baltimore, Md.: Johns Hopkins University Press, 2004).

8. For a shorter version of this material, with a simpler layout, see Paul Fitzsimmons, Robert Tarule, and Donald P. White III, "The English Roots of Thomas Dennis, American Joiner," *New England Antiques Journal* (January 2010): 22–30.

9. The Family History Library search engine (www.familysearch.org) includes an extracted record for the 1635 birth of William Searle, son of John and Margaret, in Ottery St. Mary. The use of double-dating in the seventeenth century results in this record sometimes being rendered as 1635, and in other cases, such as the Chipstone chest, as 1634. It is unclear if Bennett just missed this record or had other evidence that the 1659 marriage concerned the William born in 1611. Bennett's letter, dated October 14, 1970, is in the Benno Forman Papers, Winterthur Museum.

10. Chris Currie, review, "Discovering Dennis: The Search for Thomas Dennis among the Artisans of Exeter," *Regional Furniture Society Newsletter* 52 (spring 2010): 25.

11. Anthony Wells-Cole, "An Oak Bed at Montacute: A Study in Mannerist Decoration," *Furniture History* 17 (1981): 1–19.

12. For a brief report concerning Exeter studies, see "Recent Events," *Regional Furniture Society Newsletter* 53 (autumn 2010): 7–9.

13. In addition, a believable wainscot cupboard from this shop tradition was advertised in *Antiques* 122, no. 5 (November 1982): 929.

14. The notched rear stiles of an Ipswich chest are illustrated in Fairbanks and Trent, eds., *New England Begins*, 3: 548.

15. Frances Gruber Safford, *American Furniture in the Metropolitan Museum of Art*, vol. 1, *Early Colonial Period: The Seventeenth-Century and William and Mary Styles* (New York: Metropolitan Museum of Art, 2007), pp. 202–4. Two other chests from the Thomas Dennis shop are included in this collection; see pp. 196–202.

16. Robert Blair St. George, *The Wrought Covenant: Source Material for the Study of Craftsmen and Community in Southeastern New England, 1620–1700* (Brockton, Mass.: Fuller Art Museum, 1979).

17. *A Place for Everything: Chests and Boxes in Early Colonial America*, edited by Barbara McLean Ward (Winterthur, Del.: Winterthur Museum, 1986), pp. 9–13, esp. n. 2.

18. Safford, *American Furniture in the Metropolitan Museum of Art*, pp. 200–202.

Compiled by
Gerald W. R. Ward

Recent Writing on
American Furniture:
A Bibliography

This year's list includes works published in 2009 and roughly through October 2010. As always, a few earlier publications that had escaped notice are included. The short title *American Furniture 2009* is used in citations for articles and reviews published in last year's edition of this journal, which is also cited in full under Luke Beckerdite's name.

Once again, many people have assisted in compiling this list. I am particularly grateful to Luke Beckerdite, Dennis Carr, Jonathan Fairbanks, Michelle Finamore, Nonie Gadsden, Steven M. Lash, Kelly H. L'Ecuyer, Johanna McBrien, George Shackelford, Fronia W. Simpson, Laura Fecych Sprague, and Barbara McLean Ward as well as to the scholars who have prepared reviews for this issue. I am also indebted to the librarians of the Museum of Fine Arts, Boston, the Portsmouth Athenaeum, and the Portsmouth Public Library for their ongoing assistance.

It is a pleasure to list below the new Rhode Island furniture database organized under the leadership of Patricia E. Kane for the Yale University Art Gallery. This project-based source is also a reminder that an increasing number of institutions have made their collections available on the web; links to a few of those databases are included below by institution name. There are many more such sites available to the researcher.

I would be glad to receive citations for titles that have been inadvertently omitted from this or previous lists. Information about new publications and review copies of significant works would also be much appreciated.

Ackerman, Daniel Kurt. "Living with Antiques: Shearer Energy." *Antiques* 177, no. 3 (April–May 2010): 138–45. 17 color illus.

———. "A Land of Liberty and Plenty: Georgia Decorative Arts at MESDA." *Antiques and Fine Art* 10, no. 4 (summer/autumn 2010): 214–21. Color illus.

Adamson, Glenn. "Get Out the Lead." *American Craft* 70, no. 2 (April–May 2010): 36–37. 3 color illus.

Adamson, Glenn, ed. *The Craft Reader.* Oxford and New York: Berg, 2010. xiii + 641 pp.; 56 bw illus., index.

Anderson, Jennifer L. "Nature's Currency: The Atlantic Mahogany Trade and the Commodification of Nature in the Eighteenth Century." *Early American Studies* 2, no. 1 (spring 2004): 47–80.

Angers, Shelly. "New Hampshire's New Artist Laureate." *New Hampshire Arts Journal* 2, no. 1 (summer 2010): 2–4. bw illus. (Re David Lamb, furniture craftsman.)

Archer, Sarah. Review of Janet Koplos and Bruce Metcalf, *Makers: A History of American Studio Craft.* In *American Craft* 70, no. 4 (August–September 2010): 17–18.

Arnold, Mark. "2009 Cartouche Award Recipient: Dennis Bork." *American Period Furniture: Journal of the Society of American Period Furniture Makers* 9 (2009): 60–62. Color illus.

Art Institute of Chicago. *Collections Database.* www.artic.edu/aic/collections/amer.

Ayres, James. Review of The Knight of Glin and James Peill, *Irish Furniture: Woodworking and Carving in Ireland from the Earliest Times to the Act of Union.* In *Winterthur Portfolio* 44, no. 1 (spring 2010): 132–34.

Bailey, Chris H. *Fifty Years of Time: The First Fifty Years of the American Clock and Watch Museum.* Bristol, Conn.: American Clock and Watch Museum, 2009. 164 pp.; illus.

Baker, Peggy M. "William Brewster at Pilgrim Hall Museum." *Pilgrim Society News* (February 2010): 14–15. 4 bw illus.

Barter, Judith A., ed., with essays by Sarah E. Kelly, Ellen E. Roberts, Brandon K. Rudd, and Monica Obniski. *Apostles of Beauty: Arts and Crafts from Britain to Chicago.* Chicago: Art Institute of Chicago, 2009. 208 pp.; numerous color and bw illus., bibliography, index. Distributed by Yale University Press, New Haven and London.

Bascom, Mansfield. *Wharton Esherick: The Journey of a Creative Mind.* New York: Abrams, 2010. 275 pp.; numerous color and bw illus.

———. *Wharton Esherick: Studio and Collection.* Ed. Paul Eisenhauer. Atglen, Pa.: Schiffer, 2010. 96 pp.; color illus.

[Bayou Bend Collection and Gardens]. *The Intelligencer, Bayou Bend Collection and Gardens* (fall/winter 2010–2011): 1–74. Color and bw illus. (Special issue re opening of Kilroy Visitor and Education Center.)

Beckerdite, Luke. "American Rococo Looking Glasses: From Maker's Hand to Patron's Home." In *American Furniture 2009,* 2–27. 30 color and bw illus.

Beckerdite, Luke, ed. *American Furniture 2009.* Milwaukee, Wis.: Chipstone Foundation, 2009. vii + 192 pp.; numerous color illus., bibliography, index.

Bell, Nicholas R. "An Ark of the New Republic." In *American Furniture 2009,* 28–41. 18 color and bw illus.

Bennett, Jane. *Vibrant Matter: A Political Economy of Things.* Durham, N.C.: Duke University Press, 2010. xxiv + 176 pp.; bibliography, index.

Bergdoll, Barry, and Leah Dickerman. *Bauhaus 1919–1933: Workshops for Modernity.* New York: Museum of Modern Art, 2009. 344 pp.; numerous color and bw illus., chronology, index.

Berwick, Carly. "Into the Woods." *ARTnews* 109, no. 2 (February 2010): 54–57. Color illus.

Bias, Jerome. "The Trust's MESDA Scholar for 2009." [Newsletter of the] *Decorative Arts Trust* 19, no. 1 (winter 2010): 8–9. 4 bw illus. (Re Thomas Day.)

Blackburn, Roderic H. *Old Homes of New England: Historic Houses in Clapboard, Shingle, and Stone.* New York: Rizzoli, 2010. 256 pp.; numerous color illus., appendix, index. (With many images of interiors with furniture.)

Blaszczyk, Regina Lee. *American Consumer Society, 1865–2005: From Hearth to HDTV.* Wheeling, Ill.: Harlan Davidson, 2009. 330 pp.; 74 bw illus., bibliography, index.

Boradkar, Prasad. *Designing Things: A Critical Introduction to the Study of Objects.* Oxford: Berg, 2010. 320 pp.; 100 bw illus.

Bowett, Adam. *Early Georgian Furniture, 1715–1740.* Woodbridge, Eng.: Antique Collectors' Club, 2009. 328 pp.; 750 color and bw illus., appendixes, bibliography, index.

Bowker, Michael. "French Renaissance." *American Craft* 70, no. 5 (October–November 2010): 28–29. 4 color illus. (Re studio furniture-maker Patrice Pinaquy.)

Brock, Horace Wood, Martin P. Levy, and Clifford S. Ackley. *Splendor and Elegance: European Decorative Arts and Drawings from the Horace Wood Brock Collection.* Boston: MFA Publications, 2009. 160 pp.; 164 color illus.

Brown, Michael K. "Early Rhode Island Table Significant Addition to Bayou Bend Collection." *The Intelligencer, Bayou Bend Collection and Gardens* (winter 2009–2010): 15–16. 2 color illus.

Brownstein, Joan, and Peter Eaton. "A Contemporary Home for a Classic Collection." *Antiques and Fine Art* 10, no. 4 (summer/autumn 2010): 154–69. Color illus.

Bryson, Bill. *At Home: A Short History of Private Life.* New York: Doubleday, 2010. 497 pp.; bw illus., bibliography, index.

Buck, Susan L. "Early Polychrome Chests from Hadley, Massachusetts: A Technical Investigation of Their Paint and Finish." In *American Furniture 2009,* 42–61. 23 color and bw illus.

Burkette, Allison. "The Lion, the Witch, and the Armoire: Lexical Variation in Case Furniture Terms." *American Speech* 84, no. 3 (fall 2009): 315–39.

Busch, Jason, ed. *Decorative Arts and Design: Collection Highlights*. Pittsburgh: Carnegie Museum of Art, 2010. 224 pp.; numerous color illus., index.

Cahan, Richard. "Edgar Miller: Total Art Environments." *Modernism* 13, no. 2 (summer 2010): 56–67. Color illus.

Callahan, Ashley, ed. *A Colorful Past: Decorative Arts of Georgia*. The Fourth Henry Green Symposium of the Decorative Arts. Athens: Georgia Museum of Art, 2008. 149 pp.; numerous color and bw illus. (See, in particular, Ashley Callahan and Dale L. Couch, "New Discoveries in Georgia Painted Furniture," 107–48.)

Carlisle, Nancy, and Peter Gittleman. "Four Centuries at Historic New England." *Antiques and Fine Art* 10, no. 1 (winter/spring 2010): 272–79. 16 color illus.

Carr, Dennis, and Derin Bray. "The Ingenious Patent Extension Tables of Cornelius Briggs." *Antiques and Fine Art* 10, no. 2 (spring 2010): 202–5. 7 color and bw illus.

Carroll, Abigail. "Of Kettles and Cranes: Colonial Revival Kitchens and the Performance of National Identity." *Winterthur Portfolio* 43, no. 4 (winter 2009): 335–64. 22 color and bw illus.

[Castle, Wendell]. *Wendell Castle: Rockin'*. New York: Barry Friedman, 2010. 88 pp.; color illus. (With essay by Robert C. Morgan.)

Chapman, Carol Flake. "Gathering Texas History, Piece by Piece: Bill Hill." *Antiques* 177, no. 5 (September–October 2010): 127–29. 4 color illus.

Chew, Elizabeth V. "New Perspectives on Domestic Life at Monticello." *Antiques and Fine Art* 10, no. 5 (autumn/winter 2010): 142–49. 11 color illus.

Chicirda, Tara L. Gleason. Review of Dean T. Lahikainen, *Samuel McIntire: Carving an American Style*. In *Winterthur Portfolio* 43, no. 4 (winter 2009): 414–16.

Chipstone Foundation. *Collections*. www.chipstone.org/framesetcollection.html.

Clark, Hazel, and David Brody, eds. *Design Studies: A Reader*. Oxford: Berg, 2009. 608 pp.; 50 bw illus.

Clowes, Jody. Exhibition review of "The Artistic Furniture of Charles Rohlfs." In *American Craft* 69, no. 6 (December 2009–January 2010): 36–37. 4 color illus.

Coleman, Brian. Review of Joseph Cunningham, *The Artistic Furniture of Charles Rohlfs*. In *Nineteenth Century* 29, no. 2 (winter 2009): 36–37.

Connors, Michael W. *Caribbean Houses: History, Style, and Architecture*. New York: Rizzoli, 2009. 272 pp.; color illus., map.

Cooper, Wendy A., Patricia Edmonson, and Lisa M. Minardi. "The Compass Artist of Lancaster County, Pennsylvania." In *American Furniture 2009*, 62–87. 47 color and bw illus., maps.

[Crom, Ted, collection]. *Science, Technology, and Clocks, Featuring the Ted Crom Horological Tool Collection and Library*. Sale 2502. Boston: Skinner, May 1, 2010. 150 pp.; numerous color illus.

Culp, Brandy S. "Grandeur Preserved: Historic Charleston Foundation's House Museums and Collection." *Antiques and Fine Art* 10, no. 5 (autumn/winter 2010): 182–89. 12 color illus.

Currie, Chris. Review of Paul Fitzsimmons, Robert Tarule, and Donald P. White III, *Discovering Dennis: The Search for Thomas Dennis among the Artisans of Exeter*. In *Regional Furniture Society Newsletter* 52 (spring 2010): 25.

Czerwinski, Michael. *Fifty Chairs That Changed the World*. London: Conrad Octopus, 2009. 106 pp.; color and bw illus., index.

[Dallas Museum of Art]. "Dallas Museum of Art Acquires Charles Rohlfs' Corner Chair." *Antiques and the Arts Weekly* (December 4, 2009): 34. 1 bw illus.

Dapkus, Mary Jane. "'Henry Terry vs. Matthews et al.': Order and Work Rules in an Antebellum Connecticut Clock Factory." *NAWCC Bulletin* 52, no. 2 (April 2010): 207–9. 1 bw illus.

Davis, Elliot Bostwick, Dennis Carr, Nonie Gadsden, Cody Hartley, Erica H. Hirshler, Heather Hole, Kelly H. L'Ecuyer, Karen E. Quinn, Dorie Reents-Budet, and Gerald W. R.

Ward. *A New World Imagined: Art of the Americas*. Boston: MFA Publications, 2010. 360 pp.; 285 color and 4 bw illus., bibliography, index. (Includes some furniture.)

Davison, Elizabeth A. "Images of Loyalism and Heritage in John Shearer's Furniture." *Antiques* 177, no. 3 (April–May 2010): 146–53. 6 color illus.

Dejean, Joan. *The Age of Comfort: When Paris Discovered Casual and the Modern Age Began*. New York: Bloomsbury, 2009. 295 pp.; color and bw illus., bibliography, index.

Dervan, Andrew H. "Mt. Vernon Tablets on Full-Size Waltham Clocks." *NAWCC Bulletin* 52, no. 2 (April 2010): 169–72. 12+ color illus.

Deutsch, Alexandra. "With an Artistic Eye: Folk Art at the Maryland Historical Society." *Antiques and Fine Art* 10, no. 2 (spring 2010): 212–19. Color illus.

Dietz, Ulysses G. [Untitled note re lady's secretary of 1878 reattributed by the author from Herter Brothers to Pottier and Stymus, New York; acquired by the Newark Museum]. *Antiques* 177, no. 5 (September–October 2010): 70. 1 color illus. [See also detail on p. 72.]

DiNoto, Andrea. "Mining the Beauty of Coal." *American Craft* 70, no. 1 (February–March 2010): 30–31. 4 color illus.

"'Dominy Craftsmen' on View at Clinton Academy Museum." *Antiques and the Arts Weekly* (June 11, 2010): 27. 1 bw illus.

Duncan, Alastair. *Art Deco Complete: The Definitive Guide to the Decorative Arts of the 1920s and 1930s*. New York: Abrams, 2009. 544 pp.; numerous color and bw illus.

Evans, Jeffrey S., with contributions by W. Wayne Anderson and Scott Hamilton Suter. *Come In and Have a Seat: Vernacular Chairs of the Shenandoah Valley*. Winchester, Va.: Museum of the Shenandoah Valley, 2010. 84 pp.; color and bw illus.

Fallan, Kjetil. *Design History: Understanding Theory and Method*. Oxford: Berg, 2010. 242 pp.; 20 bw illus.

Fenster, Julie M. *The Spirit of Invention: The Story of the Thinkers, Creators, and Dreamers Who Formed Our Nation*. New York: HarperCollins. 2009. xiii + 209 pp.; numerous bw illus., bibliography, index.

[Fine Collection]. *The M. Austin and Jill R. Fine Collection*. Portsmouth, N.H.: Northeast Auctions, August 7, 2010. 132 pp.; numerous color illus.

Fischer, Claude S. *Made in America: A Social History of American Culture and Character*. Chicago: University of Chicago Press, 2010. x + 511 pp.; bibliography, index. (With some references to furnishings.)

Fiske, John, and Peter Eaton. "What's New Hampshire about New Hampshire Furniture?" *New England Antiques Journal* 29, no. 2 (August 2010): 22–27. Color illus.

Fitzgerald, Oscar P. *New Masters of the Wooden Box: Expanding the Boundaries of Box Making*. East Petersburg, Va.: Fox Chapel, 2009. 208 pp.; illus., bibliography, index.

Fitzsimmons, Paul, Robert Tarule, and Donald P. White III. *Discovering Dennis: The Search for Thomas Dennis among the Artisans of Exeter*. Exeter, Eng.: Marhamchurch Antiques, 2009. 50 pp.; color illus.

———. "The English Roots of Thomas Dennis, American Joiner." *New England Antiques Journal* (January 2010): 22–30. Illus.

Fort, Megan Holloway. "Current and Coming: Georgia on Our Minds." *Antiques* 176, no. 4 (October 2009): 16–17. 2 color illus.

———. "Current and Coming: Virginia Vernacular." *Antiques* 176, no. 6 (December 2009): 20–22. 1 color illus.

[Foster-Lemmens Collection]. *The Foster-Lemmons Collection*. Portsmouth, N.H.: Northeast Auctions, August 8, 2010. 104 pp.; numerous color illus.

Friedel, Robert. *A Culture of Improvement: Technology and the Western Millennium*. Cambridge, Mass.: MIT Press, 2007. 588 pp.; bw illus., index.

Frost, Randy O., and Gail Steketee. *Stuff: Compulsive Hoarding and the Meaning of Things*. Boston: Houghton Mifflin Harcourt, 2010. 290 pp.; reference list. (Sheds light on some collectors.)

[Gendron Collection]. *Annual Summer Americana Auction*. Portsmouth, N.H.: Northeast Auctions, August 6–8, 2010. 164 pp.; numerous color illus. (See pp. 90–109.)

Gontar, Cybèle T. "New Light: Spanish Chairs in the New Republic." *Antiques* 177, no. 4 (summer 2010): 78–82. 7 color illus.

———. "Furniture Collecting in Louisiana." *Antiques and Fine Art* 10, no. 4 (summer/autumn 2010): 206–13. Color illus.

Gordon, Glenn. "Plane Views." *American Craft* 70, no. 2 (April–May 2010): 28–29. 3 color illus.

Greenfield, Briann G. *Out of the Attic: Inventing Antiques in Twentieth-Century New England*. Amherst and Boston: University of Massachusetts Press, 2009. xii + 265 pp.; 31 bw illus., index.

Gustafson, Eleanor H. "Living with Antiques: One House, Two Worlds." *Antiques* 177, no. 3 (April–May 2010): 104–13. 13 color illus.

Hamilton, Timothy. "A Fine Chippendale Mahogany Desk-and-Bookcase, Philadelphia, 1760–1775." *Arader Galleries Director's Report* (September–October 2009): 1. 1 color illus.

[Henderson, William P.] *An American Journey: The Art of William P. Henderson*. Santa Fe: Owings Gallery, 2010. 64 pp.; color and bw illus. (Essay by Karl L. Horn.)

Historic New England. *Collections Access*. www.historicnewengland.org/collections-archives-exhibitions/collections-access. (Includes many categories of library, archives, and museum collections.)

Hosley, William. "Inspired Innovations: A Celebration of Shaker Ingenuity." *Antiques and the Arts Weekly* (March 12, 2010): 1, 50–51. 15 bw illus.

Huggins, Maryalice. *Aesop's Mirror: A Love Story*. New York: Farrar, Straus and Giroux, 2009. xii + 270 pp.; bw illus., bibliography.

Hussey, David, and Margaret Ponsonby, eds. *Buying for the Home: Shopping for the Domestic from the Seventeenth Century to the Present*. Aldershot, Eng., and Burlington, Vt.: Ashgate, 2008. 218 pp.; 20 bw illus., index.

Jaffee, David. *A New Nation of Goods: The Material Culture of Early America*. Philadelphia: University of Pennsylvania Press, 2010. xv + 400 pp.; 108 color and bw illus., index.

Jellinek, Tobias. *Early British Chairs and Seats, 1500 to 1700*. Woodbridge, Eng.: Antique Collectors' Club, 2009. 328 pp.; 500+ color illus.

Johnson, Kathleen Eagen. *The Hudson-Fulton Celebration: New York's River Festival of 1909 and the Making of a Metropolis*. Tarrytown, N.Y.: Historic Hudson Valley and Fordham University Press, 2009. 202 pp.; 132 color and 107 bw illus., bibliography, appendixes, index.

Johnston, Nancy N. "A Way of Life: Adventures in Collecting." *Antiques and Fine Art* 10, no. 1 (winter/spring 2010): 228–39. Color illus.

Kaminsky, Christine. "Judy Kensley McKie." *American Craft* 70, no. 2 (April–May 2010): 72. 3 color illus.

Kammen, Michael. "Moving Forward at Bayou Bend." *Antiques* 177, no. 5 (September–October 2010): 120–26. 15 color illus.

Kane, Patricia E. "A Newly Discovered Rhode Island Cabinetmaker: Thomas Spencer of East Greenwich." *Antiques* 177, no. 3 (April–May 2010): 114–19. 5 color illus.

Keno, Leigh, and Leslie Keno. "My Favorite Things." *Historic New England* 10, no. 3 (winter/spring 2010): 32–33. 4 color illus.

Kirtley, Alexandra Alevizatos. "Contriving the Madisons' Drawing Room: Benjamin Henry Latrobe and the Furniture of John and Hugh Finlay." *Antiques* 176, no. 6 (December 2009): 56–63. 13 color illus.

———. "Living with Antiques: Pennsylvania Style." *Antiques* 177, no. 1 (January 2010): 216–25. 17 color illus.

———. "The Ties That Bind: New Light on Philadelphia Cabinetmaker Thomas Affleck." *Antiques* 177, no. 5

(September–October 2010): 150–57. 11 color illus.

Klanton, Robert, Sven Ehmann, Andrej Kupetz, and Shonquis Moreno, eds. *Once upon a Chair: Design beyond the Icon*. Berlin: Gestolten, 2009. 272 pp.; numerous color illus., index. (Re modern European design.)

Kolosek, Lisa Schlansker. "Helen Appleton Read: Tastemaker." *Antiques* 177, no. 1 (January 2010): 242–47. 11 color and bw illus.

Koplos, Janet, and Bruce Metcalf. *Makers: A History of American Studio Craft*. A Project of the University of North Carolina Center for Craft, Creativity, and Design. Durham: University of North Carolina Press, 2010. xi + 529 pp.; 409 color and 50 bw illus., index.

Koverman, Jill Beute. Review of Patricia Phillips Marshall and Jo Ramsay Leimenstoll. *Thomas Day: Master Craftsman and Free Man of Color*. In *American Craft* 70, no. 5 (October–November 2010): 12. 2 color illus.

Krashes, David. "Collecting Fifty Years Ago." *Maine Antique Digest* 38, no. 8 (August 2010): 21C. 4 bw illus.

Krill, Rosemary Troy. *Early American Decorative Arts, 1620–1860: A Handbook for Interpreters*. Rev. ed. Walnut Creek, Calif.; AltaMira Press, 2010. 324 pp.; illus. (Includes a CD of illustrations.)

Krohn, Deborah, and Peter N. Miller, eds., with Marybeth De Filippis. *Dutch New York between East and West: The World of Margrieta van Varick*. New Haven and London: Yale University Press for the Bard Graduate Center; Decorative Arts, Design History, Material Culture, New York, 2009. 424 pp.; 336 color and 3 bw illus., 3 appendixes, glossary, bibliography, index.

Lang, Brian J. "Columbia Museum of Art Unveils New American Art Galleries." *Antiques and Fine Art* 10, no. 1 (winter/spring 2010): 164–66, 194. Color illus.

Lapp, Herb. "Early American Comb-Back Windsor Chairs." *American Period Furniture: Journal of the Society of American Period Furniture Makers* 9 (2009): 42–50. 25 color illus.

Larson, Frances. *An Infinity of Things: How Sir Henry Wellcome Collected the World*. New York: Oxford University Press, 2009. xiii + 343 pp.; bw illus., bibliography, index. (Of interest re the history of collecting in general and period-room displays of artifacts.)

Lauria, Jo. "Expanding the Toolbox." *American Craft* 70, no. 2 (April–May 2010): 50–57. Color illus.

Leach, Ralph Denton, Jr., and Andrew H. Dervan. "Unraveling the Mysteries of Killam & Co." *NAWCC Bulletin* 52 (October 2010): 531–35. 7+ bw and color illus.

Lees-Maffer, Grace, and Rebecca Houze, eds. *The Design History Reader*. Oxford: Berg, 2010. 544 pp.; 70 bw illus.

Lemire, Elise. *Black Walden: Slavery and Its Aftermath in Concord, Massachusetts*. Philadelphia: University of Pennsylvania Press, 2009. 233 pp.; 10 bw illus., bibliography, index.

Lidz, Maggie. "English Regency Wrought Iron Garden Furniture." *Antiques and Fine Art* 10, no. 2 (spring 2010): 200–201. 2 color illus.

Linley, David, Charles Cator, and Helen Chislett. *Star Pieces: The Enduring Beauty of Spectacular Furniture*. New York: Monacelli Press, 2009. 256 pp.; numerous color illus., bibliography, index.

Long, Christopher. "Design and Reform: The Making of the Bauhaus." *Antiques* 176, no. 4 (October 2009): 78–87. 17 color and bw illus.

– – –. Review of Phyllis Ross, *Gilbert Rohde: Modern Design for Modern Living*. In *American Furniture 2009*, 159–62.

Lovell, Sophie. *Limited Edition: Prototypes, One-Offs, and Design Art Furniture*. Basel, Boston, and Berlin: Birkhauser, 2009. 256 pp.; numerous color illus.

Lucas, June. "Paint-Decorated Furniture from Piedmont North Carolina." In *American Furniture 2009*, 88–139. 81 color and bw illus., maps.

Luhrs, Kathleen. "Museum Accessions." *Antiques* 177, no. 1 (January 2010): 46–50. 8 color illus.

Luse, Mimi. "Matthew Fairbank: Furniture to Keep." *American Craft* 70,

no. 4 (August–September 2010): 42–49. Color illus.

Lutz, Brian. *Knoll: A Modernist Universe*. New York: Rizzoli, 2010. 299 pp.; numerous color and bw illus.

Mack, Daniel. *The Hammock: A Celebration of a Summer Classic*. New York: Stewart, Tabori, and Chang, 2008. 128 pp.; numerous color and bw illus.

MacLeish, A. Bruce. "New Acquisitions." *Antiques and Fine Art* 10, no. 4 (summer/autumn 2010): 50. 2 color illus. (Re desk with initials of John Townsend and a writing table, ca. 1740–1760, both acquired by the Whitehorne House of Newport Restoration Foundation.)

[*Maine Antique Digest* staff]. Review of Philip D. Zimmerman, *Harmony in Wood: Furniture of the Harmony Society*. In *Maine Antique Digest* 38, no. 12 (December 2010): 38B. 1 bw illus. (Signed A. C. V.)

Mair, Victor H., and Erling Hoh. *The True History of Tea*. New York: Thames and Hudson, 2009. 280 pp.; 82 bw illus., 3 appendixes, bibliography, index.

Mansfield, Howard. "Living with Antiques: Two of a Kind." *Antiques* 177, no. 5 (September–October 2010): 158–67. 16 color illus.

Marshall, Patricia Phillips, and Jo Ramsay Leimenstoll. *Thomas Day: Master Craftsman and Free Man of Color*. The Richard Jenrette Series in Architecture and the Decorative Arts. Chapel Hill: University of North Carolina Press, in association with the North Carolina Museum of History, 2010. xii + 289 pp.; numerous color and bw illus., 2 appendixes, bibliography, index.

Matthias, David. *Greene & Greene Furniture: Poems of Wood and Light*. Cincinnati, Ohio: Betterway Home, 2010. 175 pp.; numerous color and bw illus., line drawings, index.

May, Stephen. "Gustav Stickley and the American Arts and Crafts Movement at Newark Museum." *Antiques and the Arts Weekly* (September 3, 2010): 1, 30–31. 14 bw illus.

Mayer, Roberta. *Lockwood de Forest: Furnishing the Gilded Age with a Passion for India.* Newark: University of Delaware Press, 2009. 283 pp.; 60 color and 132 bw illus., bibliography, index.

McBrien, Johanna. "The Dynamics of Collecting." *Antiques and Fine Art* 10, no. 1 (winter/spring 2010): 198–211. Color illus.

———. "Touching History." *Antiques and Fine Art* 10, no. 5 (autumn/winter 2010): 120–31. Color illus.

McCrossen, Alexis. "The 'Very Delicate Construction' of Pocket Watches and Time Consciousness in the Nineteenth-Century United States." *Winterthur Portfolio* 44, no. 1 (spring 2010): 1–30. 25 color and bw illus., 10 tables, appendix.

Metropolitan Museum of Art. *Collections Database.* www.metmuseum.org/works_of_art/collection_database/.

Miller, Marla R. *Betsy Ross and the Making of America.* New York: Henry Holt, 2010. 467 pp.; bw illus., index. (With relevance to Philadelphia upholstery trade.)

Miller, M. Stephen. *Inspired Innovations: A Celebration of Shaker Ingenuity.* Hanover, N.H.: University Press of New England, 2010. xiv + 226 pp.; numerous color and bw illus., index.

Moore, William D. Review of Stephen Bowe and Peter Richmond, *Selling Shaker: The Commodification of Shaker Design in the Twentieth Century.* In *Winterthur Portfolio* 43, no. 4 (winter 2009): 409–11.

Moreno, Shonquis. "Quiet Riot." *American Craft* 70, no. 4 (August–September 2010): 26–27. 7 color illus. (Re Brazilian furniture-maker Rodrigo Almeida.)

Moscou, Margo Preston. *New Orleans' Free-Men-of-Color: Cabinet Makers in the New Orleans Furniture Trade, 1800–1850.* New Orleans: Xavier Review Press, 2008. xxii + 96 pp.; illus.

———. "The Rise of a Lost Generation." *Historical New Orleans Collections Quarterly* 26, no. 2 (spring 2009): 4–6. Color illus.

Museum of Fine Arts, Boston. *Collections.* www.mfa.org/collections.

Muthesius, Stefan. *The Poetic Home: Designing the Nineteenth-Century*

Domestic Interior. New York: Thames and Hudson, 2009. 352 pp.; color and bw illus., bibliography, index.

[Nakashima, George]. "Nakashima's 'Early Furniture' on View at Moderne Gallery." *Antiques and the Arts Weekly* (October 30, 2009): 20. 1 bw illus.

National Watch & Clock Museum. *Museum Collection.* www.nawcc.org/index.php/museum-collection.

Newbern, Thomas R. J., and James R. Melchor. *WH Cabinetmaker: A Southern Mystery Solved.* N.p.: Legacy Ink Publishing, 2009. ix + 294 pp.; numerous color and bw illus., maps, plans.

[New Hampshire Furniture Masters Association]. *Unsurpassed Artistry: New Hampshire Furniture Masters 2009.* Manchester, N.H.: New Hampshire Furniture Masters Association, 2009. 33 pp.; color illus.

[New Hampshire Furniture Masters]. "Currier Museum to Host NH Furniture Masters Auction." *Antiques and the Arts Weekly* (September 3, 2010): 3. 2 bw illus.

North Bennet Street School. *Annual Report 2009.* Boston: North Bennet Street School, 2009. 24 pp.; color illus. (See discussion of exhibition at Concord Museum.)

"Noteworthy Sales." *Antiques and Fine Art* 10, no. 1 (winter/spring 2010): 24. 3 color illus. (Re John Bailey Jr. tall clock sold privately, and American Centripetal spring chairs acquired by Brooklyn Museum and Victoria and Albert Museum.)

Nutt, Craig. "Brian Ferrell: Static." *American Craft* 70, no. 2 (April–May 2010): 35. 2 color illus.

Obniski, Monica, and Brandon K. Rudd. "Chicago and the Arts and Crafts Movement." *Antiques* 176, no. 4 (October 2009): 96–101. 9 color and bw illus.

O'Brien, Liz. *Ultra Modern, Samuel Marx: Architect, Designer, Art Collector.* New York: Pointed Leaf Press, 2007. 216 pp.; illus.

[Old Sturbridge Village]. "Inland Mass. Furniture, 1790–1830, at Old Sturbridge Village Museum." *Antiques and the*

Arts Weekly (October 16, 2009): 32. 2 bw illus.

O'Leary, Elizabeth, Sylvia Yount, Susan J. Rawles, and David Park Curry. *American Art at the Virginia Museum of Fine Arts.* Richmond: Virginia Museum of Fine Arts, in association with the University of Virginia Press, 2010. 432 pp.; 360 color and 60 bw illus.

O'Neill, Stephen C. "First an Owner, Now a Maker, for the Cushman Chest." *Pilgrim Society News* (February 2010): 16–17. 1 bw illus. (Re chest of drawers attributed to Robert Crossman of Taunton, Massachusetts.)

Oney, Steve. "Los Angeles Folk." *Antiques* 177, no. 4 (summer 2010): 184–92. 20 color illus.

Pearce, Clark, and Kemble Widmer II. "Mr. Luscomb's Desk." *Antiques and Fine Art* 10, no. 4 (summer/autumn 2010): 224–25. 3 color illus. (Re Salem desk of 1794 made by Elijah and Jacob Sanderson for William Luscomb.)

Pierce, Donna, and Ronald Otsuka, eds. *Asia and Spanish America: Trans-Pacific Artistic and Cultural Exchange, 1500–1850: Papers from the 2006 Mayer Center Symposium at the Denver Art Museum.* Denver: Frederick and Jan Mayer Center for Pre-Columbian and Spanish Colonial Art at the Denver Art Museum, 2009. 200 pp.; numerous color and bw illus., maps. (Includes several furniture-related articles.)

Pochada, Elizabeth. "Living with Antiques: Rohde Show." *Antiques* 177, no. 5 (September–October 2010): 142–49. 14 color illus.

Poirier, Noel. "Collection Database Accessible Online." *NAWCC Bulletin* 52, no. 5 (October 2010): 592. 1 bw illus. (Can be accessed through the museum's website or at http://nawcc.pastperfect-online.com; with references to ca. 12,000 objects and 5,000 images.)

Polan, Judy. "Milo Baughman Revealed." *Modernism* 13, no. 2 (summer 2010): 46–54. Color illus.

Prickett, C. L. *Fine Authenticated American Antiques from the C. L. Prickett Collection.* Yardley, Pa.: C. L. Prickett, 2010. 36 pp.; color illus.

Priddy, Sumpter, III. "Regional Matters: Roddy and Sally Moore, Collectors." *Antiques* 177, no. 3 (April–May 2010): 120–31. 19 color illus.

Prioleau, Robert Means, Harriott Cheves Leland, and Dianne Watts Ressinger. *Huguenot Footprints: The Journey to America*. Charleston: Huguenot Society of South Carolina, 2010. vii + 49 pp.; 37 bw illus., bibliography.

Pulinka, Steven M. "Dedication to Preservation: One Couple's Mission." *Antiques and Fine Art* 10, no. 1 (winter/spring 2010): 212–27. Color illus.

Pynt, Jennifer, and Joy Higgs. "Nineteenth-Century Patent Seating: Too Comfortable to Be Moral?" *Journal of Design History* 21, no. 3 (autumn 2008): 277–88.

Raizman, David. *History of Modern Design: Graphics and Products since the Industrial Revolution*. 2nd ed. London: Laurence King, 2010. 432 pp.; numerous illus.

Riegler, Shax. "The Legacy of Henry Davis Sleeper." *Antiques* 176, no. 6 (December 2009): 49–55. 7 color illus.

Ross, Phyllis. "Gilbert Rohde: Innovations for Modern Living." *Modernism* 12, no. 4 (winter 2009–2010): 45–55. Color and bw illus.

Routhier, Jessie Skwire. "Making History: Art and Industry in the Saco River Valley." *Antiques and Fine Art* 10, no. 3 (summer 2010): 158–63. (Includes tall-case clock by Moulton and Forsskol of Saco, ca. 1810–1820.)

Salm, Betsy Krieg. *Women's Painted Furniture, 1790–1830: American Schoolgirl Art*. Hanover, N.H., and London: University Press of New England, 2010. xvii + 223 pp.; numerous color and bw illus., 9 appendixes, glossary, bibliography, index.

Scheller, W. G. *America, a History in Art: The American Journey Told by Painters, Sculptors, Photographers, and Architects*. New York: Black Dog and Leventhal, 2008. 320 pp.; numerous color and bw illus., index. (Includes some furniture.)

Scherer, Barrymore Laurence. "Destination Pittsburgh." *Antiques* 177, no. 1 (January 2010): 206–15. Color illus.

Schinto, Jeanne. "'Miss Edgerton's Ye Colonial Shoppe' or Women in the Trade, Part II." *Maine Antique Digest* 38, no. 8 (August 2010): 36B–38B. 6 bw illus.

———. Review of Chris H. Bailey, *Fifty Years of Time: The First Fifty Years of the American Clock and Watch Museum*. In *Maine Antique Digest* 38, no. 8 (August 2010): 18F–19F. 1 bw illus.

Shallcross, Gilian. *The MFA Handbook: A Guide to the Collections of the Museum of Fine Arts, Boston*. Rev. ed. Boston: MFA Publications, 2009. 400 pp.; 500 color illus., index.

Smith, David S. Review of "Apostles of Beauty: Arts and Crafts from Britain to Chicago." In *Antiques and the Arts Weekly* (January 1, 2010): 1, 24–25. 15 bw illus.

Smith-Rosenberg, Carroll. *This Violent Empire: The Birth of an American National Identity*. Chapel Hill: University of North Carolina Press for the Omohundro Institute of Early American History and Culture, Williamsburg, Virginia, 2010. xxii + 484 pp.; 22 bw illus., index.

Snodin, Michael, ed., with the assistance of Cynthia Roman. *Horace Walpole's Strawberry Hill*. New Haven and London: Lewis Walpole Library, Yale University; Yale Center for British Art; and Victoria and Albert Museum, in association with Yale University Press, 2009. xv + 368 pp.; numerous color illus., bibliography, index.

Snyder, Alan. "Patriotic Eagle Inlays on Federal Furniture." *Maine Antique Digest* 38, no. 6 (June 2010): 26B–30B. 23+ bw illus.

Society of American Period Furniture Makers. *American Period Furniture: Journal of the Society of American Period Furniture Makers* 9 (2009): 1–108. Color and bw illus.

Solis-Cohen, Lita. "A Spirit of Simplicity." *Maine Antique Digest* 37, no. 12 (December 2009): 10A. 1 bw illus. (Re exhibition of Rudy Ciccarello collection of arts and crafts material at Flagler Museum, Palm Beach, Florida.)

———. "Early Work of Nakashima at Moderne Gallery in Philadelphia." *Maine Antique Digest* 37, no. 12 (December 2009): 12A. 1 bw illus.

———. "The Carnegie Museum Celebrates Decorative Arts." *Maine Antique Digest* 38, no. 6 (June 2010): 10B–12B. bw illus.

———. Review of Luke Beckerdite, ed., *American Furniture 2009*. In *Maine Antique Digest* 38, no. 6 (June 2010): 20C–21C. 1 bw illus.

———. Review of Roberta A. Mayer, *Lockwood de Forest*. In *Maine Antique Digest* 38, no. 6 (June 2010): 22C–23C. 1 bw illus.

———. "Fake Rose Valley Table Exposed." *Maine Antique Digest* 38, no. 8 (August 2010): 20D–21D. 11 bw illus.

Sparke, Penny, Anne Weallens, Trevor Keeble, and Brenda Martin. *Designing the Modern Interior: From the Victorians to Today*. Basingstoke, Eng., and New York: Palgrave Macmillan, 2009. 311 pp.; 77 bw illus., bibliography, index.

Sperling, David A. "The War of 1812: Timely Reflections: Part 1, 1812." *NAWCC Bulletin* 51, no. 6 (December 2009): 657–64. Color and bw illus.

———. Review of Frank L. Hohmann III et al., *Timeless: Masterpiece American Brass Dial Clocks*. In *Maine Antique Digest* 37, no. 12 (December 2009): 39D. 1 bw illus.

———. "The War of 1812: Timely Reflections: Part 2, 1813–1815." *NAWCC Bulletin* 52, no. 1 (February 2010): 25–32. Color and bw illus.

———. "A Willard Banjo Clock circa 1982: When Old Becomes New Again." *NAWCC Bulletin* 52, no. 4 (August 2010): 388–92. 10 bw illus.

———. "Johnson Clockmakers of Sanbornton: Highly Regarded, Little Known." *Maine Antique Digest* 38, no. 10 (October 2010): 44C–47C. 24 bw illus.

———. "Will the Real John Adams Please Stand Up?" *Maine Antique Digest* 38, no. 12 (December 2010): 8C–10C. 10+ bw illus.

Spittler, Tom. "'Boston' Dials." *NAWCC Bulletin* 52, no. 2 (April 2010): 168. 1 color illus.

———. "William Jones of Philadelphia Dials." *NAWCC Bulletin* 52, no. 5 (October 2010): 536. 1 color illus.

Sprague, Laura Fecych. "Sit Down! Chairs from Six Centuries." *Antiques and Fine Art* 10, no. 5 (autumn/winter 2010): 204–9. 10 color and bw illus.

———. *Sit Down! Chairs from Six Centuries*. Brunswick, Maine: Bowdoin College Museum of Art, 2010. Unpaged brochure; color and bw illus.

Stillinger, Elizabeth. "Isabel Carleton Wilde." *Antiques* 177, no. 1 (January 2010): 234–41. 14 color illus.

Stout, Brian E. "American China Cased Clocks." *NAWCC Bulletin* 52 (October 2010): 515–20. 12 color illus., bibliography.

Stuart, Susan E. *Gillows of Lancaster and London, 1730–1840: Cabinetmakers and International Merchants, A Furniture and Business History*. 2 vols. Woodbridge, Eng., and Easthampton, Mass.: Antique Collectors' Club, 2008. Vol. 1: 448 pp.; 367 color and 228 bw illus. Vol. 2: 415 pp.; 290 color and 105 bw illus., glossary, 5 appendixes, bibliography, index. (See also review by Martin Levy in *Studies in the Decorative Arts* 17, no. 1 [fall/winter 2009–2010]: 208–13.)

[Suffolk County (New York) Historical Society]. "Victorian Parlor Furniture on View at Suffolk County Historical Society." *Antiques and the Arts Weekly* (February 5, 2010): 76. 3 bw illus.

Symons, Allan. "The House of Snider: Harry Snider's Clock Companies in Toronto, 1950–1976." *NAWCC Bulletin* 52, no. 2 (April 2010): 173–81. 35 color and bw illus.

Thompson, Jane, and Alexandra Lange. *Design Research: The Store That Brought Modern Living to American Homes*. San Francisco: Chronicle Books, 2010. 192 pp.; numerous color and bw illus.

Tucker, Kevin W. "A Well-Crafted Table: Gustav Stickley's Model Dining Room of 1893." *Antiques* 177, no. 5 (September–October 2010): 104–11. 14 color and bw illus.

Tucker, Kevin W., with essays and contributions by Beverly K. Brandt,

David Cathers, Joseph Cunningham, Beth Ann McPherson, Tommy McPherson, and with contributions by Sally-Anne Huxtable. *Gustav Stickley and the American Arts and Crafts Movement*. New Haven, Conn.: Yale University Press, in association with Dallas Museum of Art, 2010. 271 pp.; numerous color and bw illus., catalogue, bibliography, index.

Valluzzo, Andrea. "Convenient and Fashionable: Furniture of Inland Massachusetts Showcases Federal Furniture at Old Sturbridge Village." *Antiques and the Arts Weekly* (January 8, 2010): 1, 40–41. 10 bw illus.

Vogt, Rick. "A Conservation Collaboration: The James Monroe Gilded Ceremonial Armchair." *Antiques* 177, no. 2 (March 2010): 80–83. 5 color illus. (Re an Italian upholstered chair of ca. 1806.)

Ward, Gerald W. R., comp. "Recent Writing on American Furniture: A Bibliography." In *American Furniture 2009*, 175–81.

Waterhouse, George, and Peter Schreiner. "A Clock of the State of Georgia Governor's Mansion." *NAWCC Bulletin* 52 (October 2010): 526–30. 9 color illus.

Wharton, Edith, and Ogden Codman. *The Decoration of Houses*. 1897. Reprint. New York: Rizzoli and the Mount Press, 2007. xxii + 204 pp.; bw illus., bibliography, index. (New foreword by Richard Guy Wilson.)

Widmer, Kemble, and Joyce King. "The Cabots of Salem and Beverly: A Fondness for the Bombé Form." *Antiques and Fine Art* 10, no. 2 (spring 2010): 166–75. 11 color and bw illus., tables.

Wilkinson, Randy. "New London County Connecticut Furniture." *American Period Furniture: Journal of the Society of American Period Furniture Makers* 9 (2009): 78–85. 18 color and bw illus., bibliography.

Williams, Donald C. "The Art of Japanning." *American Period Furniture: Journal of the Society of American Period Furniture Makers* 9 (2009): 4–11. 31 color and bw illus.

Williams, Gareth. *Telling Tales: Fantasy and Fear in Contemporary Design*. London: V&A Publications, 2009. 128 pp.; 78 color illus., catalogue, bibliography, index.

Williamson, Leslie. *Handcrafted Modern: At Home with Mid-Century Designers*. New York: Rizzoli, 2010. 224 pp.; illus.

Wilson, Kristina. "Saarinen's Womb Chair and the Mainstreaming of American Modernism." *Antiques* 177, no. 3 (April–May 2010): 132–37. 7 color illus.

[Winterthur Museum]. "Recent Acquisitions." In *Winterthur in Review*, 26–31. Winterthur, Del.: Winterthur Museum and Country Estate, 2009. 19 color illus.

Wood, David F. Review of George Kubler, *The Shape of Time: Remarks on the History of Things*. In *American Furniture 2009*, 163–69.

Wood, Lucy. *The Upholstered Furniture in the Lady Lever Art Gallery*. 2 vols. New Haven and London: Yale University Press, 2009. 1,200 pp.; 140 color and 2,000 bw illus., 10 appendixes, bibliography, index. (See also review by Geoffrey Beard in *Studies in the Decorative Arts* 17, no. 1 [fall/winter 2009–2010]: 206–7.)

Yale University Art Gallery. *Collections Database*. http://ecatalogue.art.yale.cdu/search.htm (Provides access to some 86,400 objects in the museum's collection.)

Yale University Art Gallery. *Rhode Island Furniture Archive at the Yale University Art Gallery*. Patricia E. Kane, project director. http://rifa.art.yale.edu/. (As noted on its website, this large new archive "documents furniture and furniture making in Rhode Island from . . . 1636 through the early nineteenth century. Bringing together records of surviving furniture, individuals who owned it, and known furniture makers, this archive aims to provide a complete account of the specific culture, local variations, and artistic practices surrounding the first two centuries of furniture making in Rhode Island.")

[Yale University Art Gallery]. "Yale University Art Gallery Seeks Info on 'Dan Spencer' Desk and Bookcase." *Antiques and the Arts Weekly* (December 4, 2009): 8. 1 bw illus.

Zimmerman, Philip D. "The 'Boston Chairs' of Mid-Eighteenth-Century Philadelphia." In *American Furniture 2009*, 140–58. 22 color and bw illus.

———. Review of Frank L. Hohmann III et al., *Timeless: Masterpiece American Brass Dial Clocks*. In *American Furniture 2009*, 169–73.

———. *Harmony in Wood: Furniture of the Harmony Society*. Ambridge, Pa.: Friends of Old Harmony Village, 2010. x + 214 pp.; numerous color and bw illus., bibliography, index. Distributed by University Press of New England.

———. "Notes on the Furniture at Boscobel." *Antiques* 177, no. 3 (April–May 2010): 154–61. 7 color illus.

Index

98–99; stone carvers and, 100–1; stone carvings, 113(fig. 59); view of, 76(fig. 2)

U.S. Census of Manufactures, 127

U.S. Senate, stone carving, 101(figs. 42, 44)

User, physical relationship to object, 55–68, 74–75*n*4

Valaperta, Giuseppe, 112, 113(fig. 59), 129, 137*n*70

Value, defining, 242

Vander Sande, John D., 178

Varrin, Thomas, 202

Vasiform banisters, 149(&fig. 20), 153, 182–83

Victoria and Albert Museum, 262

View from the Window of My Chamber at Tremoulet's Hotel, New Orleans (Latrobe), 37(fig. 13)

A View of New Orleans . . . (Boqueta de Woiseri), 35(fig. 11)

Vincent, Robert, 99(fig.), 134*n*38

Virginia red cedar (*Juniperus virginiana*), 226

Virginia State Capitol, 79, 81

Virginia walnut, 222

Volutes, 146

Vose, Isaac, 26*n*7, 26*n*12

Voussoirs, 217

Voyseyan home, Rohlfs and, 250

V-V-ogee molding, 264, 267

Wainscot fleets, 209

Wakfeld, Obediah, 235*n*20

Waln, William, 4, 25*n*4

Walnut: armchair, 65(fig. 14); cabinet, 222(fig. 31); Campeche chairs and, 31(fig. 5); catafalque, 87(fig. 18); chests, 216(fig. 22), 217(fig. 24); chests of drawers, 224(fig. 35), 225(fig. 37); cupboard with drawers, 214(fig.); desk-and-bookcase, 80(fig. 5); side chairs, 59(fig.), 63(fig. 9), 91(fig. 25), 149(fig. 21); *sillon da cadera*, 31(fig. 4); sofa, 114(fig. 61)

Walters, William, 135*n*50

Warren, James, 24

Warren, Mercy Otis, 24

Washington, D.C. *See* District of Columbia

Washington, George, 38, 77, 84; casket and catafalque for, 87; Ingle and, 82; sculpture of, 79

Washington, Martha, 132*n*21

Washington Building Company, 131*n*8

Washington family, 78

Washington Gazette, 135*n*45

Washington Historical Society, 132*n*13

Waters, Elizabeth (Shaw), 102

Waters, Somersett, 135*n*50

Waters, Walter, 135*n*50

Waters, William, 102–7, 119, 135*n*45; advertisements, 102; civic positions, 102–3; mercantile pursuits and, 106; sofas, 103–5(&figs. 45–48)

Waters, William, Sr., 135*n*50

Watkins, C. Malcolm, 246–47

Weare, Meschach, 184(fig. 71)

Webb, John, 79

Webster, Daniel, 125–26, 126, 138*n*83

Wells-Cole, Anthony, 261

Whitaker, Thomas, 139*n*85

White, Donald P., III, 256–70

White, J., 4–5

White, John, 235*n*20

White, Lyman, 6(&fig.), 26*n*6, 26*n*10

White ash, pier table, 2(fig.)

The White House and Capitol (Baker), 76(fig. 2)

White oak: Campeche chair, 31(fig. 5); chest of drawers with doors, 194(fig.); chests of drawers, 228(fig.); side chairs, 18(figs.), 19(fig.), 130(fig.); sofa, 97(fig. 38)

White pine: breakfast table, 126(fig. 89); cabinets, 221(fig. 29), 222(figs.); card tables, 9(fig.), 13(fig.); chest of drawers with doors, 194(fig.); chests, 216(figs.), 218(fig.); chests of drawers, 213(fig.), 224(figs.), 226(fig.), 228(fig.); cupboard with drawers, 214(fig.); dressing tables, 15(fig.), 17(fig.); pier table, 2(fig.); side chairs, 115(fig.), 125(fig. 87), 130(fig.); sofas, 97(fig. 38), 119(fig. 70), 120(fig. 73); worktable, 16(fig. 22)

Wightman, Thomas, 14

Wilde, Oscar, 249

Wilkinson, William L., 136*n*53

Willard, Aaron, Jr., 25*n*2; portrait of, 21–22(&fig. 29)

Willard, Aaron, Sr., 20(fig.), 22, 27*n*22

Willard, Nancy, 22

Willard, Simon, 27*n*22

Willard, Susan (Bartlett), 22

William and Mary style, 228

Williamson, Collen, 98, 134*n*37

William Worthington, 105(fig. 49)

Winslow, Edward, 211–12

Winslow, Kenelm, 212(&figs.), 234*n*6

Winterthur Museum, 261, 262

Wise, Ann (Bolling), 135*n*48

Wise, John, 104–5, 135*n*48

Wise, Peter, 135*n*48

Wistar, Caspar, 34

Wood: ash as secondary, 6, 26*n*7; exotic, 222–27, 239*n*53; reused, 225, 225(fig. 38); sources in Boston, 209; sources in

London, 209; timber in London records, 232–33; tropical, 201

Woodlands, 81, 81(fig. 8), 96

Woods, John, 113, 137*n*71

Workbox, 14(&fig. 20)

Worktable, Penniman-decorated, 16(&figs.)

Worrall, John, 25*n*5

Worshipful Company of Carpenters, 234*n*11, 235*n*21

Worshipful Company of Joiners and Ceilers, 198–99(&fig.), 201, 234*n*6

Worshipful Company of Turners, 205

Worthington, Ann, 135*n*50

Worthington, Harriet, 127

Worthington, John, III, 105

Worthington, Ruth, 135*n*50

Worthington, William, Jr., 51*n*14, 105–107; apprentices, 135*n*50, 136*n*53, 139*n*87; civil affairs, 136*n*54; crown bedstead, 109, 136*n*62; French bedstead, 110(fig. 51); government commissions, 127, 138–39*n*85; Madisons and, 106–7; Monroes and, 109; portrait of, 105(fig. 49); side chairs, 116(fig. 63), 117–19(&figs. 65–67, 69); sofas, 103(fig.), 104(figs.), 119–22(&figs. 70–79); Spanish (Campechy) chairs, 123–25(&figs. 81–83, 85–86); Waters and, 103

Worthington, William, Sr., 105

Wren, Eleanor, tombstone, 99–100(&fig. 41), 122, 123(fig. 80), 138*n*79

Wren, Sarah, tombstone, 99–100(&fig. 40), 124(fig. 84)

Yellow pine: chests of drawers, 228(fig.); desk-and-bookcase, 80(fig. 5); French bedstead, 110(fig. 51); side chairs, 94(fig. 30), 116(fig. 63), 117(fig. 65); sofas, 97(fig. 38), 103(fig.), 104(figs.), 114(fig. 61); Campechy chairs, 123(fig. 81), 124(fig. 85), 125(fig. 86)

Yen-yen banisters, 147